1993 Traveler's Guide to Art Museum Exhibitions

Museum Guide Publications, Inc.

distributed by
Harry N. Abrams, Inc., New York

Front Cover:

The Seed of the Areoi (Te aa no areois), 1892, Paul Gauguin.
Courtesy The Museum of Modern Art, New York. From "The William S. Paley Collection," organized by The Museum of Modern Art, New York.
A traveling exhibition: Seattle Art Museum, WA: thru Feb. 7; San Diego Museum of Art, CA: June 12–Sept. 26; The Baltimore Museum of Art, MD: Oct. 31, 1993–Jan. 9, 1994.

Acknowledgments

Special thanks to Kate Hensler, associate editor; Nina Hall, contributing editor; Anne Delphenich and Paul Clements, production; and to the supportive public relations and press representatives in the museums across the country and abroad.

 Distributed by Harry N. Abrams, Inc., New York. A Times Mirror Company.

ISBN 0-8109-2522-2
Printed in the U.S.A.

Table of Contents

How to Use

The *Traveler's Guide to Art Museum Exhibitions* is an annual index to national and international exhibitions. It is also a guide to the permanent collections of museums throughout the United States, and selected museums in Canada and Europe.

The guide begins with Major Traveling Exhibitions, where the reader will find exhibitions listed alphabetically, with itinerary. Individual entries for each museum follow, organized by state (and by city within state) in the United States, and by country in Europe. Each entry lists exhibition schedules for the entire year, highlights from permanent collections, information on the architecture of the building, and on hours, admissions, and tours. The Color Section includes images from both traveling exhibitions and permanent collections.

Be sure to note the many excellent exhibitions organized by the American Federation of Arts, each marked with an asterisk (*).

Every effort has been made to ensure accuracy, but exhibition dates are subject to change; be sure to double check by telephoning museums before a visit.

Editor's Choice

Talk abounds of funding cutbacks, retrenchment, and the end of the "blockbuster" exhibition. But many museums are opening innovative new gallery spaces and even entire new buildings. These are undoubtedly projects begun in the affluent eighties, but the fulfillment of artful housekeeping will be enjoyed in 1993.

New Spaces

The Guggenheim expansion and its new facility in SoHo head the list of new museum facilities. The Institute of Contemporary Art in Philadelphia, the Davis Museum and Cultural Center at Wellesley College are new spaces; extensive renovations in Cincinnati, Toledo, New Orleans, and Denver and at The Jewish Museum and the Brooklyn Museum will all be completed in 1993.

Museum Collections Travel

The 1993 schedule features several traveling exhibitions drawn from individual museum collections, such as "The William S. Paley Collection" from the Museum of Modern Art, "Highlights From the Butler Institute of American Art" (Youngstown, Ohio); "Facing the Past: 19th-Century Portraits from the Pennsylvania Academy of the Fine Arts" (AFA); and "Free Within Ourselves: African American Art From the National Museum of American Art." Masterpieces from European collections including drawings from the National Gallery of Ireland, treasures of the Russian Museum, St. Petersburg, and Marc Chagall's murals for Moscow's State Jewish Kamerny Theatre will all visit American museums. Opening in 1993 is "Great French Paintings From the Barnes Foundation," to be viewed for the first time outside Philadelphia.

One-Person Exhibitions

Photography by Annie Leibovitz and Alfred Stieglitz, whose images are featured in both "Stieglitz in the Darkroom" at the National Gallery and the traveling exhibition "Two Lives: Georgia O'Keeffe and Alfred Stieglitz," are exhibits of note. Other single-artist shows feature modern works by Joseph Beuys, Jeff Koons, Max Ernst (paintings and sculpture), Red Grooms, Anish Kapoor, Eva Hesse, Jacob Lawrence, and Roy Lichtenstein. Not to miss is the enormous and enticing Matisse retrospective at the Museum of Modern Art, closing January 11th.

Single Museum Exhibitions

Several exhibitions at museums featuring works from their own collections promise to be fascinating: "What's New: Prague," at the Art Institute of Chicago, "Willem de Kooning: Selections from the Hirshhorn Museum," and "A Breadth of Vision: The Ritz Collection" (Milwaukee). And....come spring, the Miró Foundation in Barcelona will mount a retrospective celebrating the centennial of the world-renowned artist.

There is infinite variety and quality in exhibitions across the country and abroad, so make plans now for many 1993 museum visits.

1993 Major Traveling Exhibitions

Africa Explores: 20th Century African Art
The Carnegie Museum of Art, Pittsburgh, PA: thru Jan. 10;
The Corcoran Gallery of Art, Washington, DC: Feb. 6–Apr. 4;
Center for the Fine Arts, Miami, FL: May 15–July 18;
Fundació Antoni Tàpies, Barcelona, Spain: Sept.–Nov.

****American Abstraction at the Addison Gallery of American Art***
Newport Harbor Art Museum, CA: Mar. 6–May 29;
Terra Museum of American Art, Chicago, IL: May 15–Aug. 1.

****American Prints in Black and White, 1900–1950: Selections from the Collection of Reba and Dave Williams***
Heckscher Museum, Huntington, NY: thru Jan. 10;
Dallas Museum of Art, TX: Feb. 7–Apr. 4.

The Ancient Americas: Art from Sacred Landscapes
The Art Institute of Chicago, IL: thru Jan. 3;
Museum of Fine Arts, Houston, TX: Feb. 14–Apr. 18;
Los Angeles County Museum of Art, CA: June 6–Aug. 15.

Art of the American Indian Frontier, 1800–1900: The Chandler/Pohrt Collection
National Gallery of Art, Washington, DC: thru Jan. 24;
Seattle Art Museum, WA: Mar. 11–May 9;
Buffalo Bill Historical Center, Cody, WY: June 18–Sept. 12;
The Detroit Institute of Arts, MI: Oct. 17, 1993–Feb. 6, 1994.

The Art of Seeing: John Ruskin and the Victorian Eye
Phoenix Art Museum, AZ: Mar. 6–May 23;
Indianapolis Museum of Art, IN: June 26–Aug. 29.

The Arts and Crafts Movement in California: Living the Good Life
The Oakland Museum, CA: Feb. 27–May 23;
Renwick Gallery, Washington, DC: Oct. 8, 1993–Jan. 9, 1994.

Jean Michel Basquiat
Whitney Museum of American Art, New York, NY: thru Feb. 14;
The Menil Collection, Houston, TX: Mar. 11–May 9.

Frederic Bazille: Prophet of Impressionism
The Brooklyn Museum, NY: thru Jan. 24;
The Dixon Gallery and Gardens, Memphis, TN: Feb. 14–Apr. 25.

Max Beckmann Prints from the Collection of The Museum of Modern Art
Toledo Museum of Art, OH: Mar. 14–May 2;
San Francisco Museum of Modern Art, CA: Sept. 10–Dec. 15.

Thinking is Form: The Drawings of Joseph Beuys
The Museum of Modern Art, New York, NY: Feb. 21–May 4;
Los Angeles County Museum of Art, CA: May 30–Aug. 1;
Philadelphia Museum of Art, PA: Sept. 19, 1993–Jan. 2, 1994;
The Art Institute of Chicago, IL: Feb. 15–Apr. 25, 1994.

Julie Bozzi: American Food
University of Massachusetts–Amherst, MA: Jan. 30–Mar. 12;
Modern Art Museum of Fort Worth, TX: Apr. 18–June 13.

Brushstrokes: Styles and Techniques of Chinese Painting
Asian Art Museum of San Francisco, CA: thru Jan. 4;
Santa Barbara Museum of Art, CA: Feb. 13–Apr. 25.

Vija Celmins: Mid-Career Retrospective
Institute of Contemporary Art, Philadelphia, PA: thru Jan. 17;
Henry Art Gallery, Seattle, WA: Mar. 31–May 23;
Whitney Museum of American Art, New York, NY: Sept. 15–Nov. 29.

Marc Chagall and the Jewish Theater
Guggenheim Museum SoHo, NY: thru Jan. 17;
The Art Institute of Chicago, IL: Jan. 30–May 10.

Classical Taste in America 1800–1840
The Baltimore Museum of Art, MD: June 27–Sept. 26;
Mint Museum of Art, Charlotte, NC: Nov. 20, 1993–Mar. 13, 1994.

Common Ground/Uncommon Vision: The Michael and Julie Hall Collection of American Folk Art
Milwaukee Art Museum, WI: Apr. 16–June 20;
The Nelson-Atkins Museum of Art, Kansas City, MO: July 16–Sept. 5;
Albright-Knox Art Gallery, Buffalo, NY: Nov. 12, 1993–Jan. 2, 1994.

Concept/Construct: Los Angeles Art and the Photograph, 1960–1980
Laguna Art Museum, Laguna Beach, CA: thru Jan. 17;
Ansel Adams Center for Photography, San Francisco, CA: June 23–Aug. 22;
Montgomery Museum of Fine Arts, AL: Sept. 12–Nov. 7.

Robert Cumming
Museum of Contemporary Art, San Diego (downtown), CA: May 28–Aug. 7;
Museum of Fine Arts, Boston, MA: Sept. 4–Nov. 28.

****The Drawings of Stuart Davis: The Amazing Continuity***
Terra Museum of American Art, Chicago, IL: thru Feb. 7;
Middlebury College Art Museum, Middlebury, VT: Mar. 30–May 2;
Marion Koogler McNay Art Museum, San Antonio, TX: May 23–July 18.

Dutch and Flemish Seventeenth Century Paintings: The Harold Samuel Collection
The Frick Art Museum, Pittsburgh, PA: thru Feb. 14;
Museum of Fine Arts, Boston, MA: Mar. 13–May 9;
Seattle Art Museum, WA: June 3–July 25.

The Earthly Paradise: Arts and Crafts by William Morris and his Circle from Canadian Collections
Art Gallery of Ontario, Toronto, Ontario, Canada: July;
National Gallery of Canada, Ottawa, Ontario, Canada: Oct. 22, 1993–Jan. 16, 1994.

Egypt's Dazzling Sun: Amenhotep III and his World
Kimbell Art Museum, Fort Worth, TX: thru Jan. 31;
Galeries Nationales du Grand Palais, Paris, France: Mar. 2–May 31.

Max Ernst: Dada and the Dawn of Surrealism
The Museum of Modern Art, New York, NY: Mar. 12–May 2;
The Menil Collection, Houston, TX: May 27–Aug. 29;
The Art Institute of Chicago, IL: Sept. 15–Nov. 30.

Max Ernst: The Sculpture
University Art Museum, Berkeley, CA: thru Mar. 7;
Indianapolis Museum of Art, IN: Apr. 3–May 30.

****Richard Estes: The Complete Prints***
The Canton Art Institute, Canton, OH: Jan. 17–Mar. 14;
Middlebury College Art Museum, Middlebury, VT: June 22–July 25;
Louisiana Arts and Science Center, Baton Rouge, LA: Aug. 8–Oct. 3;
Columbia Museum of Art, SC: Oct. 31, 1993–Jan. 1, 1994.

****Facing the Past: 19th-Century Portraits from the Collection of the Pennsylvania Academy of the Fine Arts***
Pennsylvania Academy of the Fine Arts, Philadelphia, PA: thru Apr. 11;
Museum of Arts & Sciences, Macon, GA: Sept. 18–Nov. 13;
Joslyn Art Museum, Omaha, NE: Dec. 11, 1993–Jan. 30, 1994.

Flags of the Fante Asafo
Museum of Modern Art, Oxford, England: Apr. 4–June 20;
University Art Museum, Berkeley, CA: July 7–Sept. 27.

Free Within Ourselves: African-American Art from the National Museum of American Art
Wadsworth Atheneum, Hartford, CT: thru Jan. 10;
IBM Gallery of Science and Art, New York, NY: Feb. 9–Apr. 10;
Crocker Art Museum, Sacramento, CA: Nov. 5–Dec. 30.

The French Drawing: Masterpieces from the Collection of the Pierpont Morgan Library
Musée du Louvre, Paris, France: June 2–Aug. 30;
The Pierpont Morgan Library, New York, NY: Sept. 15, 1993–Jan. 2, 1994.

Gates of Mystery: The Art of Holy Russia from the Russian Museum, St. Petersburg
Dallas Museum of Art, TX: Feb. 14–Apr. 11;
The Art Institute of Chicago, IL: July 1–Sept. 15.

Frank Gehry: New Bentwood Furniture Designs
The Saint Louis Art Museum, MO: thru Feb. 16;
The Carnegie Museum of Art, Pittsburgh, PA: Sept. 11–Nov. 7.

Emmet Gowin: Photographs
Museum of Contemporary Art, Chicago, IL: thru Jan. 17;
Columbus Museum of Art, OH: Mar. 14–Apr. 25.

The Graphic Art of Les XX and the Belgian Avant-Garde
Spencer Museum of Art, Lawrence, KN: Jan. 24–Mar. 21;
Sterling and Francine Clark Art Institute, Williamstown, MA: Apr. 17–June 13.

The Greek Miracle: Classical Sculpture from the Dawn of Democracy, The Fifth Century B.C.
National Gallery of Art, Washington, DC: thru Feb. 7;
The Metropolitan Museum of Art, New York, NY: Mar. 11–May 23.

***Red Grooms:* Ruckus Rodeo**
Modern Art Museum of Fort Worth, TX: thru Feb. 14;
Joslyn Art Museum, Omaha, NE: Aug. 14–Sept. 26.

Hand-Painted Pop: American Art in Transition, 1955–62
The Museum of Contemporary Art, Los Angeles, CA: thru Mar. 7;
Museum of Contemporary Art, Chicago, IL: Apr. 3–June 20;
Whitney Museum of American Art, New York, NY: July 16–Oct. 3.

The Still-Life Paintings of William M. Harnett
The Fine Arts Museums of San Francisco (de Young Museum), CA: thru Feb. 14;
National Gallery of Art, Washington, DC: Mar. 14–June 13.

John Heartfield: Photomontages
The Museum of Modern Art, New York, NY: Apr. 15–July 6;
San Francisco Museum of Modern Art, CA: July 22–Sept. 19.

Eva Hesse: A Retrospective
Hirshhorn Museum and Sculpture Garden, Washington, DC: thru Jan. 10;
Galerie Nationale du Jeu de Paume, Paris, France: Apr. 27–June 20.

Highlights from the Butler Institute of American Art, Youngstown
IBM Gallery of Science and Art, New York, NY: Feb. 9–Apr. 10;
Brandywine River Museum, Chadds Ford, PA: Sept. 11–Nov. 21.

I Dream a World: Portraits of Black Women Who Changed America (marked *)
Fort Wayne Museum of Art, IN: Jan. 2–Feb. 20;
Museum of Photographic Arts, San Diego, CA: Mar. 17–Apr. 28;
New York State Museum, Albany, NY: Mar. 22–July 3;
Indianapolis Museum of Art, IN: July 31–Sept. 11;
Milwaukee Art Museum, WI: Oct. 9–Nov. 20;
Dayton Art Institute, OH: Dec. 18, 1993–Jan. 29, 1994.

Imperial Painting from the Ming Dynasty: The Zhe School
The Metropolitan Museum of Art, New York, NY: Mar. 10–May 9;
Dallas Museum of Art, TX: May 16–July 11.

The Impressionist and the City: Late Series Paintings by Pissarro
Dallas Museum of Art, TX: thru Jan. 10;
Philadelphia Museum of Art, PA: Mar. 7–June 6.

In Medusa's Gaze: Still-Life Painting in Upstate New York Collections
The Albany Institute of History and Art, NY: thru Feb. 14;
Albright-Knox Art Gallery, Buffalo, NY: Mar. 20–May 2.

In the Spirit of Fluxus
Walker Art Center, Minneapolis, MN: Feb. 14–June 6;
Whitney Museum of American Art, New York, NY: July 9–Oct. 17.

Louis I. Kahn: In the Realm of Architecture
The Museum of Contemporary Art, Los Angeles, CA: Feb. 28–May 30;
Kimbell Art Museum, Fort Worth, TX: July 3–Oct. 10.

Anish Kapoor
Des Moines Art Center, IA: Jan. 30–Apr. 25;
National Gallery of Canada, Ottawa, Ontario, Canada: July 9–Sept. 19;
The Power Plant, Toronto, Ontario, Canada: Nov. 1993–Jan. 1994.

Karsh: American Legends
International Center of Photography, New York, NY: thru Jan. 24;
The Corcoran Gallery of Art, Washington, DC: Feb. 27–Apr. 18.

On Kawara: Date Paintings in 89 Cities
Museum of Fine Arts, Boston, MA: thru Feb. 7;
San Francisco Museum of Modern Art, CA: Feb. 25–Apr. 11.

Jeff Koons
San Francisco Museum of Modern Art, CA: thru Feb. 7;
Walker Art Center, Minneapolis, MN: July 10–Oct. 3.

Latin American Artists of the Twentieth Century
Musée d'Art Moderne, Paris, France: thru Jan. 11;
Museum of Modern Art, New York, NY: June 5–Sept. 7;
Museum Ludwig, Cologne, Germany: Mar.–May.

Jacob Lawrence: The Frederick Douglass and Harriet Tubman Series of Narrative Paintings
Joslyn Art Museum, Omaha, NE: Feb. 13–Apr. 25;
The Fine Arts Museums of San Francisco, CA: Sept. 15, 1993–Jan. 2, 1994.

Sir Thomas Lawrence: Portrait of an Age, 1790–1830
Yale Center for British Art, New Haven, CT: Feb. 27–Apr. 25;
Kimbell Art Museum, Fort Worth, TX: May 15–July 11;
Virginia Museum of Fine Arts, Richmond, VA: Aug. 3–Sept. 26.

Annie Leibovitz: Photographs 1970–1990
Ansel Adams Center for Photography, San Francisco, CA: Jan. 27–Mar. 14;
High Museum of Art, Atlanta, GA: Sept. 21–Nov. 28;
Museum of Fine Arts, Houston, TX: Dec. 19, 1993–Jan. 30, 1994.

Roy Lichtenstein
The Solomon R. Guggenheim Museum, New York, NY: May–Aug.;
The Museum of Contemporary Art, Los Angeles, CA: Oct. 24, 1993–Jan. 9, 1994.

****Light, Air, and Color: American Impressionist Paintings from the Collection of the Pennsylvania Academy of the Fine Arts***
Memorial Art Gallery of the University of Rochester, NY: thru Feb. 7;
Beaverbrook Art Gallery, Frederickton, New Brunswick, Canada: Mar. 7–May 2;
Huntsville Museum of Art, AL: May 30–July 18.

Fables and Fantasies: The Art of Felix Lorieux
Crocker Art Museum, Sacramento, CA: thru Jan. 10;
Delaware Art Museum, Wilmington, DE: Jan. 29–Mar. 14.

The Lure of Italy: American Artists and the Italian Experience, 1760–1914
The Cleveland Museum of Art, OH: Feb. 3–Apr. 11;
The Museum of Fine Arts, Houston, TX: May 23–Aug. 8.

René Magritte
The Menil Collection, Houston, TX: thru Feb. 21;
The Art Institute of Chicago, IL: Mar. 16–May 30.

Agnes Martin
Whitney Museum of American Art, New York, NY: thru Jan. 31;
Milwaukee Art Museum, WI: Feb. 12–Apr. 4;
Center for the Fine Arts, Miami, FL: May 22–July 11;
Contemporary Arts Museum, Houston, TX: Sept. 11–Oct. 31.

Master European Paintings from The National Gallery of Ireland: Mantegna to Goya
Museum of Fine Arts, Boston, MA: Jan. 13–Mar. 28;
IBM Gallery of Science and Art, New York, NY: Apr. 27–June 26.

Master European Drawings from Polish Collections: Fifteenth through Eighteenth Centuries
The Nelson-Atkins Museum of Art, Kansas City, MO: Apr. 17–June 6;
Milwaukee Art Museum, WI: July 9–Aug. 29.

Masterworks of American Impressionism from the Pfeil Collection
Phoenix Art Museum, AZ: thru Feb. 14;
Center for the Fine Arts, Miami, FL: Mar. 6–May 9;
The Dixon Gallery and Gardens, Memphis, TN: June 6–Aug. 8;
Honolulu Academy of Arts, HI: Sept. 2–Oct. 17;
Birmingham Museum of Art, AL: Nov. 6, 1993–Jan. 2, 1994.

Masterworks from Lille: Old Master Paintings and Drawings from the Musée des Beaux Arts, Lille
The Metropolitan Museum of Art, New York, NY: thru Jan. 17;
The National Gallery, London, England: Mar. 24–July 11.

Ralph Eugene Meatyard: An American Visionary
Newport Harbor Art Museum, CA: thru Feb. 14;
High Museum of Art, Atlanta, GA: Mar. 3–May 30.

Motion and Document—Sequence and Time: Eadweard Muybridge and Contemporary American Photography
Henry Art Gallery, Seattle, WA: Jan. 22–Mar. 21;
Wadsworth Atheneum, Hartford, CT: May 9–Aug. 8.

****Ottocento: Romanticism and Revolution***
Worcester Art Museum, MA: Jan. 16–Feb. 26;
The Frick Art Museum, Pittsburgh, PA: Mar. 12–Apr. 23.

The William S. Paley Collection
Seattle Art Museum, WA: thru Feb. 7;
San Diego Museum of Art, CA: June 12–Sept. 26;
The Baltimore Museum of Art, MD: Oct. 31, 1993–Jan. 9, 1994.

Duncan Phillips Collects: Paris Between the Wars
The Dixon Gallery and Gardens, Memphis, TN: Aug. 15–Oct. 10;
The Carnegie Museum of Art, Pittsburgh, PA: Nov. 6, 1993–Jan. 16, 1994.

Duncan Phillips Collects: Augustus Vincent Tack
The Phillips Collection, Washington, DC: Apr. 24–Aug. 15;
Sheldon Memorial Art Gallery, Lincoln, NE: Nov. 13, 1993–Jan. 23, 1994.

Photography in Contemporary German Art 1960–1990
The Saint Louis Art Museum, MO: thru Jan. 3;
Guggenheim Museum SoHo, NY: Jan. 22–May 2.

Pleasures and Terrors of Domestic Comfort
Los Angeles County Museum of Art, CA: thru Jan. 24;
Contemporary Arts Center, Cincinnati, OH: Apr. 3–May 29.

A Private View: Small Paintings in the Manoogian Collection
Yale University Art Gallery, New Haven, CT: Apr. 3–July 31;
The Detroit Institute of Arts, MI: Sept. 11–Nov. 14;
High Museum of Art, Atlanta, GA: Dec. 18, 1993–Mar. 6, 1994.

Rolywholyover: A Circus
The Museum of Contemporary Art, Los Angeles, CA: Sept. 12–Nov. 28;
The Menil Collection, Houston, TX: Jan. 14–Apr. 3, 1994;
Guggenheim Museum SoHo, NY: Apr.–Aug. 1994.

Rookwood Pottery: The Glorious Gamble
The Nelson-Atkins Museum of Art, Kansas City, MO: thru Feb. 7;
Cincinnati Art Museum, OH: Mar. 17–May 30;
Sterling and Francine Clark Art Institute, Williamstown, MA: July 3–Sept. 12.

Susan Rothenberg: Paintings and Drawings
Albright-Knox Art Gallery, Buffalo, NY: thru Jan. 3;
Hirshhorn Museum and Sculpture Garden, Washington, DC: Feb. 10–May 9;
The Saint Louis Art Museum, MO: May 28–July 25;
Museum of Contemporary Art, Chicago, IL: Aug. 20–Oct. 24.

Seeing Straight: The f.64 Revolution in Photography
The Oakland Museum, CA: thru Jan. 10;
Akron Art Museum, OH: Jan. 30–Mar. 28;
Santa Barbara Museum of Art, CA: Apr. 22–July 8;
Center for Creative Photography, Tucson, AZ: Sept. 19–Nov. 14;
Minnesota Museum of Art, St. Paul, MN: Dec. 12, 1993–Feb. 27, 1994;
Worcester Art Museum, MA: Mar. 29–May 29, 1994.

Lorna Simpson: For the Sake of the Viewer
Museum of Contemporary Art, Chicago, IL: thru Mar. 14;
Contemporary Arts Museum, Houston, TX: Mar. 20–May 30;
Henry Art Gallery, Seattle, WA: Nov. 24, 1993–Feb. 6, 1994.

Sisley, Master Impressionist
Musée d'Orsay, Paris, France: thru Feb. 15;
The Walters Art Gallery, Baltimore, MD: Mar. 14–June 13.

Sites of Recollection: Four Altars and a Rap Opera
Dayton Art Institute, OH: Mar. 21–May 8;
Memorial Art Gallery of the University of Rochester, NY: Oct. 9–Dec. 5.

Jaune Quick-to-See Smith
The Chrysler Museum, Norfolk, VA: Jan. 17–Mar. 28;
Smith College Museum of Art, Northampton, MA: Apr.–May.

Songs of My People
The Oakland Museum, CA: Jan. 30–Mar. 7;
Arkansas Arts Center, Little Rock, AK: Apr. 1–May 16;
The Detroit Institute of Arts, MI: June 21–Aug. 29;
Memphis Brooks Museum of Art, Memphis, TN: Oct. 31–Dec. 12.

Clyfford Still: The Buffalo & San Francisco Collections
Albright-Knox Art Gallery, NY: Jan. 16–Mar. 7;
San Francisco Museum of Modern Art, CA: Mar. 25–June 13.

Louis H. Sullivan: Unison with Nature
Sheldon Memorial Art Gallery, Lincoln, NE: Feb. 23–Apr. 24;
Arkansas Arts Center, Little Rock, AK: May 13–July 11.

****Donald Sultan: A Print Retrospective***
Butler Institute of American Art, Youngstown, OH: thru Jan. 31;
The Museum of Fine Arts, Houston, TX: June 26–Aug. 22.

Tales of Japan: Three Centuries of Japanese Painting from the Chester Beatty Library, Dublin
Indianapolis Museum of Art, IN: thru Jan. 10;
The Dayton Art Institute, OH: Feb. 13–Mar. 28;
Hood Museum of Art, NH: Sept. 26–Nov. 28.

Mark Tansey
Los Angeles County Museum of Art, CA: June 17–Aug. 29;
Milwaukee Art Museum, WI: Sept. 10–Nov. 2;
Modern Art Museum of Fort Worth, TX: Dec. 9, 1993–Feb. 20, 1994.

****Telling Tales: 19th Century Narrative Painting from the Collection of the Pennsylvania Academy of the Fine Arts***
Greenville County Museum of Art, Greenville, SC: Jan. 7–Feb. 28;
The Chrysler Museum, Norfolk, VA: Mar. 13–May 9;
The Dixon Gallery and Gardens, Memphis, TN: Dec. 5, 1993–Jan. 30, 1994.

Theme and Improvisation: Kandinsky and the American Avant-Garde 1912–1950
The Dayton Art Institute, OH: thru Jan. 31;
Terra Museum of American Art, IL: Feb. 13–Apr. 25;
Amon Carter Museum, TX: May 15–Aug. 1.

This Sporting Life, 1878–1991
Delaware Art Museum, Wilmington, DE: Apr. 30–June 26;
Albright-Knox Art Gallery, Buffalo, NY: June 26–Aug. 29.

Three Centuries of Roman Drawings from the Villa Farnesina, Rome
The Nelson-Atkins Museum of Art, Kansas City, MO: Apr. 17–June 6;
The Frick Art Museum, Pittsburgh, PA: Sept. 4–Oct. 24.

Two Lives: Georgia O'Keeffe and Alfred Stieglitz—A Conversation in Paintings and Photographs
The Phillips Collection, Washington, DC: thru Apr. 4;
IBM Gallery of Science and Art, New York, NY: Apr. 27–June 26;
The Minneapolis Institute of Arts, MN: July 18–Sept. 12;
Museum of Fine Arts, Houston, TX: Oct. 3–Nov. 28.

A Privileged Eye: The Photography of Carl Van Vechten
The Nelson-Atkins Museum of Art, Kansas City, MO: thru Jan. 10;
The Detroit Institute of Arts, MI: May 12–July 3.

Visions of the People: A Pictorial History of Plains Indian Life
The Saint Louis Art Museum, MO: Feb. 2–Apr. 18;
Joslyn Art Museum, Omaha, NE: May 22–July 25.

Max Weber: The Cubist Decade, 1910–20
The Brooklyn Museum, NY: thru Jan. 10;
Los Angeles County Museum of Art, CA: Feb. 18–Apr. 25.

Carrie Mae Weems
National Museum of Women in the Arts, Washington, DC: Jan. 7–Mar. 21;
San Francisco Museum of Modern Art, CA: June 10–Aug. 4;
Institute of Contemporary Art, Philadelphia, PA: fall.

With Grace and Favour: Fashion From the Victorian and Edwardian Eras
Cincinnati Art Museum, OH: May 22–Sept. 5;
The Chrysler Museum, Norfolk, VA: Oct. 24, 1993–Jan. 3, 1994.

UNITED STATES MUSEUMS

Galleries of Modern Art
1900–1950, The Art
Institute of Chicago.
Tom Cinoman, photo.

Birmingham Museum of Art

2000 Eighth Ave. North, Birmingham, Ala. 35203-2278
(205) 254-2566; 254-2565 (recording)

1993 Exhibitions

NOTE: The museum is closed through Oct. 2, 1993, for expansion, but has organized exhibitions at other venues. Call (205) 254-2566 for information.

Thru Feb. (Brookwood Women's Medical Pavilion)
Ceramic Vessels from Many Cultures
A cross-cultural look at vessels from the museum collection.

Thru Feb. 25 (Visual Arts Gallery, University of Alabama at Birmingham)
Picture Relations: Photo Essays from the South by Debbie Fleming Caffery and Birney Imes

Thru summer (Museum of Art/Civic Center Annex, 1001 19th St. North)
Art of the Americas
Art of the Western hemisphere from 1200 B.C. to the present, drawn from the museum's permanent collection.

Mar.–May (Brookwood Women's Medical Pavilion)
Light at Play: Art Glass from the Turn of the Century
A selection of art glass from the museum collection.

Nov. 6, 1993–Jan. 2, 1994
Masterworks of American Impressionism from the Pfeil Collection
More than 100 paintings by three generations of American Impressionists, including Cassatt, Sargent, and lesser-known figures. Catalogue.

Permanent Collection

Over 15,000 objects, including contemporary Chinese paintings, collections of Oriental, Native American, African, and Pre-Columbian art, art of the Old West. **Highlights:** Kress collection of Renaissance art; Beeson Wedgwood collection; Hitt collection of 18th-century French furniture and decorative objects; recent library gift of 1,200 Wedgwood books, letters, and catalogues. **Architecture:** 1959 original building; 1965, 1967, 1974, and 1980 additions by Warren, Knight, and Davis; 1993 expansion and renovation by Edward Larrabee Barnes.

Chilcat Blanket, Kitchikan, Alaska (Tlingit). From "Art of the Americas." Birmingham Museum of Art.

Admission: Free; donations accepted. Handicapped accessible.
Hours: Annex gallery open Wed.–Sat., 10–5.
Tours: Call (205) 254-2318 two weeks in advance.
Food & Drink: Hours to be determined.

Montgomery Museum of Fine Arts

One Museum Dr., Montgomery, Ala. 36123
(205) 244-5700

1993 Exhibitions

Thru Jan. 10
AFRIKA
Multimedia works by Russian conceptual artist Sergei Bugaev ("AFRIKA").
Jan. 10–Feb. 21
In Good Conscience: The Radical Tradition in 20th-Century American Illustration
Examines American artists' involvement in politics, social concerns, and war efforts.
Jan. 17–Mar. 7
A Graphic Odyssey: Romare Bearden as Printmaker
Over 100 prints by the 20th-century artist.
Mar. 21–May 9
Before Discovery: Artistic Development in the Americas before the Arrival of Columbus
Showcases the cultural and artistic achievements of ancient civilizations in Mexico, Central America, Colombia, Ecuador, and Peru.
May 21–July 3
The John F. Eulich Collection of American Western Art
Works chronicling the history of the settlement of the American West.
July 14–Sept. 1
Fluxus: A Conceptual Country
Commemorates the 30th anniversary of the international movement.
Sept. 4–Oct. 24
Guerilla Girls Talk Back: A Retrospective, 1985–1990
First appearance in the South of posters and banners by this anonymous collective of women, committed to combating sexism and racism in galleries and museums.
Sept. 12–Nov. 7
Concept/Construct: Los Angeles Art and the Photograph, 1960–1980
Influential photography-based works by such artists as John Baldessari, Robert Heinecken, and Ed Ruscha. Catalogue.

Permanent Collection

Eighteenth-, 19th-, and 20th-century American painting, sculpture, and graphic arts; Old Master prints; works by

Southern historical and contemporary artists. **Highlights:** The Blount Collection of American Art; First Period Worcester porcelains from the Loeb Collection. **Architecture:** 1988 building by Barganier, McKee Sims Architects Associated.

Admission: Free. Handicapped accessible.
Hours: Tues.–Sat., 10–5; Thurs., 10–9; Sun., noon–5. Closed Mon.
Tours: Call tour coordinator at (205) 244-5700.
Food & Drink: The Terrace Café open Tues.–Sat., 11–2. For private luncheons and dinner parties, call (205) 244-5747.

Anchorage Museum of History and Art

121 W. Seventh Ave., Anchorage, Alaska 99501
(907) 343-4326

1993 Exhibitions

Jan. 10–Feb. 7
Oceanic Ceremonial Objects
Shields, masks, and figurines collected in the 1920s from New Guinea and the Marquesas.
Mark Zirpel Solo Exhibition
Prints by the Alaskan artist.
Jan. 10–Mar. 7
Earth, Fire, and Fibre
Biennial juried craft exhibition.
Feb. 14–Mar. 14
Robby Mohatt Solo Exhibition
Abstract paintings and works on paper by the Alaskan artist.
Feb. 14–Mar. 28
The New Whitney Dissenters
Works by artists to express dissatisfaction with the Whitney Museum's Biennial exhibitions.
Mar. 21–Apr. 18
Kenneth de Roux Solo Exhibition
Paintings by the Alaskan artist.
Apr. 6–May 9
Barry Moser: Wood Engravings
Sixty wood engravings composed of prints used to illustrate children's literature.
Oct. 3–Nov. 28
More Than One: Contemporary Studio Production
Survey of contemporary craft production in all media and forms. Catalogue.

Permanent Collection

Traditional and contemporary Alaskan art; objects from the Athapaskan, Aleut, Tlingit, Haida, Eskimo peoples, the Russian period, American whaling, the Gold Rush, World

War II, contemporary life. **Architecture:** 1968 building and 1975 addition by Maynard & Partch; 1986 addition by Mitchell/Giurgola.

Admission: Adults, $4; senior citizens, $3.50; Anchorage Museum Association members, free. Handicapped accessible.
Hours: Mid-May–mid-Sept: 9–6. Mid-Sept.–mid-May: Tues.–Sat., 10–6; Sun., 1–5. Closed Mon.
Tours: Summer: Alaska Gallery, 11, 2. Call (907) 343-4326.
Food & Drink: Museum Café open museum hours.

The Heard Museum

22 E. Monte Vista Rd., Phoenix, Ariz. 85004-1480
(602) 252-8840

1993 Exhibitions

You Follow a Chief, Cliff Whiting. From "Te Waka Toi: Contemporary Maori Art of New Zealand." The Heard Museum.

Thru Jan. 3
Te Waka Toi: Contemporary Maori Art of New Zealand
Painting, sculpture, and textiles by leading Maori artists.
Thru Jan. 31
Objects of Myth and Memory: American Indian Art from the Brooklyn Museum
Thru Mar. 28
Native Mosaic Musical Instruments
Thru Apr. 18
¡Chispas! Cultural Warriors of New Mexico
Latin American art from northern New Mexico, including religious carvings, furniture, textiles, and frescoes.
Thru Sept. 19
Me Korero A Tatou Tamariki (Our Children Speak): Maori Photography Exhibit
Black-and-white photography takes visitors on a historical trip through Maori culture.
Jan. 16–Mar. 28
Counter Colon-ialismo
Addresses and interprets the quincentenary of America from an indigenous viewpoint.
Apr. 17, 1993–Apr. 1994
For the Love of It: Albion and Lynne Fenderson Collection of Native American Fine Art
May 15–Sept. 5
The Submoluc Show/Columbus Wohs (...Who's Columbus?)
Thirty-eight American Indian artists respond to the quincentennial Columbus "celebration."

Permanent Collection

Extensive collection of Native American art, jewelry, textiles, ceramics, quillwork, beadwork, baskets; Hispanic traditional arts; African and Oceanic tribal art. **Highlights:** 1,200 kachina dolls from the past 100 years. **Architecture:**

1929 Spanish Colonial Revival building by Herbert Green; 1984 wing following original design.

Admission: Adults, $5; senior citizens 65+, students with ID, $4; juniors 13–18, $3; children 4–12, $2; children under 4, free. Wed., 5–9, free. Handicapped accessible.
Hours: Mon.–Sat., 10–5; Wed., 10–9; Sun., noon–5. Closed holidays.
Tours: Sept.–May: Mon.–Sat., noon, 1:30, 3; Sun., 1:30, 3. June–Aug: Mon.–Fri., 1:30; Sat., 11, 1:30; Sun., 1:30, 3. For group tours, reserve three weeks in advance; call (602) 251-0262.

Phoenix Art Museum

1625 N. Central Ave., Phoenix, Ariz. 85004
(602) 257-1880; 257-1222 (recording)

1993 Exhibitions
Thru Feb. 14
Masterworks of American Impressionism from the Pfeil Collection
More than 100 paintings by three generations of American Impressionists, including Cassatt, Sargent, and lesser-known figures. Catalogue.
Thru Feb. 28
1920s Capes and Cloaks
Thru Mar. 14
The Artist's Hand
Fifty-six contemporary drawings by artists including David Hockney and Claes Oldenburg.
Thru Mar. 21
Russian Boxes
Over 60 lacquer boxes decorated with Russian fairy tales.
Thru May 2
Get a Clue
Offers clues to children and adults on understanding art.
Jan. 9–Mar. 7
The American West: Legendary Artists of the Frontier
Paintings from 1830 to 1930 ranging from the earliest exploration of the American West to the first generation of Taos painters; includes works by Remington, Catlin, and Wyeth.
Mar. 6–May 23
The Art of Seeing: John Ruskin and the Victorian Eye
More than 150 paintings, watercolors, and drawings by such 19th-century artists as Turner, Whistler, and Rossetti.
Mar. 16–Aug. 22
Fans & Fashion
Explores the role of the fan as a fashion accessory.
Mar. 27–May 9
Revelaciones: The Art of Manuel Alvarez Bravo
Features over 100 black-and-white photographs by the artist, taken in Mexico between 1927–1987.

La hija de los danzantes (The Daughter of the Dancers), 1933, Manuel Alvarez Bravo. From "Revelaciones: The Art of Manuel Alvarez Bravo." A traveling exhibition.

Permanent Collection

Exceptional collection of Western American art, including earliest paintings of Arizona (Stanley, *Chains of Spires Along the Gila River*; Hennings, *The Drummers*), works by Remington, Russell. European works from the16th to 19th centuries; contemporary art; Asian art; Thorne Miniature Rooms replicating American and European interiors.
Highlights: Picasso, *Nude Female Bather with Raised Arms*; O'Keeffe, *Pink Abstraction*; costume collection.
Architecture: 1959 building; addition and renovation scheduled for completion in 1995.

Admission: Adults, $4; senior citizens, $3; students, children 6+, $1.50; children under 6, free. Wed., free; donation suggested. Handicapped accessible.
Hours: Tues.–Sat., 10–5; Wed., 10–9; Sun., noon–5. Closed Mon., major holidays.
Tours: Tues.–Sun., 2; Wed. eve., 6. Call (602) 258-5269 at least three weeks in advance for group tours.

Arkansas Arts Center

Ninth & Commerce, Little Rock, Ark.
(501) 372-4000

1993 Exhibitions

Thru Jan. 24
Rodin: Sculpture from the B. Gerald Cantor Collections
Thru Jan. 31
The Sleep of Reason: Reality and Fantasy in the Print Series of Goya
Jan. 2–Feb. 1
The Definitive Contemporary American Quilt
Feb. 4–Feb. 28
James Hicks: A Southern Tour
Feb. 4–Mar. 28
Theodore Roszak: The Drawings
French Drawings from the Permanent Collection
Mar. 4–Mar. 28
23rd Annual Mid-Southern Watercolorists
Mar. 4–Apr. 11
Elaine de Kooning
The first painting retrospective for de Kooning (1919–1989), featuring 70 works. Catalogue.
May 20–July 4
John Newman: Sculpture and Works on Paper
22nd Prints, Drawings, and Photographs Exhibition
Apr. 1–May 16
Songs of My People
The regional traditions and lifestyles of African Americans as recorded on film by 50 black photojournalists in summer 1990. Catalogue.

May 13–July 11
Louis H. Sullivan: Unison with Nature
The artists's architectural features, including chimney caps, door panels, and plates, viewed as works of art.

Permanent Collection
Works by Rembrandt, van Gogh, Degas, Cézanne, Tiepolo Delacroix, and others typefy large collection of Old Master and modern European drawings; 750 American drawings.

Admission: Free. Handicapped accessible.
Hours: Mon.–Sat., 10–5; Sun., noon–5.
Tours: Call (501) 372-4000.
Food & Drink: Vineyard in the Park restaurant open 11:30–1:30, Mon.–Fri.

University Art Museum
University of California, 2626 Bancroft Way, Berkeley, Calif. 94720
(415) 642-0808

1993 Exhibitions
Thru Jan. 31
Hans Hofmann: Selected Works
A survey of works from the 1930s through the 1960s.
Cecilia Vicuña
Installation of sculpture by the Chilean artist.
Thru Feb. 7
Contemporary California Art from the Collection, Part II
Thru Mar. 7
Max Ernst: The Sculpture
Concentrates on the Surrealist artist's metal pieces, reliefs, jewelry, and *Chess Set* of 1929–30. Catalogue.
Jan. 20–mid-Mar.
Edvard Munch and His Models, 1912–1943
Focus on the complex relationship between the artist and his female models during the last 30 years of his life, through watercolors, drawings, and prints.

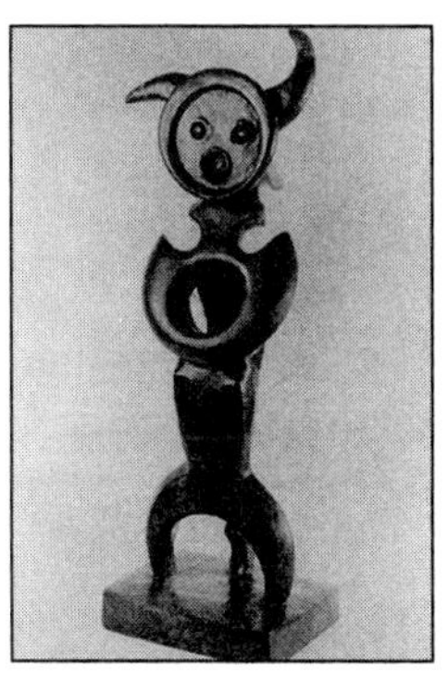

Moonmad, 1944, Max Ernst. From "Max Ernst: The Sculpture." A traveling exhibition.

Feb. 10–Apr. 18
Jonathan Hammer
Examples of the San Francisco artist's bookbinding with a contemporary edge.
Lutz Bacher
An installation by the Berkeley artist entitled *Jim and Sylvia.*
Spring
The University of California's 125th Anniversary Exhibition: Ansel Adams Photographs UC Berkeley
Apr.–June
Linda Roush
A site-specific installation combining light and space art with found objects and everyday materials.

July 7–Sept. 27
Flags of the Fante Asafo
Exhibition of large, brightly colored, appliquéd flags from the Fante Asafo people of south-central Ghana. Catalogue.
Fall
The Moore International I: Terry Fox
Explores the conceptual artist's complex work, which incorporates his identities as avant-garde musician and performance artist. Catalogue.

Permanent Collection

Paintings, photographs, prints, drawings, conceptual art, including 16th- to 19th-century European works by Cézanne, Renoir, Rubens, Bierstadt; Asian art; 20th-century works by Bacon, Calder, Frankenthaler, Rothko, Still; Pacific Film Archive of over 6,000 international films. **Highlights:** Borofsky, *Hammering Man*; Hofmann collection and archive; Modersohn-Becker, *Head of Peasant Woman*; newly opened Asian art galleries; newly installed European and American collections. **Architecture:** 1970 building by Mario Ciampi.

Admission: Adults, $5; senior citizens, students, $4; UC Berkeley students, children under 6, free. Handicapped accessible.
Hours: Wed.–Sun., 11–5. Closed Mon.–Tues., holidays.
Tours: Thurs., Sun. afternoons. Call (415) 642-2403, Mon.–Fri, for reservations.
Food & Drink: Swallow Restaurant open Wed.–Sat., 11–8; Tues., Sun., 11–5. Closed Mon.

Laguna Art Museum

307 Cliff Dr., Laguna Beach, Calif. 92651
(714) 494-6531

1993 Exhibitions

Thru Jan. 17
Concept/Construct: Los Angeles Art and the Photograph, 1960–1980
Influential photography-based works by such artists as John Baldessari, Robert Heinecken, and Ed Ruscha. Catalogue.
Jan. 22–Mar. 28
From Watkins to Weston: 101 Years of California Photography
More than 160 images of the state by three generations of photographers (1849–1950). Catalogue.
Apr. 2–June 13
75 Works, 75 Years: From the Permanent Collection
June 18–Sept. 5
Custom Culture: Von Dutch, "Big Daddy," Robert Williams and their Influence
Focus on the three underground cult figures who were the central progenitors of the custom-car culture.

Sept. 10–Nov. 7
Art in Los Angeles Before 1900
Features works produced by residents and touring artists in Southern California. Catalogue.
Nov. 26, 1993–Jan. 20, 1994
John McLaughlin: A Retrospective
Examines the career of the 20th-century painter. Catalogue.

Permanent Collection

American art, with a particular focus on the development of art in California. Strengths include Southern California between the world wars, early 20th-century photography, contemporary art. **Highlights:** Group of prints by photographers Outerbridge and Hurrell; works by Arnoldi, Brandt, Burkhardt, Dixon, Kauffmann, McLaughlin, Moses, Oliveira, Park, Rose, Ruscha, Teraoka. **Architecture:** 1929 building; 1986 renovation.

Admission: Adults, $3; senior citizens, students with ID, $1.50; members, children under 12, free. Handicapped accessible.
Hours: Tues.–Sun., 11–5. Closed Mon.
Tours: Sun., Tues., Wed., 2. Call (714) 494-8971, Mon.–Fri.

Museum of Contemporary Art, San Diego

700 Prospect St., La Jolla, Calif. 92037
(619) 454-3541

Downtown: 1001 Kettner Blvd., San Diego, Calif. 92101
(619) 234-1001

1993 Exhibitions

NOTE: The museum will close for renovations in late 1993. The downtown location is scheduled to open in Feb. 1993.
Thru Feb. 28
Jana Sterbak: States of Being/Corps á Corps
Canadian artist addresses stereotypical practices associated with food, sex, dress, and the boudoir.
Mar. 5–May 22 (Downtown)
La Frontera/The Border: Art About the Mexican/United States Border Experience
Work in various media by artists who live on, are influenced by, or address the United States–Mexico border, with an emphasis on the San Diego and Tijuana region. Catalogue.
May 28–Aug. 7 (Downtown)
Robert Cumming
Forty works in various media from the mid-1970s to the present, displaying the artist's gently skeptical vision of post-industrial society. Catalogue.

Aug. 13–Oct. 23 (Downtown)
Bill Viola: Slowly Turning Narrative
A new video work exploring the theme of self-annihilation.
Group Material
The New York-based collective of artists will create a new work for this exhibition-project.
Oct. 29, 1993–Jan. 8, 1994 (Downtown)
Edward and Nancy Reddin Kienholz
First U.S. showing of *The Hoerengracht* (1984–88), a large installation by the internationally recognized artists.

Permanent Collection
Twentieth-century holdings spanning a variety of media with particularly strong Minimalist, Pop, Postmodern work. **Highlights:** André, *Magnesium-Zinc Plain*; Kelly, *Red Blue Green*; Ruscha, *Ace*; Oldenburg, *Alphabet* and *Good Humor*; Warhol, *Flowers*; Stella, *Sinjerli I* and *Sabra III*; Long, *Baja California Circle*; Kapoor, *Angel* and *The Healing of St. Thomas*. **Architecture:** 1916 building by Gill; 1959, 1979 expansions by Mosher; 1993 renovation by Venturi. 1993 downtown location is part of America Plaza complex designed by Helmut Jahn; interiors by Robert Irwin and Richard Fleischner.

Admission: Adults, $4; senior citizens, students, $2; children 5–12, 50¢; children under 5 and members, free. Handicapped accessible.
Hours: Tues.–Sun., 10–5; Wed., 10–9; call for downtown location hours.
Tours: Wed., 5:30; Sat.–Sun., 1:30, 2:30; call (619) 454-3541 for group tours.

Los Angeles County Museum of Art

5905 Wilshire Blvd., Los Angeles, Calif. 90036
(213) 857-6111

1993 Exhibitions
Thru Jan. 17
A Mirror of Nature: Dutch Paintings from the Collection of Mr. and Mrs. Edward William Carter
Thirty-six landscapes and still-lifes from the Dutch golden age; includes works by Hendrick Avercamp, Clara Peeters, and Jacob van Ruisdael. Catalogue.
Thru Jan. 24
The Arts of the Persian Court: Selections from the Art and History Trust
Paintings and manuscripts trace the evolution of Persian art from prehistory to the 19th century. Catalogue.
Pleasures and Terrors of Domestic Comfort
Documentary and staged photographs explore the settings, rituals, and moods of domestic experience. Catalogue.

Soap Bubbles, c. 1733–1734, Jean-Siméon Chardin. Los Angeles County Museum of Art.

Thru Feb. 2
When Art Became Fashion: Kosode in Edo-Period Japan
Feb. 18–Apr. 25
Max Weber: The Cubist Decade, 1910–1920
About 70 Cubist still-lifes, figure studies, and New York scenes by this American, who was instrumental in bringing Modernist ideas to the United States.
June 6–Aug. 15
The Ancient Americas: Art from Sacred Landscapes
Approximately 300 objects, focusing on the intellectual and aesthetic structures of ancient civilizations in Mesoamerica, the American Southwest, Central America, and the Andes.
June 17–Aug. 29
Mark Tansey
Retrospective of the career of the New York figurative painter, featuring works from the late 1970s through early 1993.

Permanent Collection

Ancient, Egyptian, Far Eastern, Indian, Southeast Asian art; Islamic art; Pre-Columbian Mexican pottery, textiles; European and American paintings, sculptures, prints, drawings, decorative arts; glass from antiquity to the present; costumes, textiles; photographs. **Highlights:** B. Gerald Cantor Sculpture Garden; Gilbert collection of mosaics and monumental gold and silver; Heeramaneck collection of art from India, Nepal, Tibet; de La Tour, *Magdalen with the Smoking Flame*; Matisse, *Tea*; Rodin bronzes. **Architecture:** 1965 Ahmanson, Bing, and Hammer buildings by William Pereira; 1986 Anderson building and central court by Hardy Holzman Pfeiffer Associates; 1988 Shin'enkan Pavilion for Japanese Art by Goff and Prince.

Admission: Adults, $5; senior citizens, students with ID, $3.50; children 6–17, $1; museum members, children under 6, free. Second Tues. of month, free except for special exhibitions. Handicapped accessible; wheelchairs available.
Hours: Tues.–Thurs., 10–5; Fri, 10–9; Sat.–Sun., 11–6. Closed Mon., Jan. 1, Thanksgiving, Dec. 25.
Tours: Daily. Call (213) 857-6108 for information.
Food & Drink: Plaza Café open Tues.–Thurs., 10–4:30; Fri., 10–8:30; Sat.–Sun., 11–5:30. Times Mirror Central Court Café open seasonally Tues.–Sun., 11–5.

The Museum of Contemporary Art

MOCA at California Plaza
250 S. Grand Ave., Los Angeles, Calif. 90012
(213) 626-6222

MOCA at the Temporary Contemporary
152 N. Central Ave., Los Angeles, Calif. 90013
(213) 626-6222

1993 Exhibitions
NOTE: The Temporary Contemporary is closed and will reopen in spring 1994.
Thru Feb. 7
Focus Series: Wolfgang Laib
Site-specific installation by the German artist. Catalogue.
Thru Mar. 7
Hand-Painted Pop: American Art in Transition, 1955–62
Explores the evolution of Pop Art from the stylistic techniques used by first-generation Abstract Expressionists of the New York School; artists include Jim Dine, Jasper Johns, and Cy Twombly. Catalogue.
Feb. 28–May 30
Louis I. Kahn: In the Realm of Architecture
Drawings, models, and photographs for 60 projects by the American architect. Catalogue.
Mar. 28–May 16
Focus Series: Renée Green
Lee Bontecou
Reexamines the American sculptor's work from the 1960s.
May 30–Aug. 1
Thinking is Form: The Drawings of Joseph Beuys
A range of Beuys' drawings—from highly finished renderings to sketches on the backs of envelopes—that attest to his conception of drawing as a reservoir of ideas. Catalogue.
June 20–Aug. 15
Robert Irwin
Paintings, sculptures, installations, and a site-specific work by this key figure of the Light and Space movement. Catalogue.

Sept. 12–Nov. 28
Rolywholyover: A Circus
A major exhibition, with accompanying performances and events, based on the life of composer, writer, and artist John Cage. Catalogue.
Oct. 24, 1993–Jan. 9, 1994
Roy Lichtenstein
An in-depth survey of the works of one of the most influential artists of the American Pop Art movement and entire postwar era. Catalogue.

Permanent Collection

Art from 1940 to the present, featuring paintings, sculpture, works on paper, photographs, and environmental work of regional and international importance; also explores new art forms combining dance, theater, film, and music.
Highlights: Heizer, *Double Negative*; Kline, *Black Iris*; Rauschenberg, *Interview*; Rothko, *Red & Brown*; Rothenberg, *The Hulk*; Ruscha, *Annie*; Syrop, *Treated and Released*; works by Nevelson, Twombly, Warhol.
Architecture: 1983 Temporary Contemporary warehouse renovation by Frank Gehry; 1986 California Plaza building by Arata Isozaki.

Admission: Adults, $4; senior citizens, students with ID, $2; members, children under 12, prescheduled accredited school groups, free. Thurs., 5–8, free. Handicapped accessible.
Hours: Tues.–Sun., 11–5; Thurs., 11–8. Closed Mon., Jan. 1, Dec. 25.
Tours: California Plaza: Thurs.–Sun., 1, 2.
Food & Drink: Moca Café (MOCA) open Tues.–Fri, 11–4; Sat.–Sun, 11:30–4:30.

Library, Philips Exeter Academy, New Hampshire, 1965–72, Louis I. Kahn. From "Louis I. Kahn: In the Realm of Architecture." A traveling exhibition.

The J. Paul Getty Museum

17985 Pacific Coast Hwy., Malibu, Calif. 90265
(310) 458-2003

1993 Exhibitions

Thru Jan. 17
Art and Science: Joris Hoefnagel and the Representation of Nature in the Renaissance
The artist's extraordinary illuminations for *Mira calligraphiae monumenta* (Model Book of Calligraphy) as seen in the lively context of 16th-century scientific inquiry.

Thru Feb. 21
In the Tomb of Nefertari: Conservation of the Wall Paintings
Explores the six-year conservation process of the wall paintings of the Egyptian tomb; features a full-scale replica of one of the tomb's six chambers.

Thru Feb. 28
Silvy's River Scene*: The Story of a Photograph*
Celebrates the recent acquisition of Camille Silvy's 1858 photograph.

Thru Feb. 28
16th- and 17th-Century Italian Drawings
Drawings from the High Renaissance, Mannerist, and Baroque periods, including works by Raphael, Vasari, and Guercino.

Thru Apr. 11
Early Medieval and Romanesque Manuscripts
A selection of manuscripts from the 9th to 12th centuries.

Feb. 2–Apr. 11
Illuminating the Past: Historical Texts of the Middle Ages and Renaissance

Mar. 2–May 9
Central European Drawings of the 16th and 17th Century

May 17–Aug. 1
Drawings by Giovanni Battista Tiepolo from The Metropolitan Museum of Art

Main peristyle garden, J. Paul Getty Museum.

Permanent Collection

Extensive holdings of Greek and Roman antiquities; pre-20th-century European paintings, drawings, sculpture, illuminated manuscripts, decorative arts; 19th- and 20th-century American and European photographs. **Highlights:** Greek vases, sculpture; French paneled rooms from the time of Louis XIV to the Napoleonic era; Giambologna, *Bathsheba*; Pontormo, *Portrait of Cosimo I de'Medici*; Renoir, *La Promenade*; van Gogh, *Irises*; Rembrandt, *Nude Woman with a Snake (as Cleopatra)*; masterpieces of Ottoman, Romanesque, Gothic illuminated manuscripts; photographs by Alvarez Bravo, Cameron, Evans, Man Ray, Stieglitz, Weston. **Architecture:** 1974 recreation of a first-century Roman country villa with gardens.

Admission: Free; parking by prior reservation; no walk-ins. Call museum daily, 9–5. Handicapped accessible.
Hours: Tues.–Sun., 10–5. Entrance closes at 4:30. Closed Mon., holidays.
Tours: Call (310) 458-2003 for information. In Spanish: (310) 458-1104.
Food & Drink: Garden Tea Room open Tues.–Sun.: light refreshments, 9:30–4:30; lunch, 11–2:30.

Monterey Peninsula Museum of Art

559 Pacific St., Monterey, Calif. 93940
(408) 372-7591

1993 Exhibitions

Continuing
The Collector's Eye: The Barbara and Bill Hyland Collection
Selected Works: William R. Ritschel
Works by Charles M. Russell and Frederic Remington: Permanent Collection
Thru Oct.
Works on Paper: Permanent Collection
Jan. 23–Apr. 18
Photogravures from Cameraworks
Jan. 23–May 9
Long Nguyen: Paintings on Paper
Jan. 25–Mar. 26
Mary Buskirk Textiles
Jan. 30–Apr. 25
Paris Connections: African and Caribbean Artists
Jan. 30–May 2
Wonderful Colors: The Paintings of August Gay
Apr. 6–May 28
Barry Masteller Paintings
Apr. 24–Sept. 26
New Acquisitions

May 1–Sept. 12
John Sexton: Photographs
May 15–Sept. 19
The Crafts of Monterey Bay
May 15–Sept. 26
Ancestral Memories
Aug. 8–Oct. 1
Jef Workman: Mixed Media
Sept. 18, 1993–Jan. 23, 1994
The Solitary Figure
Oct. 1, 1993–Jan. 23, 1994
Takako Yamaguchi: Paintings on Paper
Oct. 1, 1993–Jan. 30, 1994
Julius Hatofsky: Against the Grain
Oct. 1, 1993–Feb. 6, 1994
Ansel Adams: Working Prints of Yosemite

Permanent Collection
American art, with emphasis on regional and California art; Asian and Pacific Rim art; international folk, ethnic, and tribal arts; graphics; photography. **Highlights:** Monterey Peninsula artists including Adams, Bierstadt, Fortune, Gray, Hansen, Keith, Ritschel, Shore, Weston; graphics by Utamaro, Rembrandt, Piranesi, Manet, Picasso, Rauschenberg.

Admission: $2 donation requested. Handicapped accessible.
Hours: Tues.–Sat., 10–4; Sun., 1–4. Closed Mon.
Tours: Sun., 2. Call (408) 372-5477 for special arrangements.

Newport Harbor Art Museum

850 San Clemente Dr., Newport Beach, Calif. 92660
(714) 759-1122

1993 Exhibitions
Thru Feb. 14
Ralph Eugene Meatyard: An American Visionary
A retrospective featuring 125 black-and-white photographs by this American photographer, who pioneered "no-focus" shots and arranged tableaux.
Thru Feb. 21
El Corazón Sangrante/The Bleeding Heart
The bleeding heart is a recurrent motif in Mexican history. This show explores the heritage of contemporary Mexican, Chicano, and Cuban artists.
Mar. 6–May 2
New California Art

Mar. 6–May 9
**American Abstraction at the Addison Gallery of American Art*
Celebrates a 60-year commitment to non-objective art; 90 works in a variety of media by 70 noted artists.
May 6–June 6
New Acquisitions: Beyond the Bay

Permanent Collection
Post-1945 California art. **Highlights:** Work by Baldessari, Bengston, Burden, Celmins, Diebenkorn, Goode, Ruscha; room-size installations by Burden, Kienholz, Stone, Viola.
Architecture: Opened in 1977; 1994 building planned.

Admission: Adults, $4; senior citizens and students, $2; children under 12, free. Handicapped accessible.
Hours: Tues.–Sun., 10–5; July–Aug.: Fri., 10–8.
Tours: Tues.–Fri., 12:15, 1:15; Sat.–Sun., 2. Call (714) 759-1122 for group tours.
Food & Drink: Sculpture Garden Café open Mon.–Fri., 11:30–2:30.

The Oakland Museum

1000 Oak St., Oakland, Calif. 94607
(510) 238-3401; 834-2413 (recording)

1993 Exhibitions
Thru Jan. 10
Between Two Worlds: The People of the Border
More than 70 black-and-white photographs by Don Barteletti, documenting immigrants in shantytowns along the U.S.-Mexican border.
Seeing Straight: The f.64 Revolution in Photography
Eighty works by group members including Ansel Adams, Imogen Cunningham, and Edward Weston, who searched for "observable essence" through their sharp-focus images.

Blossom, 1931, Sonya Noskowiak. From "Seeing Straight: The f.64 Revolution in Photography." A traveling exhibition.

Jan. 9–Mar. 28
Carmen Lomas Garza: Pedacito de mi Corazón (A Little Piece of My Heart)
This Bay Area narrative artist portrays Mexican-American life during her South Texas childhood.
Jan. 30–Mar. 7
Songs of My People
The regional traditions and lifestyles of African Americans as recorded on film by 50 black photojournalists in summer 1990. Catalogue.
Feb. 27–May 23
The Arts and Crafts Movement in California: Living the Good Life
About 200 objects, including art pottery, architectural elements and renderings, furniture, and textiles.

June 26–Sept. 12
Imogen Cunningham: Ideas Without End
More than 80 works spanning the 70-year career of the photographer, internationally known for her fine-art photography and as a member of Group f.64.
Sept. 11, 1993–Mar. 20, 1994
To See the Sea: The Underwater Vision of Al Giddings
Retrospective of the marine explorer's underwater film and still photography.
Oct. 23, 1993–Feb. 6, 1994
Raymond Saunders: New Work
Mixed-media installation by the East Bay artist.

Permanent Collection
Three galleries in one museum: **Gallery of California Art** contains works in all media by California artists or artists dealing with California themes; **Cowell Hall of California History** features Indian arts (prehistoric to Colonial), the Spanish-Mexican period, the American period, and the 20th century; and the **Hall of California Ecology** depicts the interrelated life activites of plants and animals. This guide lists art exhibitions. **Architecture:** 1969 building by Roche, Dinkeloo & Associates.

Admission: Free. Fee for selected exhibitions. Handicapped accessible.
Hours: Wed.–Sat., 10–5; Sun., noon–7. Closed Mon.–Tues., Jan. 1, July 4, Thanksgiving, Dec. 25.
Tours: Weekday afternoons; weekends upon request. Call (510) 238-3514 for information.
Food & Drink: Museum Café open Wed.–Sat., 10–4; Sun., noon–5.
Branch: Oakland Museum Sculpture Court at City Center, 1111 Broadway, Oakland.

Norton Simon Museum
411 W. Colorado Blvd., Pasadena, Calif. 91105
(818) 449-6840; 449-3730

1993 Exhibitions
Thru Jan. 17
The Painter-Printmaker and the Art of Book Illustration
European and American etchings and lithographs created for the purpose of book illustration.
Thru Mar. 14
Sculpture in Two Dimensions: The Prints of Moore and Nevelson
Works on paper by two of the century's leading sculptors.

Thru May 9
Eugène Bléry: Views of the French Countryside
Prints by the artist that portray the countryside of Central France.
Lewis Baltz: The Tract Houses
Twenty-five photographs from the artist's series examining a complex of prefab houses under construction.
Thru July 18
The Nabis
Paintings, prints, sculpture, and furniture created by the Nabis and their circle; artists include Denis, Bonnard, and Maillol.

Permanent Collection

European art from the Renaissance through the 20th century, including works by Raphael, Lippi, Rembrandt, Zurbarán, Goya, Monet, Degas, van Gogh, Picasso, Klee, Kandinsky; sculpture from the Indian Subcontinent and Southeast Asia; sculpture garden. **Highlights:** Raphael, *Madonna*; Zurbarán, *Still Life with Lemons, Oranges, and a Rose*; Dieric Bouts, *Resurrection of Christ*; Manet, *Ragpicker*. **Architecture:** 1969 building by Ladd and Kelsey.

Admission: Adults, $4; senior citizens and students, $2; members and children under 12, free. Handicapped accessible.
Hours: Thurs.–Sun., noon–6. Closed Mon.–Wed., Jan. 1, Thanksgiving.
Tours: Call (818) 449-6840 for information.

L'Espeigle (The Flute Player), Rembrandt. Norton Simon Museum.

Crocker Art Museum

216 O St., Sacramento, Calif. 95814
(916) 264-5423

1993 Exhibitions

Thru Jan. 10
Fables and Fantasies: The Art of Felix Lorieux
First exhibition of the French children's book illustrator outside of France.
Thru Jan. 17
Table Manners
Scenes of eating and drinking from the museum's collection of 16th- and 17th-century Dutch and Flemish drawings.
Jan. 10–Mar. 7
**Ceramic Figures from Ancient America*
More than 150 miniatures, dating as early as 3500 B.C., from Mexico, Guatemala, Costa Rica, Venezuela, Ecuador, and Peru.
Jan. 21–Apr. 4
Galeria Posada
Celebrates the 20th anniversary of Galeria Posada/La Raza Bookstore.
Apr. 2–May 23
68th Annual Crocker-Kingsley Open Art Exhibition
Apr. 9–June 13
French Prints
A selection of prints from the museum's collection, recreating the Belle Époque of late–19th-century France; works by Charles Daubigny, Mary Cassatt, Berthe Morisot, and others.
June 11–Aug. 8
Greg Kondos: A Retrospective
Paintings and works on paper by the Sacramento-area artist.
June 18–Aug. 22
Olivia Parker
A 1970 portfolio of the artist's photographs recently donated to the museum, juxtaposed with her recent works.
Aug. 20–Oct. 17
Chiura Obata: Yosemite Views
Works documenting the artist's experience in Yosemite in 1927, and the subsequent transformation of paintings into woodblock prints by Japanese artists between 1928 and 1930.
Aug. 27–Oct. 31
Master Drawings
Nov. 5–Dec. 30
Free Within Ourselves: African-American Art from the National Museum of American Art
Showcases works from one of the premier collections of African-American art.

Permanent Collection

Old Master paintings; 19th-century California art; 19th-century German painting; Northern California art since 1945; American Victorian furniture and decorative arts, photography, Asian art; arts of the Americas. **Highlights:** Hill, *Great Canyon of the Sierras, Yosemite*; Nahl, *Sunday Morning in the Mines* and *The Fandango*; Thiebaud, *Boston Cremes*. **Architecture:** 1873 Crocker Art Gallery by Seth Babson; 1969 Herold wing; 1989 Crocker mansion wing by Edward Larrabee Barnes.

Admission: Adults, $3; children 7–17, $1.50; children 6 and under, free. Handicapped accessible.
Hours: Wed.–Sun., 10–5. Closed Mon., Tues., major holidays.
Tours: By reservation. Call (916) 264-5537 or 264-5423, Mon.–Fri., 10–noon.

San Diego Museum of Art

1450 El Prado, Balboa Park, San Diego, Calif. 92101
(619) 232-7931

1993 Exhibitions

Thru Jan. 31
Pacific Parallels: Artists and the Landscape in New Zealand
Commemorates New Zealand's sesquicentennial celebration.
Feb. 13–Mar. 28
NCECA Clay National Juried Exhibition
San Diego Crafts
Apr. 29–May 1
Art Alive
June 12–Sept. 26
The William S. Paley Collection
Paintings, drawings, and sculpture by Bonnard, Cézanne, Degas, Gauguin, Matisse, Toulouse-Lautrec, and others. Catalogue.
June–July
Artist Guild Open Exhibition
Sept.–Nov.
Helen Frankenthaler
Oct.–Dec.
Bruno Shultz

Permanent Collection

European painting and sculpture from the Renaissance to the 20th century, including notable Italian Renaissance, Dutch, and Spanish Baroque works; American paintings by Chase, Eakins, Homer, O'Keeffe, Peale; Indian and Persian paintings; Asian art, including Buddhist sculptures and ritual bronzes, Japanese prints; largest collection of contemporary California art. **Highlights:** Beckmann, *Moon Landscape*;

ter Borch, *The Love Letter*; Bougereau, *The Young Shepherdess*; Braque, *Still Life*; Rembrandt, *Young Man with a Cock's Feather in His Cap*; Rubens, *Allegory of Eternity*; Sanchez Cotán, *Quince, Cabbage, Melon, and Cucumber*; sculpture garden with works by Hepworth, Moore, Rickey, Rodin. **Architecture:** 1926 Spanish Colonial Plateresque–style building by William Templeton Johnson and Robert W. Snyder.

Admission: Adults, $5; seniors, $4; military, $3; students with ID, children 6–17, $2; children under 6, free. Handicapped accessible.
Hours: Tues.–Sun., 10–4:30. Closed Mon., Jan. 1, Thanksgiving, Dec. 25.
Tours: Tues.–Thurs., 10, 11, 1, 2; Fri.–Sun., 1, 2. Call (619) 232-7931 for information.
Food & Drink: Sculpture Garden Café open Tues.–Sun. Call (619) 232-7931, ext. 250.

Ansel Adams Center for Photography

250 Fourth St., San Francisco, Calif. 94103
(415) 495-7000

1993 Exhibitions

Thru Jan. 17
Flesh and Blood: Photographers' Images of Their Families
Photographers, including David Hockney, Sally Mann, and Emmet Gowin, photographing their own families.
Open Space/John Wilson White
The contemporary artist's installation, focusing on the water-delivery system of San Francisco.
Thru Feb. 14
Ansel Adams Portraits
Jan. 27–Mar. 14
Annie Leibovitz: Photographs 1970–1990
Images spanning the photographer's career, from early black-and-white portraits for *Rolling Stone* to recent advertising work.
George Hurrell
Celebrity portraits by photographer Hurrell, whose career spanned the 1930s to the 1980s.
Feb. 18–Apr. 25
Yosemite before Ansel Adams
Nineteenth-century precursors to Adams' images of Yosemite; artists include Eadweard Muybridge and Carleton Watkins.
Apr. 29–Sept. 5
Yosemite after Ansel Adams
Scenes of Yosemite today, from works by Bruce Davidson to fashion photography shot on-site.

Mar. 19–Apr. 25
Body Doubles
Recent work by David Levinthal and Cindy Sherman, together with Surrealist vintage prints by Hans Belmer.
May 5–June 13
Constantin Brancusi
The artist's self-portraits and photos of his sculpture.
June 23–Aug. 22
Concept/Construct: Los Angeles Art and the Photograph, 1960–1980
Influential photography-based works by such artists as John Baldessari, Robert Heinecken, and Ed Ruscha. Catalogue.

Permanent Collection
Over 130 vintage Ansel Adams prints; historic and contemporary photographic work. **Highlights:** *Moonrise, Hernandez, New Mexico*; *Clearing Winter Storm*; *Yosemite National Park, California*. **Architecture:** 1989 building by Robinson, Mills & Williams Architectural Firm.

Admission: Adults, $4; students, $3; senior citizens, children 12–17, $2; members, children under 12, free. Handicapped accessible.
Hours: Tues.–Sun., 11–6. Closed Mon.
Tours: Sat., 1:15; call (415) 495-7000 for information.

Asian Art Museum of San Francisco

The Avery Brundage Collection
Golden Gate Park, San Francisco, Calif. 94118
(415) 668-8921

1993 Exhibitions
Thru Jan. 4
Brushstrokes: Styles and Techniques of Chinese Painting
Paintings, ceramics, jades, and hand scrolls from China, Japan, and Tibet. Catalogue.
Thru Mar. 14
Beauty, Wealth, and Power: Jewels and Ornaments of Asia
About 250 ornaments, from earrings to eating sets, from Mongolia to Southeast Asia, used for adornment in both life and death. Many have never before been displayed.

Permanent Collection
Art of China, Japan, Korea, India, Southeast Asia, India, the Himalayas; sculptures, paintings, bronzes, jades, ceramics, textiles, decorative objects, architectural elements representing all stylistic movements of Asian art.
Highlights: Newly reinstalled Chinese, Indian, Korean galleries displaying objects from the permanent collection; oldest-known dated Chinese Buddha (338 A.D.); largest collection of Gandharan sculpture in North America; collection of Japanese *netsuke* and *inro*.

Manchu woman's headdress, Qing dynasty, late 19th c. From "Beauty, Wealth, and Power: Jewels and Ornaments of Asia." Asian Art Museum of San Francisco.

Admission: Adults, $5; senior citizens, $3; children 12–17, $2; children under 12, free. Handicapped accessible; wheelchairs available.
Hours: Wed.–Sun., 10–5. Closed Mon.–Tues., some holidays.
Tours: Six tours daily; call (415) 750-3638 for reservations.

The Fine Arts Museums of San Francisco

California Palace of the Legion of Honor
Lincoln Park, near 34th Ave. & Clement St., San Francisco, Calif. 94121
(415) 863-3330 (recording)

The M. H. de Young Memorial Museum
Golden Gate Park, Eighth Ave. & JFK Dr., San Francisco, Calif. 94118
(415) 863-3330 (recording)

1993 Exhibitions

NOTE: The Legion of Honor is closed until Apr. 1994 for renovations and expansion.

Thru Jan. 3
Dior's Basic Black
Six ensembles by fashion designer Christian Dior from 1949 through 1956 from the permanent collection.

Thru Feb. 14
The Still-Life Paintings of William M. Harnett
Approximately 50 works—including the renowned group of four paintings, After the Hunt—by this late–19th–century American trompe l'oeil master. Catalogue.

Thru June 27
Unravelling the Yarns: The Art of Everyday Life
Explores how textiles document the art and culture of a society; includes nomad and village weavings from the Far East and Central Asia, 20th-century Pygmy bark cloths from Central Africa, and Pre-Columbian textiles.

Jan. 20–May 30
Viewpoints XX: Louis Comfort Tiffany and Art Glass from Europe and the United States
Features art glass by Tiffany and other major European glass factories of the late-19th and early 20th centuries.
May 26–Oct. 31
City of the Gods: Teotihuacan
Two hundred objects, including stone sculptures, figurines, and painted wall murals, from the most visited archaeological site in Mexico. Catalogue.
Sept. 15, 1993–Jan. 2, 1994
Jacob Lawrence: The Frederick Douglass and Harriet Tubman Series of Narrative Paintings
African-American artist Lawrence's 1938–1940 paintings depicting the lives of abolitionists. The 63 works here reflect his concern with the human struggle. Catalogue.

Permanent Collection

Outstanding holdings in American paintings, sculpture and decorative arts. Arts of Oceania, Africa, the Americas; jewelry from the ancient world; Egyptian mummies.
Highlights: American paintings by Bingham, Cassatt, Church, Copley, Harnett, Sargent; Revere silver.
Architecture: 1921 building by Mullgardt.

Admission: Both museums: adults, $5; senior citizens, $3; students 12–17, $2; children under 12, free. First Wed. and Sat. of month, 10–noon, free.
Hours: Wed.–Sun., 10–5. Closed Mon.–Tues.
Tours: Call (415) 750-3638.
Food & Drink: Café de Young and Café Chanticleer open Wed.–Sun., 10–4.

Ease, 1887, William M. Harnett. From "The Still-Life Paintings of William M. Harnett." A traveling exhibition.

San Francisco Museum of Modern Art

401 Van Ness Ave., San Francisco, Calif. 94102
(415) 252-4000

1993 Exhibitions

Thru Jan. 24
Richard Diebenkorn
Works include the artist's early abstractions from 1948 to 1955, works from his Bay Area Figurative period (1955–67), and selections from his "Ocean Park" series.

Thru Feb. 7
Jeff Koons
Comprehensive presentation featuring 65 mixed-media sculpture and wall pieces by the controversial contemporary artist. Catalogue.
California Graphic Designers
Details the evolution of California's design community, featuring the work of four acclaimed designers.

Feb. 25–Apr. 11
On Kawara: Date Paintings in 89 Cities
Retrospective of the Japanese-American artist with paintings from each of the 89 cities in which he has worked.

Mar. 3–June 6
Shin Takamatsu

Mar. 25–June 13
Clyfford Still: The Buffalo & San Francisco Collections
Brings together two collections of the abstract painter's work; features masterpieces from 1936 to 1963. Catalogue.

Apr. 29–July 25
Richard Prince

May 6–July 11
Thresholds and Enclosures

June 10–Aug. 4
Carrie Mae Weems
Photographs and installations reveal the artist's use of photographic imagery and text to comment on issues of identity, race, gender, and class. Catalogue.

Deuce, 1954, Stuart Davis. San Francisco Museum of Modern Art.

July 22–Sept. 19
John Heartfield: Photomontages
Over 100 works from 1930 to 1939 by the German artist.
Sept. 9–Nov. 28
Cady Noland: New Work
Sept. 10–Dec. 15
Max Beckmann Prints from the Collection of The Museum of Modern Art
One-third of the artist's graphic works is represented, capturing dramatic high points in 20th-century art.

Permanent Collection

Twentieth-century works of international scope in all media. **Highlights:** Gorky, *Enigmatic Combat*; Matisse, *The Girl with Green Eyes*; Pollock, *Guardians of the Secret*; Rauschenberg, *Collection*; Rivera, *The Flower Carrier*; Tanguy, *Second Thoughts*; paintings by Bay Area artists Diebenkorn, Neri, Oliveira, Thiebaud; exceptional selection of photographs by Adams, Stieglitz, Weston. **Architecture:** Located in San Francisco War Memorial Veterans Building; new building by Mario Botta scheduled for 1995 completion.

Admission: Adults, $4; senior citizens, students, $2; children under 13, free. Thurs., 5–9, reduced admission. First Tues. of each month, free. Handicapped accessible.
Hours: Tues.–Fri., 10–5; Thurs., 10–9; Sat.–Sun., 11–5. Closed Mon., Jan. 1, Thanksgiving, Dec. 25.
Tours: Call (415) 252-4096 for information.

The Huntington

Library, Art Collections, and Botanical Gardens
1151 Oxford Rd., San Marino, Calif. 91108
(818) 405-2141

Snowy Owl, in *The Birds of America*, 1785–1851, John James Audubon. The Huntington.

1993 Exhibitions

Thru Apr. 25
The Legacy of the Wilderness: Photographs by Robert Glenn Ketchum
Retrospective of work by the Los Angeles environmentalist-photographer, from 1960 to the present.
Thru Apr.
Beyond the Western Star: Conflicting Visions of the American West
Original manuscripts, diaries, drawings, and rare books document the history of westward movement.
Apr.–Aug.
British Mezzotints from the Permanent Collection
May–Aug.
Constructing the Heavens
Examines changing conceptions of the universe through manuscripts, rare books, and photographs.

Sept. 1993–Feb. 1994
The Age of Hogarth
A satirical look at 18th-century politics and society as observed by the British painter and engraver.
Sept. 1993–Aug. 1994
"The Last Best Hope of Earth": Abraham Lincoln and the Promise of America
Large exhibition on Lincoln drawn from the Huntington and other collections.

Permanent Collection
Library collection of rare books, manuscripts from the 11th century to the present; Renaissance paintings and bronzes; important 17th-century works by Claude, Van Dyck; 18th-century French paintings by Boucher, Nattier, Watteau; British 18th- and 19th-century painting; European decorative arts; 18th- to 20th-century American art by Cassatt, Copley, Hopper; decorative art objects by California architects Greene & Greene. **Highlights:** Cassatt, *Breakfast in Bed*; Church, *Chimborazo*; Constable, *View on the Stour*; Gainsborough, *The Blue Boy*; Hopper, *The Long Leg*; Lawrence, *Pinkie*; Van der Weyden, *Madonna and Child*; Gutenberg Bible; Chaucer's *Canterbury Tales*; early editions of Shakespeare; letters and papers of the Founding Fathers; botanical gardens including the Japanese, Desert, Rose, Jungle gardens. **Architecture:** 1909–11 Huntington mansion by Hunt and Grey; 1984 Scott Gallery of American Art by Warner and Grey.

Admission: Donation suggested: adults, $5; children and students, $3. Handicapped accessible.
Hours: Tues.–Fri., 1–4:30; Sat.–Sun., 10:30–4:30. Closed Mon., holidays.
Tours: Garden tours, Tues.–Sun. For group-tour reservations call (818) 405-2127.
Food & Drink: Patio Restaurant open Tues.–Fri., 1–4; Sat.–Sun., 11–4. English tea: Tues.–Fri., 1–3:30; Sat.–Sun., noon–3:30. For reservations call (818) 584-9337.

Santa Barbara Museum of Art
1130 State St., Santa Barbara, Calif. 93101
(805) 963-4364

1993 Exhibitions
Thru Jan. 17
Santa Barbara's Own: The Architecture of Lutah Maria Riggs
Twenty Montecito and Los Angeles projects by the female architect, who made a significant contribution to the Spanish Colonial Revival style.

Thru Jan. 24
Mexican Colonial Paintings: From the Old World to the New
Works from the invasion of Mexico by Cortés in 1519 to Mexican independence in 1921.
Thru Feb. 7
Cambios: The Spirit of Transformation in Spanish Colonial Art
Religious painting, silver, sculpture, textiles, and other objects from the Colonial period (1521–1850).
Feb. 9–Mar. 28
Ed Moses: Two Decades of Works on Paper
Retrospective of the career of the contemporary California abstract painter.
Feb. 13–Apr. 25
Brushstrokes: Styles and Techniques of Chinese Painting
Paintings, ceramics, jades, and hand scrolls from China, Japan, and Tibet. Catalogue.
Feb.–Apr.
Egypt Through the Lens
More than 30 works dating from the 1850s that capture the wonders of Egypt.
Mar. 6–May 30
Auguste Rodin: Selections from the Fine Arts Museums of San Francisco
More than 80 sculptures in plaster, terracotta, marble, and bronze; works include *The Thinker.*
Apr. 22–July 8
Seeing Straight: The f.64 Revolution in Photography
Eighty works by group members including Ansel Adams, Imogen Cunningham, and Edward Weston, who searched for "observable essence" through their sharp-focus images.
June 26–Sept. 5
Werner Bischof, 1916–1954
Comprehensive exhibition of 152 photographs takes the viewer on a journey to India, Japan, Korea, and other locations.

Farmer's Inn in the Puszta, Hungary, 1947, Werner Bischof. From "Werner Bischof, 1916–1954." A traveling exhibition.

Oct. 9, 1993–Jan. 3, 1994
The Splendid Century: 18th- and 19th-Century French Paintings from the Fine Arts Museums of San Francisco

Permanent Collection
Houses more than 15,000 works; important holdings of American and Asian art, classical antiquities, European paintings, 19th-century French art, 20th-century art, photography, works on paper. **Architecture:** 1914 Neoclassical building by John Taylor Knox; 1941 redesign by David Adler; 1991 addition by Paul Gray.

Admission: Adults, $3; children 6–16, $1.50; children under 6, free. Thurs. and first Sun. of the month, free. Handicapped accessible.
Hours: Tues., Wed., 11–5; Thurs., 11–9; Fri., Sat., 11–5; Sun., noon–5.
Tours: Tues.–Sun., 1; focus tours on changing subjects, selected Wed., noon; Spanish-English tours on changing subjects one Sat. a month, 3. Call (805) 963-4364.

Stanford University Museum of Art

Window, 1967, Richard Diebenkorn. Stanford University Museum of Art.

Lomita Dr. & Museum Way, Stanford, Calif. 94305-5060
(415) 723-4177

1993 Exhibitions
NOTE: The museum is temporarily closed due to damage suffered in the 1989 earthquake. Exhibitions continue in the T. W. Stanford Art Gallery near Hoover Tower.
Jan. 12–Apr. 25
Frank Lobdell: Selected Works, 1947–1991
Catalogue.
Jan. 26–Apr. 25
William Trost Richards: A Selection
July 6–Oct. 3
Edward Weston/Ansel Adams: Personal Porfolios
Oct. 19–Dec. 12
Nuclear Enchantment: Photographs by Patrick Nagatani

Permanent Collection
Closed except for Rodin sculpture garden and outdoor art. **Architecture:** 1890–94 building by Percy & Hamilton; modeled on the National Museum of Athens.

Admission: Free. Partial handicapped facilities.
Hours: Tues.–Fri., 10–5; Sat.–Sun., 1–5. Closed Mon., holidays.
Tours: Call (415) 723-3469.

Denver Art Museum

100 W. 14th Ave. Pkwy., Denver, Colo. 80204
(303) 640-2793

1993 Exhibitions

NOTE: Renovated galleries reopen Feb. 6, 1993.
Thru Jan. 10
Joellyn Duesberry
Works by the Colorado landscape painter.
Thru Oct. 17
Sze Hong—Ritual Offerings: Early Chinese Art
Ceramics and bronzes from the Neolithic period through the Tang dynasty, emphasizing the role of the object in rituals.
Feb. 13–Mar. 6
A Mighty Fortress: The Denver Art Museum
Focuses on the museum's building as a work of art.

The Immaculate Conception Surrounded by Angels, 1590–1620, Baltasar de Echeva Ibia. Denver Art Museum.

Permanent Collection

Holdings of ancient to contemporary art. Extensive North American Indian collection, African, Oceanic, Northwest Coast, Eskimo arts; Renaissance and Baroque painting; 19th- and early 20th-century painting; period rooms of English Tudor, Spanish Baroque, French Gothic styles; art of the American West; Neusteter Gallery of costumes and textiles. **Highlights:** Remington, *The Cheyenne*; O'Keeffe, *Petunia and Glass Bottle*; Farny, *Laramie Creek.* **Architecture:** 1971 building by Ponti and Sudler; 1988 Native American gallery; 1989 Western and American art galleries; 1993 Pre-Columbian, Spanish Colonial, and Asian galleries.

Admission: Adults, $3; senior citizens, students, $1.50; children under 5, free. Sat., free. Handicapped accessible.
Hours: Tues.–Sat., 10–5; Sun., noon–5. Closed Mon., major holidays.
Tours: Tues.–Sat., 10:30, 1:30; Sun., 1:30. Call (303) 640-2794 for arranged tours.
Food & Drink: Museum Café open Tues.–Sat., 11–2.

Wadsworth Atheneum

600 Main St., Hartford, Conn. 06103
(203) 278-2670; 247-9111 (recording)

1993 Exhibitions

Thru Jan. 3
"The Spirit of Genius": Art at the Wadsworth Atheneum
The history of the museum told through works and documents from the collection.
Thru Jan. 3; Feb. 2–28
Facing the Rising Sun, 1842–1992: 150 Years of the African-American Experience
Works from the Amistead Foundation Collection, which contains over 6,000 documents, books, photographs, and objects that chronicle the lives of African Americans.

Thru Jan. 10
Free Within Ourselves: African-American Art from the National Museum of American Art
Showcases works from one of the premier collections of African-American art.
Thru Feb. 7
Ball Gowns: Bravo! Brava!
Women's gowns from the museum collection.
Feb. 7–Apr. 4
Portsmouth Furniture: Masterworks from the New Hampshire Seacoast
Introduces the viewer to aspects of furniture style, production, and culture in 18th-century Portsmouth; features 12 Hadley chests.
May 9–Aug. 8
Motion and Document—Sequence and Time: Eadweard Muybridge and Contemporary American Photography
Traces the influence of the 19th-century photographer's ideas and experimental working methods on other artists. Catalogue.

A Boy with a Hat, 1656, Michael Sweerts. Wadsworth Atheneum.

Permanent Collection

Sixteenth- and 17th-century Old Master, Hudson River School, and Impressionist paintings; Nutting Collection of Pilgrim-century furniture and two restored period rooms; African-American, 20th-century art. **Highlights:** Caravaggio, *Ecstasy of Saint Francis;* landscapes by Church, Cole; Goya, *Gossiping Women*; Pollock, *Number 9*; Rembrandt, *Portrait of a Young Man*; Renoir, *Monet Painting in His Garden at Argenteuil*; Zurbarán, *Saint Serapion.* **Architecture:** 1844 Neo-Gothic Wadsworth building by Davis; 1907 Tudor-style Colt Memorial; 1907 Renaissance Revival Morgan Memorial; 1934 Avery Memorial with International-style interior; 1969 Goodwin building.

Admission: Adults, $3; senior citizens, students, $1.50; members and children under 13, free. Thurs., free. Sat., 11–1, free. Handicapped accessible.
Hours: Tues.–Sun., 11–5. Closed Mon., holidays.
Tours: Thurs., 1; Sat.–Sun., 2. Call (203) 278-2670, ext. 323.
Food & Drink: Museum Café open Tues.–Fri., 11:30–2:30; Sat.–Sun., noon–3. For reservations, call (203) 728-5989.

Yale Center for British Art

1080 Chapel St., New Haven, Conn. 06520
(203) 432-2800

1993 Exhibitions

Thru Jan. 31
Martin Naylor
Feb. 27–Apr. 25
Sir Thomas Lawrence: Portrait of an Age, 1790–1830
About 50 paintings and 20 drawings by the leading society portraitist of the Regency age. Catalogue.
Sept. 21–Nov. 28
Horatio Ross
Oct. 2–Dec. 5
Turner Prints

Permanent Collection

The most comprehensive collection of English paintings, drawings, and rare books outside Great Britain. Focuses on British art, life, and thought beginning with the Elizabethan period; emphasis on work created between the birth of Hogarth in 1697 and the death of Turner in 1851, considered the golden age of English art. **Highlights:** Constable, *Hadleigh Castle*; Gainsborough, *The Gravenor Family*; Reynolds, *Mrs. Abington as Miss Prue in Congreve's "Love for Love"*; Rubens, *Peace Embracing Plenty*; Stubbs, *A Lion Attacking a Horse*; Turner, *Dort or Dor-drecht: The Dort Packet-Boat from Rotterdam Becalmed.* **Architecture:** 1977 building by Louis I. Kahn.

Admission: Free. Handicapped accessible.
Hours: Tues.–Sat., 10–5; Sun., noon–5. Closed Mon., Jan. 1, July 4, Thanksgiving, Dec. 24–25, 31.
Tours: Scheduled Tues.–Fri. between 10–4; call (203) 432-2858.

Yale University Art Gallery

1111 Chapel St. at York, New Haven, Conn. 06520
(203) 432-0600

1993 Exhibitions

Thru Jan. 3
Discovered Lands, Invented Places: Transforming Visions of the American West
Examines the interplay between discovery, invention, and erasure in artists' depictions of the exploration and settlement of America. Ninety works by such artists as Catlin, Bierstadt, Remington, O'Keeffe, Church, Cole, and Hartley. Catalogue.

Jan. 5–Mar. 7
At the Dragon Court: Chinese Embroidered Mandarin Squares from the Schuyler V.R. Camman Collection
Over 100 large embroidered badges of rank sewn onto officials' robes during the Ming and Qing dynasties.
Prints, Drawings, and Photographs: Recent Acquisitions
Feb. 6–Apr. 11
The Cosmic Dancer: Shiva Nataraja
Fifty objects centering around one of the great masterpieces of Indian bronze sculpture, a late–10th-century dancing Shiva.
Apr. 3–July 31
A Private View: Small Paintings in the Manoogian Collection
Masterpieces include informal portraits by Sargent, genre scenes by Millet, and still-lifes by Harnett. Catalogue.
Apr. 30–July 31
Yale Collects Yale
Contemporary painting and sculpture by graduates of Yale Art School, from the collections of Yale alumni.
Sept. 4–Nov. 21
South of the Border: Mexico in the American Imagination, 1917–1947
Works by American and Mexican artists from the three decades between the Mexican Revolution and World War II; includes paintings by Motherwell, Hartley, and Rivera. Catalogue.
Dec. 1993–Mar. 1994
Colonial Massachusetts Silversmiths
Charles Demuth: Poster Portraits, 1923–29

Permanent Collection

Works from ancient Egyptian dynasties to the present. Asian art, including Japanese screens, ceramics, prints; artifacts from ancient Dura-Europos; Italian Renaissance art; 19th- and 20th-century European paintings; early modern works by Kandinsky, Léger, Picasso; American art through the 20th century, featuring paintings, sculptures, furniture, silver, pewter. **Highlights:** Reconstructed Mithraic shrine; Van Gogh, *The Night Café*; Malevich, *The Knife Grinder*; Smibert, *The Bermuda Group*; Trumbull, *The Declaration of Independence*; contemporary sculpture by Moore, Nevelson, Smith. **Architecture:** 1928 Italianate building by Edgerton Swartout; 1953 building by Louis I. Kahn.

Admission: Free. Handicapped accessible.
Hours: Tues.–Sat., 10–5; Sun., 2–5. Closed Aug.
Tours: Call (203) 432-0620 for information.

Delaware Art Museum

2301 Kentmere Pkwy., Wilmington, Del. 19806
(302) 571-9590

1993 Exhibitions
Thru Feb. 7
19th Century Watercolors from the Collections of the National Gallery of Canada and Mellon Bank
A survey of works by 60 British watercolorists working between 1770 and 1913.
Focus on Found
Focus on the famous painting by Pre-Raphaelite painter Dante Gabriel Rossetti.
Jan. 29–Mar. 14
Fables and Fantasies: The Art of Felix Lorieux
First exhibition of the French children's book illustrator outside of France.
Apr. 16–18
Art in Bloom
Apr. 30–June 27
This Sporting Life, 1878–1991
Survey of sports photography, featuring nearly 200 works by such artists as Adams, Avedon, and Eakins, as well as photojournalists.
Apr. 30–July 11
The Artist and the Baseball Card
Over 100 of the country's top illustrators' and designers' personal, large-format interpretations of a baseball card.
May 7–Oct. 31
Peaches at an Exhibition: A Centennial Celebration of Delaware Artists at Chicago's 1893 World Columbian Exposition
July 9–Sept. 5
Biennial '93
Dec. 10, 1993–Feb. 6, 1994
Quilt National '93
Presents the latest innovations in quilt design and reinterpretations of traditional techniques.

The Buccaneer Was a Picturesque Fellow, 1905, Howard Pyle. Delaware Art Museum.

Permanent Collection

American painting from 1840 to the present by Beal, Church, Davies, Doughty, Eakins, Hassam, Henri, Homer, Hopper, Pyle, Sloan, the Wyeth family. Pre-Raphaelite paintings by Burne-Jones, Hunt, Millais, Rossetti, Stillman.
Architecture: 1938 Georgian-style building; 1956 addition; 1987 wing by Victorine and Samuel Homsey, Inc.

Admission: Adults, $4; senior citizens, students with ID, $2.50; members, children under 9, free. Sat., 10–1, free. Handicapped accessible.
Hours: Tues., 10–9; Wed.–Sat., 10–5; Sun., noon–5. Closed Mon., Jan. 1, Thanksgiving, Dec. 25.
Tours: Tues., 10–8; Wed.–Sat., 10–4; Sun., 1–4. For reservations call (302) 571-9590. Group rates available.

The Corcoran Gallery of Art

500 17th St. NW, Washington, D.C. 20006
(202) 638-3211; 638-1439 (recording)

1993 Exhibitions

Susan on a Balcony, Holding a Dog, c. 1882, Mary Cassatt. The Corcoran Gallery of Art.

Thru Jan. 31
Reverberations: Sculpture by L. C. Armstrong, Suzan Etkin, and Lisa Hoke
Eighteen works that investigate the transitory nature of human experience.

Feb. 6–Apr. 4
Africa Explores: 20th Century African Art
African artists who confront and reinterpret Western images in light of their own culture. This exhibition features 133 works from 15 countries. Catalogue.

Feb. 13–Apr. 10
Field: An Installation by Antony Gormley
Installation by the British artist consisting of over 35,000 individually made terracotta figures.

Feb. 27–Apr. 18
Karsh: American Legends
Eighty large-format images from the past two years by the Armenian-born artist.

Aug. 14–Oct. 10
Visiones del Pueblo: The Folk Art of Latin America
Over 250 objects from 17 countries, exploring both the period between the 15th century and Colonial times and contemporary art.

Permanent Collection

American art, photography from pre-Revolutionary portraits to contemporary works; 17th-century Dutch art; 19th-century Barbizon and Impressionist painting; American sculpture by French, Powers, Remington, Saint-Gaudens.
Highlights: Bellows, *Forty-two Kids*; Bierstadt, *Mount Corcoran*; Church, *Niagara Falls*; Cole, *The Departure* and *The Return*; Eakins, *The Pathetic Song*; Glackens, *Luxembourg Gardens*; Homer, *A Light on the Sea.*
Architecture: 1897 Beaux Arts building by Flagg; 1927 Clark Wing by Platt; 1927 addition contains the 18th-century Grand Salon from the Hôtel d'Orsay in Paris.

Admission: Donation suggested: adults, $3; senior citizens, students, $1; families, groups of any size, $5; members, children under 12, free. Handicapped accessible.
Hours: Tues.–Sun., 10–5; Thurs., 10–9. Closed Mon., major holidays.
Tours: Tues.–Sun., 12:30; Thurs., 7:30. Call (202) 638-1070.
Food & Drink: Corcoran Café open Tues.–Sun., 10–4:30, Thurs., 10–8:15; Sun. brunch, 10–2:30. For reservations, call (202) 638-1590.

Folger Shakespeare Library

201 E. Capitol St. SE, Washington, D.C. 20003
(202) 544-7077

1993 Exhibitions

Thru Mar. 6
New World of Wonders: European Images of the Americas, 1492–1700
Books, engravings, drawings, and artifacts that formed the European image of the "New World." Catalogue.
Mar. 24–June 12
The Elizabethan View of Italy
Examines the active cultural exchange between Elizabethan England and Renaissance Italy.
June 24–mid-Oct.
Every Living Beast a Word: The Language and Symbolism of Animals
Hieroglyphics and the imagery on antique coins and in Aesop's fables, mythology, and proverbs.
Late Oct. 1993–Jan. 1994
Paintings from the Folger Library Collection

Illustration of Eskimo garments from the Baffin Bay area, from *The History of Barbados...And the rest of the Caribby-Islands...*, Charles de Rochefort. From "New World of Wonders: European Images of the Americas." The Folger Shakespeare Library.

Permanent Collection

A preeminent international center for Shakespeare research; rich collection of 15th–18th-century printed books; prints and engravings, manuscript materials, maps, paintings, memorabilia. **Highlights:** Copy of the 1623 First Folio, first collected edition of his plays. Also houses Elizabethan Theatre. **Architecture:** 1932 building by Paul Phillippe Cret, classical facade with Tudor–Stuart interior; 1982 addition by Hartman & Cox.

Admission: Free. Handicapped accessible.
Hours: Mon.–Sat., 10–4; closed federal holidays.
Tours: Mon.–Sat., 11. For groups, call (202) 544-7077.

Freer Gallery of Art

Jefferson Dr. at 12th St. SW, Washington, D.C. 20560
(202) 357-2700

1993 Exhibitions

NOTE: The gallery will reopen on May 9, 1993, following the completion of a 4-year renovation.

Permanent Collection

Collection of Asian art, comprising Japanese, Chinese, Korean, South and Southeast Asian, and Near Eastern; 19th- and early 20th-century American art collection, including the world's most important collection of work by Whistler. **Highlights:** Whistler interior: *Harmony in Blue and Gold*: The Peacock Room; Japanese screens; Korean ceramics; Chinese paintings; Indian bronze sculptures. **Architecture:** 1923 building by Platt; 1993 renovation.

Admission: Free. Handicapped accessible.
Hours: Daily, 10–5:30. Closed Dec. 25.
Tours: Call (202) 357-3200, Mon.–Fri.

Hirshhorn Museum and Sculpture Garden

Smithsonian Institution, Independence Ave. at Seventh St. SW, Washington, D.C. 20560
(202) 357-2700

1993 Exhibitions

Thru Jan. 10
Eva Hesse: A Retrospective
The first major retrospective for this influential artist who died in 1970, bringing together her sculptures, reliefs, and rarely seen drawings and early paintings. Catalogue.

Thru Jan. 25
Joseph Kosuth WORKS
The artist incorporates "found" texts from Kafka parables and other sources in a site-specific installation for the museum.

Thru Mar. 14
Directions—Jac Leirner
Recent found-object sculpture and installations by the Brazilian artist.

Feb. 10–May 9
Susan Rothenberg: Paintings and Drawings
A retrospective tracing the career of this American imagist painter, from her early horse images to recent autobiographical, expressionist paintings. Catalogue.

Apr. 1–June 27
Directions—Alison Saar
Mixed-media wall pieces and life-size figures by the artist, exploring themes of African-American culture, religion, and classical mythology.

June 17–Sept. 12
Jean Dubuffet 1943–1963: Paintings, Sculptures, Assemblages
Traces the artist's evolution from a crude, "Art Brut" aesthetic to his invention of the "Hourloupe," networks of interlocking cellular forms. Catalogue.

Oct. 21, 1993–Jan. 9, 1994
Willem de Kooning: Selections from the Hirshhorn Museum Collection
Fifty paintings, drawings, and sculptures from 1939 to 1985, in anticipation of the artist's 90th birthday in April 1994. Catalogue.

Permanent Collection

Comprehensive holdings of modern sculpture, painting, drawing; largest U.S. public collection of sculpture by Moore; works by Hepworth, Calder, Maillol, Tucker in the

sculpture garden and plaza; 19th- and 20th-century American paintings, works on paper; European and Latin masters. **Highlights:** De Kooning, *Queen of Hearts*; Eakins, *Mrs. Thomas Eakins*; Golub, *Four Black Men*; Kiefer, *The Book*; Manzu, *Cardinal*; Matisse, *Four Backs*; Moore, *King and Queen*; Rodin, *Monument to Balzac* and *Burghers of Calais*; outstanding group of Smiths; Rivers, *History of the Russian Revolution from Marx to Mayakovsky.*
Architecture: 1974 building by Gordon Bunshaft of Skidmore, Owings, and Merrill; 1981 sculpture garden renovation by Lester Collins; 1992 sculpture garden renovation by James Urban.

Admission: Free. Handicapped accessible.
Hours: Daily, 10–5:30; sculpture garden, daily, 7:30–dusk. Summer hours determined annually. Closed Dec. 25.
Tours: Mon.–Fri., 10:30, noon, 1:30; Sat., 10:30, noon, 1:30, 2:30; Sun., 12:30, 1:30, 2:30, 3:30. Sculpture Garden tours (May and Oct.): daily, 12:15. Call (202) 357-3235.

National Gallery of Art

Fourth St. at Constitution Ave. NW,
Washington, D.C. 20565
(202) 737-4215

1993 Exhibitions

Thru Jan. 24

Ellsworth Kelly: The Years in France, 1948–1954
Focuses on the American artist's pivotal years in France, when his style evolved from representation to the geometric abstraction for which he is known.

Art of the American Indian Frontier, 1800–1900: The Chandler/Pohrt Collection
Illustrates the close relationship between cultural and artistic changes in 19th-century Native American history. Catalogue.

Models, 1886–1888, Georges Seurat. From "Great French Paintings from the Barnes Foundation: Impressionist, Post-Impressionist, and Early Modern." A traveling exhibition.

Flirting with Stone, 1985–1990, Helen Frankenthaler. From "Helen Frankenthaler Prints." National Gallery of Art.

Thru Feb. 7
The Greek Miracle: Classical Sculpture from the Dawn of Democracy, The Fifth Century B.C.
Some of the finest examples of original sculpture from an age that transformed the history of Western art.
Thru Feb. 14
Stieglitz in the Darkroom
Demonstrates the controls a fine-art photographer employs in crafting different prints from the same negative.
Jan. 17–Apr. 11
John Singleton Copley's Watson and the Shark
Focus on Copley's vivid 1778 painting of a real-life adventure; brings together versions, studies, and related materials.
Mar. 7–Aug. 15
Drawings from the O'Neal Collection
About 60 drawings, featuring architectural and theatrical designs and Victorian and Pre-Raphaelite works. Catalogue.
Mar. 14–June 13
The Still-Life Paintings of William M. Harnett
Approximately 50 works—including the renowned group of four paintings, *After the Hunt*—by this late 19th–century American trompe l'oeil master. Catalogue.
May 2–July 25
British Watercolors: The Great Age 1750–1860
Over 200 works by Gainsborough, Constable, Turner, and lesser-known painters.
May 9–Sept. 6
Great French Paintings from the Barnes Foundation: Impressionist, Post-Impressionist, and Early Modern
Highlights of the rarely-seen collection, including works by Renoir, Matisse, Rousseau, Seurat, and Picasso. Catalogue.
June 6–Sept. 6
Helen Frankenthaler Prints
Works include 75 prints and drawings, from the artist's first prints in 1961 through the present.
Sept. 5–Dec. 5
Renaissance Portrait Medals
Significant European medals from c. 1400 to 1600. Catalogue.
Oct. 3, 1993–Jan. 2, 1994
John James Audubon
Presents a rare view of America's leading naturalist as an important and innovative artist.

Permanent Collection

Focuses on European, American art from the 13th to 20th centuries in diverse media: paintings, sculptures, drawings, prints, decorative art, Kress collection of Renaissance and Baroque paintings, Netherlandish painting from the Golden Age, French Impressionist and Post-Impressionist paintings, Modern works. **Highlights:** Calder, *Untitled* (mobile); Moore, *Knife Edge Mirror*; Motherwell, *Reconciliation Elegy*; Rembrandt Peale, *Rubens Peale with a Geranium*;

Picasso, *Family of Saltimbanques*; Pollock, *Number 1, 1950*; Raphael, *Alba Madonna* and *Saint George and the Dragon*; Rembrandt, *Self-Portrait*; Titian, *Venus with a Mirror*; the only painting by Leonardo in this country: *Ginevra de' Benci*; Whistler, *White Girl.* **Architecture:** 1941 West Building by Pope; 1978 East Building by I.M. Pei.

Admission: Free. Handicapped accessible; wheelchairs available.
Hours: Mon.–Sat., 10–5; Sun., 11–6. Closed Jan. 1, Dec. 25.
Tours: Call (202) 737-4215 for information.
Food & Drink: Terrace Café open Mon.–Sat., 11–4; Sun., noon–4. Concourse Buffet open Mon.–Sat., 10–4; Sun., 11–5:50. Cascade Café open Mon.–Sat., 11–4:30; Sun., 11:30–3:30. Garden Café open Mon.–Sat., 11–4:30; Sun., 11–6:45.

National Museum of African Art

Smithsonian Institution, 950 Independence Ave. SW, Washington, D.C. 20560
(202) 357-4600

1993 Exhibitions

Thru Feb. 28
Elmina: Art and Trade on the West Africa Coast
Focuses on the influences that have shaped the history of the Ghana city, built by the Europeans in the 1400s to control the gold trade.
Feb. 6–Apr. 4
Olwe of Ise: Nigerian Court Artist
Apr. 28, 1993–Jan. 2, 1994
Astonishment and Power: Kongo Minkisi and a New World Resonance
Examines *minkisi* objects—carved wooden figures studded with natural or man-made components—thought by Kongo peoples of Zaïre to contain forces from the land of the dead.

Permanent Collection

Four permanent galleries serve as a comprehensive introduction to the numerous visual traditions of Africa south of the Sahara: carved wood, ivory, modeled clay, forged- or cast-metal works, including masks, jewelry, textiles, figures, everyday household objects mostly from the late 19th and 20th centuries. **Highlights:** Extensive photography collection. **Architecture:** 1988 building, part of a three-story underground museum complex by Yoshimura with Carlhian of Shepley, Bulfinch, Richardson, and Abbott.

Admission: Free. Handicapped accessible.
Hours: Daily, 10–5:30. Closed Dec. 25.
Tours: Mon.–Fri., 1:30; Sat., Sun., 11, 1, 3.

National Museum of American Art

Smithsonian Institution, Eighth and G sts. NW, Washington, D.C. 20560
(202) 357-2700

1993 Exhibitions

Thru Feb. 15
**Vision and Revision: The Hand-Colored Prints of Wayne Thiebaud* is printed as: **Vision and Revision: The Hand-Colored Prints of Wayne Thiebaud*
About 70 prints from 1964 to the present that offer an angular perspective on urban streets and objects.

Mar. 5–July 5
American Painting and Sculpture, 1870–1930: The Art Forum Collects NMAA
Approximately 60 paintings and sculptures selected from the private collections of the museum's American Art Forum members; works by Albert Bierstadt, William Merritt Chase, Edward Hopper, and others.

Permanent Collection

American painting, sculpture, folk art, photography, graphic art from the 18th century to the present. **Highlights:** Works by American Impressionists Cassatt and Twachtman; large group of Ryder paintings; Stuart, Portrait of John Adams; art of the 1930s; Catlin's Indian paintings; African-American art; Lincoln's Inaugural Reception Room. **Architecture:** 1836 Old Patent Office by Elliot and Mills; 1867 wings by Walter and Clark. Building also houses the Archives of American Art and National Portrait Gallery.

Admission: Free. Handicapped accessible.
Hours: Daily, 10–5:30. Closed Dec. 25.
Tours: Mon.–Fri., noon; Sat.– Sun., 2. For group tour reservations call (202) 357-3111.
Food & Drink: Patent Pending Café open Mon.–Sun., 11–3:30.

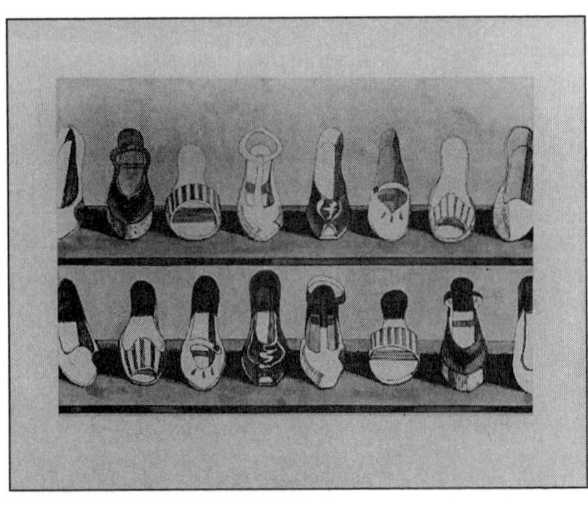

Shoe Rows, 1979, Wayne Thiebaud. From "The Prints of Wayne Thiebaud." A traveling exhibition. AFA.

National Museum of Women in the Arts

1250 New York Ave. NW, Washington, D.C., 20005-3920
(202) 783-5000

1993 Exhibitions

Thru Jan. 18
FOREFRONT: Pat Oleszko
Surveys 15 years of the artist's wearable sculpture and performance work.

Thru Jan. 31
Artists + Community: Sylvia Snowden
Features recent paintings by the artist, who is active in the D.C. community.

Thru Feb. 19
The Book as Art V
Annual exhibition, including NMWA's 1991 Library Fellows Book: *Route Book* by Mare Blocker and Katherine Dunn.

Jan. 7–Mar. 21
Carrie Mae Weems
Photographs and installations reveal the artist's use of photographic imagery and text to comment on issues of identity, race, gender, and class. Catalogue.

Feb. 18–May 2
Out of Land: Utah Women
Celebrates the rich diversity of the state's women artists and heritage. Catalogue.

Permanent Collection

More than 1,500 works by women from 28 countries, dating from the Renaissance to the present. Among the earliest: Fontana, *Portrait of a Noblewoman*; Sirani, *Virgin and Child.* Highlights: Eulabee Dix Miniature Gallery; Cassatt, *The Bath*; Kahlo, *Self-Portrait*; works by painters Chicago, Elaine de Kooning, Frankenthaler, O'Keeffe, Perry, Vigée-Lebrun; sculptor Hoffman; photographer Abbott.
Architecture: 1907 Renaissance-revival building by Waddy Wood; 1987 renovation by Scott of Keyes, Condon, and Florance.

Admission: Donation suggested: adults, $3; senior citizens, students, $2. Handicapped accessible; wheelchair available.
Hours: Mon.–Sat., 10–5; Sun., noon–5. Closed Jan. 1, Thanksgiving, Dec. 25.
Tours: Call (202) 783-5000 for information.
Food & Drink: Mezzanine Café open Mon.–Fri., 11:30–2:30.

National Portrait Gallery

**Smithsonian Institution, Eighth and F sts. NW,
Washington D.C. 20560
(202) 357-2700**

1993 Exhibitions

Thru Feb. 7

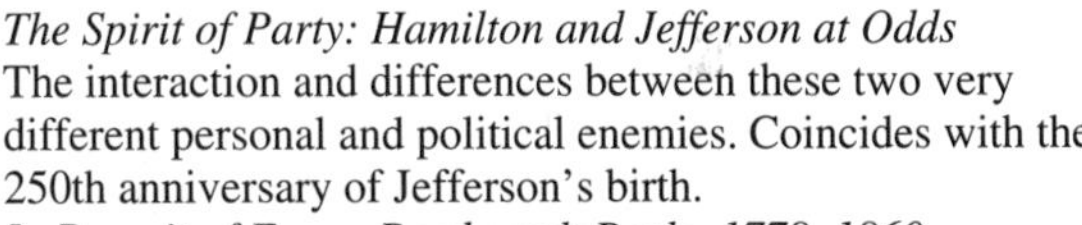

The Spirit of Party: Hamilton and Jefferson at Odds
The interaction and differences between these two very different personal and political enemies. Coincides with the 250th anniversary of Jefferson's birth.

In Pursuit of Fame: Rembrandt Peale, 1778–1860
Approximately 75 paintings, letters, and publications tracing the career of this Peale family member from the Federal period to the brink of the Civil War.

Edgehill Portrait, 1805, Gilbert Stuart. From "The Spirit of Party: Hamilton and Jefferson at Odds." The National Portrait Gallery.

Thru June 6

Recent Acquisitions

Jan. 22–June 6

The Telling Image: Photographs from the Archives of American Art
Rarely seen portraits from the collection, including self-portraits by Ansel Adams and Charles Sheeler.

Richard Avedon's Washington Portraits for Rolling Stone
Portraits taken in 1976 include such political figures as Eugene McCarthy, Henry Kissinger, and George Wallace.

Revisiting the White City: American Art from the 1893 World's Fair
Brings together 100 paintings and sculptures that were displayed in the Fine Arts Palace in Chicago; works include *The Gross Clinic* by Thomas Eakins.

June 11, 1993–Mar. 13, 1994

To the President: Presidential Portraits by the People
Forty portraits of the last 10 presidents, created by amateur artists, school children, and other citizens.

July 30–Dec. 5

Contemporary Self-Portraits from the James Goode Collection
Works from the 1970s and 1980s in styles ranging from abstraction to photorealism.

Oct. 21, 1993–Jan. 30, 1994

James Van Der Zee: Portraits
Retrospective of the artist's photographs, featuring the artists, politicians, and sportsmen of Harlem during the 1920s and 1930s.

Permanent Collection

Paintings, sculptures, prints, drawings, photographs of Americans who contributed to the history and development of the United States. **Highlights:** Portrait sculptures by Davidson; Degas, Mary Cassatt; Civil War gallery; the last photograph of Lincoln; the Hall of Presidents, including Athenaeum portraits of George and Martha Washington by Gilbert Stuart. **Architecture:** 1836 Old Patent Office by

Mills; 1867 wings by Walter and Clark. Building also houses the Archives of American Art and National Museum of American Art.

Admission: Free. Handicapped accessible. Wheelchairs available.
Hours: Daily, 10–5:30. Closed Dec. 25.
Tours: Mon.–Fri., 10–3; Sat.–Sun., holidays, 11–2. For special-subject tours call (202) 357-2920.
Food & Drink: Patent Pending Café open Mon.–Sun., 11–3:30.

The Phillips Collection

1600 21st St. NW, Washington, D.C. 20009-1090
(202) 387-0961 (recording)

1993 Exhibitions

Thru 1993
A Celebration of French Art at the Phillips Collection
Year-long series of lectures, film series, gallery talks, and other events celebrating the museum's holdings of French art.
Thru Apr. 4
Two Lives: Georgia O'Keeffe and Alfred Stieglitz—A Conversation in Paintings and Photographs
Tracks the visual and intellectual correspondences in the work of the two artists, who were artistic collaborators as well as husband and wife. Catalogue.
Thru Feb. 7
Dialogue with Nature: Nine Contemporary Sculptors
First installation in this exhibition series, featuring the work of sculptors Carol Hepper, George Lorio, and Jeff Spaulding.
Thru Feb. 14
Works on Paper: John Marin and Arthur Dove
Feb. 27–June 6
Dialogue with Nature: Nine Contemporary Sculptors
This installation in exhibition series features environmental artists Patrick Dougherty, Jim Sanborn, and Meg Webster.
Apr. 24–Aug. 15
Duncan Phillips Collects: Augustus Vincent Tack
First retrospective of the artist's work, which ranged from impressionism in his early years to spiritual abstraction. Catalogue.
June 19–Oct. 10
Dialogue with Nature: Nine Contemporary Sculptors
This installation in the series features works by multimedia artists Suzanne Anker, Robert Lobe, and Wade Saunders.
Sept. 18, 1993–Jan. 9, 1994
Jacob Lawrence's The Migration of the Negro
The artist's 60-panel series depicting African Americans' post–World War I fight from the rural South to the industrial cities of the North.

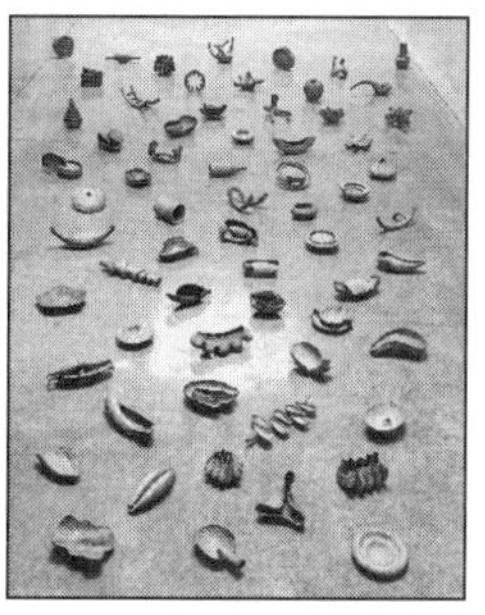

Water Drawings, 1988–1989, Wade Saunders. From "A Dialogue with Nature: Nine Contemporary Sculptors." The Phillips Collection.

Permanent Collection
Founded by Duncan Phillips, who sought to create "a museum of modern art and its sources"; late 19th- and early 20th-century European and American painting and sculpture, including Impressionist and Post-Impressionist masterpieces; major holdings of works by Bonnard, Vuillard, Cézanne, Picasso, Matisse; American artists range from Inness and Homer to American Impressionists Prendergast and Twachtman and artists of the Stieglitz circle. **Highlights:** Renoir, *Luncheon of the Boating Party*; Bonnard, *The Palm*; Cézanne, *Self-Portrait*; Chardin, *Bowl of Plums, a Peach, and a Water Pitcher*; Delacroix, *Paganini*; El Greco, *The Repentant Peter*; Ingres, *The Small Bather*; Picasso, *The Blue Room;* collections of works by Klee and Rothko. **Architecture:** 1897 building and 1907 Music Room by Hornblower and Marshall; 1920 and 1923 additions by McKim, Mead, and White; 1960 bridge and annex by Wyeth and King; 1983–84 and 1987–89 renovations by Arthur Cotton Moore Associates.

Admission: Mon.–Fri.: donation suggested; Sat.–Sun: adults, $5; senior citizens, students, $2.50; children 18 and under, free. Handicapped accessible.
Hours: Mon.–Sat., 10–5; Sun., noon–7. Closed Jan. 1, July 4, Thanksgiving, Dec. 25.
Tours: Wed., Sat., 2. Gallery talks first and third Thurs. of month, 12:30. For group-tour reservations call (202) 387-7390 one month in advance.
Food & Drink: Café open Mon.–Sat., 10:45–4:30; Sun., noon–6.

Renwick Gallery

National Museum of American Art, Smithsonian Institution, Pennsylvania Ave. at 17th St. NW, Washington, D.C. 20560
(202) 357-2700

1993 Exhibitions
Thru Jan. 10
American Crafts: The Nation's Collection
More than 120 objects in all craft media by nationally prominent artists such as Betty Woodman, Cynthia Schire, Ed Rossbach, and George Nakashima.
Albert Paley: Studies for the Renwick's Portal Gates
The artist's sketches for his award-winning, 1200-pound iron gates, installed at the Renwick Gallery in 1974.
Thru Mar. 21
Drawings by Craft Artists
Twelve drawings by six artists known primarily by their three-dimensional works: Rudy Autio, Anne Currier, Viola Frey, Tony Hepburn, Nance O'Banion, and Howard Ben Tre.

March 10–Aug. 1
American Wicker
Traces the history of American woven furniture from 1870 to1915, from the Japanese-inspired Aesthetic movement to the severe Arts and Crafts style.
Oct. 8, 1993–Jan. 9, 1994
The Arts and Crafts Movement in California: Living the Good Life
About 200 objects, including art pottery, architectural elements and renderings, furniture, and textiles.

Permanent Collection

Focus on 20th-century American crafts, decorative arts.
Architecture: 1859 Second Empire–style building by James Renwick, Jr.; Octagon Room and Grand Salon, restored and furnished in the styles of the 1860s and 1870s.

Admission: Free. Handicapped accessible.
Hours: Daily, 10–5:30. Closed Dec. 25.
Tours: Call (202) 357-2531.

Arthur M. Sackler Gallery

Smithsonian Institution, 1050 Independence Ave. SW, Washington, D.C. 20560
(202) 357-2700

1993 Exhibitions

Continuing
The Arts of China
Features jades and sculptures, Buddhist sculpture and wall paintings, glass, lacquerware, furniture, and paintings from the Neolithic period to the 20th century.
Monsters, Myths, and Minerals
Amimal imagery as expressed in jade, ceramic, and bronze from the 11th century B.C. to the 20th century.
Metalworks and Ceramics from Ancient Iran
Metal and clay artifacts created in western Iran from 2300 to 100 B.C.
Buddhist and Jain Sculpture from South Asia
Sculptures from India, Pakistan, and Tibet dating from the 2nd–17th centuries.
Thru Sept. 26
The Golden Age of Sculpture from Sri Lanka
Includes major monuments of Sri Lankan art and features Buddhist sculpture from the 3rd to 12th centuries and Hindu art of the 11th to12th centuries.
Jan. 31–Nov. 28
Joined Colors: Decoration and Meaning in Chinese Porcelain
Works of 15th–19th-century porcelain with overglaze enamel decoration from the Min Chiu Society, an organization of Hong Kong collectors. Catalogue.

Permanent Collection
Asian art spanning cultures and centuries; includes ancient Chinese bronzes and jades, contemporary Japanese ceramics, South Asian sculpture, ancient Near Eastern metalware, and Persian and Indian painting. **Highlights:** Sasanian rhyton; Shang dynasty bells; Ming dynasty paintings; Chinese furniture; Persian painting and calligraphy; ancient Near Eastern silver and gold. **Architecture:** 1987 building, part of a three-story underground museum complex by Carlhian of Shepley, Bulfinch, Richardson and Abbott.

Admission: Free. Handicapped accessible.
Hours: Daily, 10–5:30. Closed Dec. 25.
Tours: Call (202) 357-3200, Mon.–Fri.

Other Important Museums

Hillwood Museum
4155 Linnean Ave. NW, Washington, D.C. 20008
(202) 686-5800; reservations, 686-5807

National Building Museum
401 F St. at Judiciary Sq. NW, Washington, D.C. 20001
(202) 272-2448

Textile Museum
2320 S St. NW, Washington, D.C. 20008
(202) 667-0441

Washington Project for the Arts
400 Seventh St. NW, Washington, D.C. 20004
(202) 347-4813

Shiva Nataraja, 11th–12th cent. From "The Golden Age of Sculpture from Sri Lanka." Arthur M. Sackler Gallery.

Museum of Art, Fort Lauderdale

One E. Las Olas Blvd., Fort Lauderdale, Fla. 33301-1807
(305) 525-5500; 763-6464 (recording)

1993 Exhibitions
Thru Jan. 24
The Marks' Legacy: Highlights from their CoBrA Collection
Frank J. Buck: A Notable Bequest
Clyde Butcher's Florida: The Open Landscape
Thru Apr. 11
Corot to Cézanne: 19th-Century French Paintings from The Metropolitan Museum of Art
Examples of all major 19th-century French artistic styles and movements; famous works include *The Houses of Parliament*, Monet, and *The Flowering Orchard*, van Gogh.
Thru Aug. 15
Selections from the Permanent Collection, Part II
Jan. 15–Aug. 15
Linda Howard Sculpture on the Sculpture Terrace
Jan. 19–Aug. 15
CoBrA Exhibition
Feb. 5–Apr. 11
Art Spiegelman Maus Comics
Feb. 12–Aug. 15
The Magic of Line: Graphics from the Glackens Collection
Trends and Themes in American Art
Apr. 30–June 13
Contemporary Glass from South Florida Collections
Picasso Ceramics from the Bercuson Collection
Selections from the Lipschultz Donation
June 25–Aug. 15
Annual South Florida Invitational: Bonnie Clearwater Selects
Willa Shalit Sculpture for the Blind

Cape Cod Pier, 1908, William Glackens. Museum of Art, Fort Lauderdale.

Permanent Collection
European and American art with emphasis on the 20th century, including Picasso, Matisse, Calder, Moore, Dali, Warhol; impressive holdings of CoBrA paintings; comprehensive William Glackens collection; Oceanic, West African, Pre-Columbian, American Indian art; regional art. **Highlights:** Appel, *Personality*; Frankenthaler, *Nature Abhors a Vacuum*; Glackens, *Cape Cod Pier*; Warhol, *Mick Jagger*. **Architecture:** 1986 building by Edward Larrabee Barnes.

Admission: Adults, $3.25; senior citizens, $2.75; students with ID, $1.25; members, children under 12, free. Groups of 10 or more, $2.75 per person. Handicapped accessible; wheelchairs available.
Hours: Tues., 11–9; Wed.–Sat., 10–5; Sun., noon–5. Closed Mon., holidays.
Tours: Tues., Thurs., Fri., 1.

Center for the Fine Arts

101 W. Flagler St., Miami, Fla. 33130
(305) 375-3000; 375-1700 (recording)

1993 Exhibitions
Jan. 2–Feb. 21
Miami Architecture in the Tropics
Drawings, models, and photographs that establish Miami as a city whose structures set a precedent for and illustrate contemporary developments.
Feb. 13–May 2
Parameters: Philip Taaffe
Six new works by the artist that integrate motifs inspired by various Mediterranean areas.
Mar. 6–May 9
Masterworks of American Impressionism from the Pfeil Collection
More than 100 paintings by three generations of American Impressionists, including Cassatt, Sargent, and lesser-known figures. Catalogue.
May–June
Barbara Ess
A survey of the artist's work from the early 1980s, featuring 36 black-and-white images shot with a pinhole camera.
May 15–July 18
Africa Explores: 20th Century African Art
African artists who confront and reinvent Western images in light of their own culture. This exhibition features 133 works from 15 countries. Catalogue.
May 22–July 11
Agnes Martin
A major retrospective of the career of one of America's leading contemporary reductivist painters.

July 17–Sept. 26
Jim Dine: The Glyptothek Drawings
Twenty-five large-scale drawings inspired by and, in part, executed at the Glyptothek Museum, Munich, Germany.
Aug. 14–Oct. 10
**The Drawings of Stuart Davis: The Amazing Continuity*
The first such retrospective, featuring works ranging from the earliest figurative works to stylized scenes of Paris, New York, and Gloucester, Massachusetts.

Permanent Collection
No permanent collection. **Architecture:** 1983 building by Philip Johnson.

Admission: Adults, $5; children 6–12, $2. Handicapped accessible; wheelchairs available.
Hours: Tues.–Sat., 10–5; Thurs., 10–9; Sun., noon–5. Closed Mon.
Tours: Call (305) 375-1724 for information.
Food & Drink: Outdoor café open Tues.–Fri., 11–2. Metrofare snack bar open Mon.–Fri., 8–3.

Bass Museum of Art

2121 Park Ave., Miami Beach, Fla. 33139
(305) 673-7530

1993 Exhibitions
Feb. 12–Apr. 4
From Media to Metaphor: Art About AIDS
Examines the representations of AIDS in artwork in a variety of media since 1984; artists include Ross Bleckner, Keith Haring, and Robert Mapplethorpe. Catalogue.
June 18–Aug. 4
Photostroika: New Photography from the Former Soviet Union and the Baltic Republics of Lithuania, Estonia, and Latvia
Black-and-white framed photographs and hand-colored prints by various former Soviet and Lithuanian, Estonian, and Latvian photographers. Catalogue.
Oct. 15–Dec. 5
Special Collections: The Photographic Order from Pop to Now
Examines how photography influenced and was influenced by the major art movements of the last 30 years; artists include Sol LeWitt, Edward Ruscha, and Andy Warhol. Catalogue.

Permanent Collection
Features Old Master paintings, sculpture, textiles, ecclesiastical artifacts. **Highlights:** Works by Rubens, Dürer, Bol, Hopner, Delacroix, Toulouse-Lautrec, van Haarlem. **Architecture:** 1930 Art Deco building by Russell Pancoast; 1964 addition by Robert Swartburg.

Admission: Adults, $5; students with ID, $4; children 12 to 17, $3; children 6–12 with adults, $2; children under 6 and members, free; groups of 20 or more, $4 per person; groups of school children, free.
Hours: Tues.–Sat., 10–5; Sun. 1–5. Closed Mon.
Tours: Call (305) 595-2971 for information.

The Society of the Four Arts

Four Arts Plaza, Palm Beach, Fla. 33480
(407) 655-7226

1993 Exhibitions

Jan. 9–Feb. 7
Men of Rebellion: The Eight and their Associates at the Phillips
Works by the American early–20th-century group from the Phillips Collection, Washington, D.C.
Feb. 13–Mar. 14
Always in Style: French Decorative Arts from the Dalva Brothers
Eighteenth-century furniture, tapestries, and porcelain representing Regence, Louis XV, Louis XVI, Directoire, and early Empire periods.
Feb. 13–Apr. 11
**Gold Boxes from the Gilbert Collection*
Opulent gold boxes from the late 17th to early 19th centuries, including several commissioned by Frederick the Great of Prussia.
Mar. 20–Apr. 18
Fifteenth Annual Gifted Child Art Exhibition

Permanent Collection

Gallery featuring mostly traveling exhibitions is open Dec.–mid-April; society also houses the Four Arts library and gardens and the Philip Hulitar Sculpture Garden, open year-round. **Architecture:** 1929 building by Addison Mizner; 1974 renovation by John Volk.

Admission: Suggested donation: $3.
Hours: Dec.–Apr.: weekdays, 10–5; Sun., 2–5.
Tours: Call (407) 655-7226 for information.

Snuffbox, 1728–29, probably Jean-Baptiste Massé. From "Gold Boxes from the Gilbert Collection." A traveling exhibition. AFA.

Museum of Fine Arts

255 Beach Dr. N.E., St. Petersburg, Fla. 33701-3498
(813) 896-2667

1993 Exhibitions

Thru Jan. 17
Access to Art: All Creatures Great and Small
A hands-on exhibition for the sight-impaired.
Feb. 7–Mar. 14
Martin Johnson Heade: Floral and Bird Studies
Stephen Scott Young
A selection of the artist's watercolors from private collections.
Mar. 26–June 6
Paintings by American Women: The Louise and Alan Sellars Collection
June 20–Aug. 1
Florida Visual Artists Fellowships: 1992-93
Sept. 26–Nov. 7
Croatian Native Art
Nov. 21, 1993–Jan. 16, 1994
Silverpoint Etcetera: Contemporary American Metalpoint Drawing
Nov. 21, 1993–Jan. 23, 1994
Treasures of Florida: Decorative Arts in Florida Museums

Permanent Collection

Pre-Columbian gold and pottery; notable ancient and Far Eastern collection; 17th- to 20th-century European and American paintings and sculpture, including French Impressionist paintings; 19th- and 20th-century photographs, prints, decorative arts. **Highlights:** Barye, *War* and *Peace*; Cézanne, *La Côte des Boeufs Pointoise*; Monet, *Church in Springtime Giverny, Houses of Parliament, Road to Vetheuil in Snow,* and *Water Lilies*; Morisot, *La Lecture (Girl Reading)*; O'Keeffe, *Poppy*; Steuben glass gallery; Weenix, *The De Kempenaer Family*; Jacobean and Georgian period rooms. **Architecture:** 1965 Palladian-style building by Volk; 1989 expansion by Harvard, Jolly, Marcet, and Associates.

Admission: Donation suggested, $4. Handicapped accessible.
Hours: Tues.–Sat., 10–5; Sun., 1–5. Third Thurs. of month, 10–9. Closed Mon., Jan. 1, Dec. 25.
Tours: Tues.–Fri., 11, 2; Sat.–Sun., 2. Call (813) 896-2667 for group and Spanish-language tour reservations.

The John and Mable Ringling Museum of Art

5401 Bay Shore Rd., Sarasota, Fla. 34243
(813) 355-5101

1993 Exhibitions
Continuing
Permanent Collection: Old Masters
Circus Winter Quarters 1946: Photographs by Loomis Dean
Thru Feb. 28
Recent Acquisitions: Selections from the Permanent Collection
Mar. 26–June 4
Florida Statewide Exhibition

Permanent Collection

European Renaissance, Rococo paintings; Baroque art; antiquities, decorative arts, tapestries, photographs, drawings, prints; Modern and contemporary art; circus costumes, wagons, props, complete scale model of a miniature circus; circus-related fine art and memorabilia. Evolution of sculpture is traced through full-size reproductions in the Italian Renaissance–style courtyard. **Highlights:** Italian 16th–17th-century paintings; French, Dutch, Flemish, Spanish Baroque works. **Architecture:** 1924–26 Venetian Gothic Ringling residence. Ca' d'Zan; 1927–29 Renaissance-style villa museum; 1966 addition.

Admission: Adults, $8.50; senior citizens 55+, $7.50; Florida teachers, students with valid ID, children 12 and under, free; group rates available. Handicapped accessible.
Hours: Daily, 10–5:30. Closed Jan. 1, Thanksgiving, Dec. 25.
Tours: Call (813) 355-5101 for information.
Food & Drink: Banyan Restaurant open museum hours.

Norton Gallery of Art

1451 S. Olive Ave., West Palm Beach, Fla. 33401
(407) 832-5194

1993 Exhibitions
Information not available at press time.

Permanent Collection

French Impressionist and Post-Impressionist paintings by Cézanne, Matisse, Monet, Renoir, others; American art from 1900 to the present, featuring works by Davis, Hopper, Marin, Motherwell; Chinese archaic bronzes, jades, ceramics, and Buddhist sculpture. **Highlights:** Gauguin, *Agony in the Garden*; Braque, *Still Life with a Red Tablecloth*; Bellows, *Winter Afternoon;* Pollock, *Night Mist.* **Architecture:** 1941 building by Marion Syms Wyeth.

Norton Gallery of Art.

Admission: Donation requested. Handicapped accessible.
Hours: Tues.–Sat., 10–5; Sun., 1–5. Closed Mon., major holidays.
Tours: Call (407) 832-5194 for information and reservations.

Georgia Museum of Art

The University of Georgia, Athens, Ga. 30602
(404) 542-3255

1993 Exhibitions

Thru Jan. 17
Charles Meryon and Jean François Millet: Etchings of Urban and Rural 19th-Century France
Works inspired by pre-industrial Paris; Meryon fashioned romantic etchings of Parisian Medieval and Renaissance architecture; while Millet, a Barbizon painter, ennobled the lives of peasants of the forest of Fontainebleau.
Jan. 30–Mar. 21
Andrée Ruellan
First retrospective of the artist's 60-year career, spanning her early works as an American scene painter, a surrealist in the 1950s, and as an abstract expressionist. Catalogue.
Feb. 6–Mar. 21
The Art of Gerald Brockhurst
Almost 80 works by the artist, a British portrait painter and etcher. Catalogue.
Sept. 25–Nov. 21
American Impressionism in Georgia Collections
Paintings, pastels, watercolors, and drawings by masters such as Cassatt and Hassam and lesser-known artists including Theodore Butler and Agnes Richmond. Catalogue.
Faces, Facts, Fancies and Fortunes
Twenty-five paintings by American portraitists from Colonial times to the present.
Fleeting Shadows: Selected Prints by Childe Hassam
Works by the American Impressionist painter, concentrating on works produced in Easthampton, New York.
Dec. 3, 1993–Jan. 19, 1994
Adriaen van Ostade: Etchings of Peasant Life in Holland's Golden Age
An exhibition of prints by the popular 17th-century artist.

Permanent Collection

Nineteenth- and 20th-century American paintings; Kress Study Collection of Italian Renaissance paintings; prints, drawings by American, European, and Asian masters.
Architecture: 1906 Beaux Arts building by unknown architect.

Admission: Free. Handicapped accessible.
Hours: Mon.–Sat., 9–5; Sun., 1–5.
Tours: Call (404) 542-3255 for information.

High Museum of Art

1280 Peachtree St. N.E., Atlanta, Ga. 30309
(404) 892-HIGH (recording)

1993 Exhibitions

Diamond Back Chair, Maxwell Davis, 1991. High Museum of Art, Atlanta.

Thru Jan. 17
American Art, American Vision: Paintings from the Maier Museum, Randolph-Macon Woman's College
Thirty paintings ranging from the Hudson River school to American Impressionism to early Modernism.
Thru Feb. 21
Dream Makers: American Children's Book Illustrators
Original illustrations and books from the comprehensive private collection of Betsy B. Shirley of Bernardsville, N.J.
Thru May 30
Spectacles
A long-term exhibition featuring a series of room installations created by artists; visitors are able to create their own works with artists' materials.
Jan. 26–Apr. 4
Abstract Expressionist Drawings: Works on Paper, Selections from The Metropolitan Museum of Art
Sixty drawings, watercolors, and sketches by 19 of the best-known Abstract Expressionists.
Mar. 3–May 30
Ralph Eugene Meatyard: An American Visionary
A retrospective featuring 125 black-and-white photographs by this American photographer, who pioneered "no-focus" shots and arranged tableaux.
Apr. 20–July 4
African Reflections: Art from Northeastern Zaire
Art and artifacts from the Mangbetu, Azande, and Barambo people of the former Congo region in Zaire.
May 1–June 27
Art at the Edge: Alison Saar
An installation of the artist's carved figures, addressing the rich African-American legacy of Atlanta and of the South.
Sept. 21–Nov. 28
Annie Leibovitz: Photographs 1970–1990
Images spanning the photographer's career, from early black-and-white portraits for *Rolling Stone* to recent advertising work.

Oct. 16, 1993–Jan. 2, 1994
In Praise of Painting: The Art of Gerrit Dou
Dec. 18, 1993–Mar. 6, 1994
A Private View: Small Paintings in the Manoogian Collection
Masterpieces include informal portraits by Sargent, genre scenes by Millet, and still-lifes by Harnett. Catalogue.

Permanent Collection

European painting and sculpture from the Renaissance to the 20th century; sub-Saharan African art; American and European prints, photographs, decorative arts; American 18th- to 20th-century paintings and sculptures. **Highlights:** Lichtenstein, *Sandwich and Soda*; Peale, *Senator William H. Crawford of Georgia*; Prendergast, *Procession, Venice*; Rauschenberg, *Overcast III*; Stella, *Manteneia I*; Whittredge, *Landscape in the Harz Mountains*. **Architecture:** 1983 building by Richard Meier.

Admission: Adults, $5; senior citizens, students with ID, $3; students 6–17, $1; children under 6, free. Thurs, 1-5, free. Handicapped accessible.
Hours: Tues.–Thurs., Sat., 10–5; Fri., 10–9; Sun., noon–5. Closed Mon., holidays.
Tours: Available Sept.–May, Tues.–Sun.; June–Aug., Tues., Thurs., Sun. Call (404) 898-1145.
Food & Drink: Chef's Grill (Woodruff Arts Center) open Tues.–Sun., 11:30–2:30; Fri., 5–11, Sat., 5–12.

Honolulu Academy of Arts

900 S. Beretania St., Honolulu, Hawaii 96813
(808) 532-8700

1993 Exhibitions

Thru Jan. 3
Artists of Hawaii, 1992
Thru Jan. 10
Christmas Cards, Ex Libris, and Other Commemorative Prints from the Academy's Collection
Jan. 7–Jan. 31
Forever Yes: Art of the New Tattoo
Jan. 14–Mar. 7
Frederica Cassiday
Jan. 21–Feb. 28
Clarence John Laughlin
Toshiko Takaezu
Feb. 25–Mar. 11
Weaver's Hui
Mar. 18–Apr. 18
Transcending Turmoil: Painting at the Close of China's Empire, 1796–1911
Hanging scrolls, hand scrolls, and album-leaf and fan paintings from the late Qing court.

Mar. 28–Apr. 15
Honolulu Printmakers Annual Juried Exhibition
Apr. 29–June 20
Recent Print Acquisitions, 1987–1992
May 6–June 6
Reuse/Refuse
Chinese Calligraphy from the Academy's Collection
May 14–May 16
Hawaii Quilt Guild: Sixth Annual Exhibition
May 20–June 13
Photographs of Chinese Buddhist Sculpture in the Xianxi Province
June 17–Aug. 8
James Rosenquist: The Graphic Work
John Taylor Arms
June 24–Aug. 15
Howard Farrant: Recent Works on Paper
Aug. 19–Oct. 10
Mary Ellen Mark: Indian Circus Portfolio
Sept. 2–Oct. 17
Masterworks of American Impressionism from the Pfeil Collection
More than 100 paintings by three generations of American Impressionists, including Cassatt, Sargent, and lesser-known figures. Catalogue.
Nov. 18–Dec. 19
Artists of Hawaii, 1993
Jan.–Mar. 1994
Linda Butler: Rural Japan

Permanent Collection

Hawaii's only general art museum; objects from cultures around the world and throughout history. Asian art, including James A. Michener collection of Japanese woodblock prints; Kress collection of Renaissance and Baroque paintings; American paintings and decorative arts from the Colonial period to the present day; works from Africa, Oceania, the Americas; contemporary graphic arts.
Highlights: Delaunay, *The Rainbow*; van Gogh, *Wheatfields*; Ma Fen, *The Hundred Geese*; Monet, *Water Lilies*; Chinese and Persian bronzes; six garden courts.
Architecture: 1927 building by Goodhue.

Admission: Suggested donation: adults, $4; seniors, students, military, children under 12, free. Handicapped accessible.
Hours: Tues.–Sat., 10–4:30; Sun., 1–5. Closed Mon., holidays.
Tours: Tues.–Sat., 11; Sun., 1. For special tours, call 532-8726.
Food & Drink: Garden Café open Tues.–Sat.; Thurs. dinner, 6:15. For reservations call (808) 531-8865.

The Art Institute of Chicago

Michigan Ave. at Adams St., Chicago, Ill. 60603
(312) 443-3600; 443-3500 (recording)

1993 Exhibitions

Thru Jan. 3
The Ancient Americas: Art from Sacred Landscapes
Approximately 300 objects, focusing on the intellectual and aesthetic structures of ancient civilizations in Mesoamerica, the American Southwest, Central America, and the Andes.
Building in a New Spain: Contemporary Spanish Architecture
Focuses on 13 civil projects after the death of dictator Francisco Franco. Included are the housing for Olympic athletes in Barcelona and the Seville airport.
Thru Jan. 10
Photographs by Rose Mandel
A sequence of 20 photographs by the contemporary artist.
Thru Jan. 24
What's New: Prague
One hundred works from the permanent collection that survey current photographic work from Prague.
Thru Jan. 30
Rousseau's The Dream
One of Rousseau's most ambitious and most celebrated paintings will be on view. The work initiated a rich genre of fantasy art by such artists as Chagall and de Chirico.
Thru Jan. 31
Soviet Propaganda Plates from the Tuber Collection
Features plates that the post–1917 revolution Soviet government encouraged artists to decorate with propaganda.
Thru late Jan.
Translation of Forms: Modernism and a Songye Stool
Focuses on a Songye chieftain stool, a recent acquisition of the museum's Department of Africa, Oceania, and the Americas.
Thru Mar. 28
South American Textiles
Woven, embroidered, and painted or printed textiles from Peru, Mexico, and Guatemala.
Jan.–Apr.
Max Klinger's A Glove
A portfolio of 10 prints, widely known as the most innovative of the German Symbolist's career.
Jan. 30–May 10
Marc Chagall: The Moscow Jewish Theater Murals
Seven restored murals on canvas, created in 1920 for the State Jewish Kamerny Theatre in Moscow and viewed outside the Soviet Union for the first time in 1991. Catalogue.
Mar. 16–May 30
René Magritte
A retrospective featuring 120 paintings, works on paper, sculptures, and objects by the 20th-century Surrealist master.

April 1–Aug. 15
The Moscow Avant Garde: 1955–1991
Explores Moscow architects from the postwar period through the present day.

May 1–July 5
Constructing the Fair: Platinum Photographs of the World's Columbian Exposition by C. D. Arnold
A selection of large-scale photographs that document the fair's day-by-day chronology in Jackson Park; classical examples of the 19th-century architectural aesthetic. Catalogue.

June 1–Sept. 6
Thonet Furniture from the Collection of Mr. and Mrs. Manfred Steinfeld
Reexamines the output of Thonet and other bentwood furniture manufacturers from the early 19th to early 20th centuries. Catalogue.

June 10–Aug. 29
Chicago Architecture and Design, 1923–1993: Reconfiguration of an American Metropolis
Over 400 pieces, including models, furniture, and furnishings, that focus on the urban world as it changed after the Great Depression and World War II; features installation designed by eight young Chicago architects. Catalogue.

July 1–Sept. 15
Gates of Mystery: The Art of Holy Russia from the Russian Museum, St. Petersburg
Features 120 objects from the collection of the State Russian Museum, dating from the 11th to the 18th century, when Peter the Great turned artists toward Western art.

Sept. 15–Nov. 30
Max Ernst: Dada and the Dawn of Surrealism
An exploration of the artist as a Dadaist, through collages, prints, paintings, and relief sculpture. Catalogue.

Permanent Collection

Spans 40 centuries of art. Chinese bronzes, ceramics, jades; Japanese prints; works from Africa and Oceania; ancient Meso-American and Peruvian ceramics and figurative art; Harding collection of arms and armor; acclaimed Impressionist collection; American and European decorative arts; major collection of 20th-century art. **Highlights:** Caillebotte, *Paris: A Rainy Day*; Cassatt, *The Bath*; Goya, *The Capture of Maragato by Fray Pedro*; El Greco, *Assumption of the Virgin*; Monet, *The River*; large group of Picassos; Seurat, *Sunday Afternoon on the Island of La Grand Jatte*; Wood, *American Gothic*; six extraordinary panels from a large early Renaissance altarpiece by Giovanni di Paolo depicting the life of Saint John the Baptist; reconstructed Chicago Stock Exchange Trading Room designed by Adler and Sullivan. **Architecture:** 1894 Beaux Arts building by Shepley, Rutan, and Coolidge; 1986 renovation by Skidmore, Owings, and Merrill; 1988 South Building by Hammond, Beeby, and Babka; 1991 Modern Art renovation by Barnett and Smith,

Architects, and the Office of John Vinci; 1992 Chinese, Japanese, and Korean Gallery renovation by Cleo Nichols Design, with Japanese Screens Gallery by Tadao Ando.

Admission: Suggested donation: adults, $6; senior citizens, students with ID, children, $3. Tues., free. Handicapped accessible.
Hours: Mon.–Fri., 10:30–4:30; Tues., 10:30–8; Sat., 10–5; Sun., holidays, noon–5. Closed Dec. 25.
Tours: Call (312) 443-3530. For group hotel package information, call (312) 443-3944.
Food & Drink: Cafeteria open Mon.–Sat., 10:30–4; Tues., 10:30–7; Sun., noon–4. Restaurant open Mon.–Sat., 11–2:30. Garden Restaurant open June-Sept.; Mon.–Sat., 11–3; Sun., noon–3; Tues., 4–7.

Museum of Contemporary Art

237 E. Ontario St., Chicago, Ill. 60611
(312) 280-2660; 280-5161 (recording)

1993 Exhibitions

Thru Jan. 17
Emmet Gowin: Photographs
More than 120 photographs from the 25-year career of this artist, who focuses on issues involving the "changing earth." Catalogue.
Thru Jan. 23
Art at the Armory: Occupied Territory
Eighteen mixed-media, room-size installations on view at the Chicago National Guard Armory.
Thru Jan. 31
Alexander Calder from the Collection of the Ruth and Leonard J. Horwich Family
Eighteen works by the artist and inventor of the mobile.
Thru Mar. 14
Lorna Simpson: For the Sake of the Viewer
A survey of the artist's conceptual photographs, from 1985 to her most recent series. Catalogue.

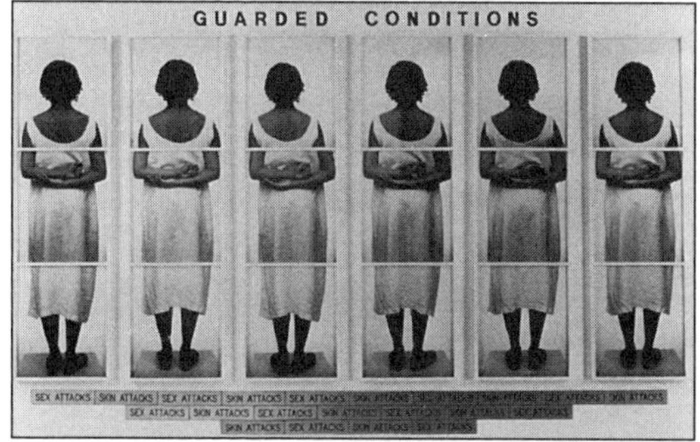

Guarded Conditions, 1989, Lorna Simpson. From "Lorna Simpson: For the Sake of the Viewer." A traveling exhibition.

Feb. 6–Mar. 21
Options 45: Libby Wadsworth
Twenty text-and-image paintings by the Chicago artist.
Conceptual Photography from the Gerald S. Elliott Collection
Features American and European works of the 1980s by pioneering conceptualists Dan Graham and Richard Long and younger, international artists Alfredo Jaar and Louise Lawler.
Apr. 3–June 20
Hand-Painted Pop: American Art in Transition, 1955–62
Examines the evolution of Pop Art from stylistic techniques used by first-generation Abstract Expressionists of the New York School; artists include Jim Dine, Jasper Johns, and Cy Twombly. Catalogue.
Aug. 10–Oct. 24
Susan Rothenberg: Paintings and Drawings
A retrospective tracing the career of this American imagist painter, from her early horse images to recent autobiographical, expressionist paintings. Catalogue.

Permanent Collection

Twentieth-century works in all media, including photographs, films, videotapes, audio pieces by Bacon, Braque, Calder, Christo, Dubuffet, Duchamp, Magritte, Oldenburg, Paschke, Rauschenberg, Segal. **Highlights:** Bacon, *Man in Blue Box*; works by Beuys, Basquiat, Jackson; Simonds, *Dwellings*. NOTE: The permanent collection is not always on view. Please call to confirm showing. **Architecture:** Former bakery renovated 1967; 1979 addition by Booth.

Admission: Adults, $4; senior citizens, students, children under 16, $2; children under 10, members, free; Tues., free. Handicapped accessible.
Hours: Tues.–Sat., 10–5; Sun., noon–5. Closed Mon., Jan. 1, Thanksgiving, Dec. 25. Galleries may be closed for installation between exhibitions.
Tours: Tues., Sun., 12:15 (call to confirm); for group-tour reservations call (312) 280-2697.
Food & Drink: Site Café Bookstore open Tues.–Sat., 11–4:45; Sun., noon–4:45.

Terra Museum of American Art

666 N. Michigan Ave., Chicago, Ill. 60611
(312) 664-3939

1993 Exhibitions

Thru Feb. 7
**The Drawings of Stuart Davis: The Amazing Continuity*
The first such retrospective, featuring works ranging from the earliest figurative works to stylized scenes of Paris, New York, and Gloucester, Massachusetts.
Feb. 13–Apr. 25
Theme and Improvisation: Kandinsky and the American Avant-Garde, 1912–1950
Traces the influence of the father of pure abstraction on American artists.
Apr. 30–May 9
Selections from the Terra Museum Permanent Collection
May 15–Aug. 1
**American Abstraction at the Addison Gallery of American Art*
Celebrates the Addison's 60-year commitment to non-objective art; 90 works in a variety of media by 70 famed artists.

Permanent Collection

Based on the personal collection of Daniel Terra, spanning two centuries of American art. **Highlights:** Bingham, *The Jolly Flatboatmen*; Morse, *Gallery of the Louvre*; works by Cassatt, Homer, Sargent, Whistler. **Architecture:** 1987 building by Booth and Hansen.

Admission: Adults, $4; senior citizens, $2.50; students, $1; children under 12, free. Handicapped accessible.
Hours: Tues., noon–8; Wed.–Sat., 10–5; Sun., noon–5. Closed Mon., holidays.
Tours: Daily, noon, 2. For school and group-tour reservations call (312) 664-3939.

A La Cremerie, 1910, Martha Walter. Terra Museum of American Art.

Indianapolis Museum of Art

1200 W. 38th St., Indianapolis, Ind. 46208
(317) 923-1331

1993 Exhibitions

Thru Jan. 10
Tales of Japan: Three Centuries of Japanese Painting from the Chester Beatty Library, Dublin
Painted hand scrolls and albums from the 16th–19th centuries illustrating famous Japanese stories and historical events.

Portrait of Leontyne Price, 1989, Brian Lanker. From "I Dream a World: Portraits of Black Women Who Changed America." A traveling exhibition. AFA.

Apr. 3–May 30
Max Ernst: The Sculpture
Concentrates on the Surrealist artist's metal pieces, reliefs, jewelry, and *Chess Set* of 1929–30. Catalogue.

June 26–Aug. 29
The Art of Seeing: John Ruskin and the Victorian Eye
More than 150 paintings, watercolors, and drawings by such 19th-century artists as Turner, Whistler, and Rossetti.

July 31–Sept. 11
**I Dream a World: Portraits of Black Women who Changed America*
Seventy-five portraits by Pulitzer Prize–winning photographer Brian Lanker of Maya Angelou, Shirley Chisholm, Odetta, Rosa Parks, Sarah Vaughan, and others. Catalogue.

Oct. 2–Nov. 21
Richard Tuttle Drawings from the Dorothy and Herbert Vogel Collection
The artist's minimalist works combine watercolors with such sculptural elements as wire, paper, and light wood.

Oct. 2, 1993–Jan. 2, 1994
Richard Tuttle: Floor Drawings
Eighteen sculptures made between 1987 and 1991 that address the value of objects that possess no material value.

Permanent Collection

J. M. W. Turner Collection of watercolors and drawings; Holliday Collection of Neo-Impressonist Art; Clowes Fund Collection; Eli Lilly Collection of Chinese Art; Eiteljorg Collection of African Art. **Architecture:** Lilly Pavilion of Decorative Arts: original J. K. Lilly mansion modeled after 18th-century French chateau; 1970 Krannert Pavilion by Ambrose Richardson; 1972 Clowes Pavilion; 1973 Showalter Pavilion; 1990 Mary Fendrich Hulman Pavilion by Edward Larrabee Barnes.

Admission: Free. Admission fee for selected exhibitions; members free to all exhibitions. Handicapped accessible.
Hours: Tues.–Sat., 10–5, Thurs., 10–8:30; Sun., noon–5. Closed Mon., major holidays.
Tours: Krannert, Clowes, and Hulman pavilions: Tues.–Sun., noon , 2:15; Thurs., 7. Call (317) 923-1331.
Food & Drink: Museum Café open Tues.–Sat., 11–2.

Cedar Rapids Museum of Art

410 Third Ave., Cedar Rapids, Iowa 52401
(319) 366-7503

1993 Exhibitions

Thru Jan. 31
John Snyder: Portraits from Society's Periphery
Works by the Iowan contemporary artist.
Thru Feb. 28
Masquerades and Demons: Tukuna Bark-Cloth Painting
Masks, costumes, and paintings by the Tukuna people of Colombia.
Jan. 30–Apr. 11
Combat Art: An Exhibition of World War II Combat Art
Watercolors, oils, and field sketches produced by soldier-artists assigned to the front lines during the war.
Feb. 17–May 30
Master Prints from Gemini G.E.L.
Forty works from the Gemini Collection of the National Gallery of Art; artists include Lichtenstein, Oldenburg, and Stella.
Mar. 15–May 2
Richard Rezac
Sixteen works, including wall and floor sculpture.
June 11–Aug. 8
La Tinaia
Artworks produced by the patients of a psychiatric clinic in Florence, Italy.
Aug. 20–Oct. 3
Tony Berlant: Recent Work
Oct. 15, 1993–Jan. 1, 1994
The People Speak: Navajo Folk Art
Collection of 100 works by Navajo artists.

Permanent Collection

Focus on Midwestern regionalism, featuring collections of works by Grant Wood, Marvin D. Cone, Mauricio Lasansky, Malvina Hoffman, James Swann, Bertha Jaques.
Architecture: 1905 Beaux Arts building; 1989 restoration, addition, and Winter Garden by Charles W. Moore.

Admission: Adults, $2.50; senior citizens, children 7–18, $1.50; children under 7, members, free. Handicapped accessible.
Hours: Tues.–Sat., 10–4, Thurs., 10–7; Sun., noon–3. Closed Mon., holidays.
Tours: Third Thurs. of the month, 5:30; fourth Fri. of the month, 11:30.

Davenport Museum of Art

1737 W. 12th St., Davenport, Iowa 52804
(319) 326-7804

1993 Exhibitions
Thru Jan. 10
The Art of Private Devotion: Retablo Painting of Mexico
Jan. 17–Mar. 18
Paul Manship: Changing Taste in America
Apr. 4–May 30
Fine Art Collectors: Connoisseurship in the Quad Cities
June 23–July 31
Quilt National '93
Aug.–Sept.
Quad Cities Regional Art Showcase 1993
Oct.–Dec.
Realism to Photo-Realism in Modern American Art

Permanent Collection
Four collections: the European Collection, with works from the Renaissance to Fauvism; the Regionalist Collection, which includes the complete lithographs of Grant Wood and John Stewart Curry; the Mexican Colonial Collection, with works from the 17th to 19th centuries; and the Haitian Collection, with over 100 works of Haitian painting and sculpture. **Architecture:** 1961 building; 1972 Weise building addition.

Admission: Donation requested. Handicapped accessible.
Hours: Tues.–Sat., 10–4:30; Sun., 1–4:30. Closed Mon., holidays.
Tours: Tues.–Fri., 10–4:30; contact education department two weeks in advance.

Des Moines Art Center

4700 Grand Ave., Des Moines, Iowa 50312
(515) 277-4405

1993 Exhibitions
Jan. 30–Apr. 25
Anish Kapoor
The Bombay-born, London-based artist, whose sculptures are characterized by biomorphic forms and tactile surfaces, will create new works in sandstone. Also earlier work. Catalogue.

Permanent Collection
Nineteenth- and 20th-century European and American paintings and sculptures; African and primitive arts. **Highlights:** Bacon, *Study after Velázquez's "Portrait of Pope Innocent X"*; Johns, *Tennyson*; Judd, *Untitled*; Kiefer, *Untitled*; Monet, *Rocks at Belle-Île*; MacDonald-Wright,

Untitled, 1990, Anish Kapoor. From "Anish Kapoor." A traveling exhibition.

Abstraction on Spectrum. **Architecture:** 1948 building by Eliel Saarinen; 1968 addition by I. M. Pei & Partners; 1985 addition by Richard Meier & Partners.

Admission: Afternoons 1–5, $2; students with ID, senior citizens, $1; mornings 11–1, free; members, children 12 and under, scheduled tours, free. Thurs., free. Handicapped accessible.
Hours: Tues.–Sat., 11–5; Thurs., 11–9; Sun., noon–5. Closed Mon., holidays.
Food & Drink: Restaurant open Tues.–Sat., 11–3; Thurs. dinner, 5:30–9.

Spencer Museum of Art

University of Kansas, Lawrence, Kan. 66045
(913) 864-4710

1993 Exhibitions
Jan. 24–Mar. 21
Les XX and the Belgian Avant-Garde: Prints, Drawings, and Books, ca. 1890
Over 125 works on paper and 25 books from Les Vingt (The Group of Twenty), a major force in the advancement of Modernism in Europe in the late 19th century. Catalogue.
Jan. 31–Mar. 14
Contact Press Images
Mar. 28–May 16
Schmidt Print Collection
Apr. 18–June 6
The New Narrative: Contemporary Fiber Art
June 4–July
Highlights of the Spencer Museum's Collections
Aug. 22–Oct. 3
Contemporary Czechoslovakian Photography
Nov. 7–Dec. 19
Always There: The African-American Presence in American Quilts

Permanent Collection

Noted holdings of European painting, sculpture; American portrait, landscape paintings, prints, quilts, photographs; Edo period paintings; Korean ceramics; Japanese prints; contemporary Chinese painting. **Highlights:** Homer, *Cloud Shadows*; Claude, *Landscape with a Draftsman*; Mitsuhiro, *Memoir from an Eastern Journey*; Riemenschneider, *Virgin and Child*; Rossetti, *La Pia de' Tolommei*; Fragonard, *Portrait of a Young Boy*; Teniers, *The Deluge;* Murray, *Chaotic Lip*, Chihuly, *Violet Persian Set.* **Architecture:** 1978 building by Jenks.

Admission: Free. Handicapped accessible.
Hours: Tues.–Sat., 8:30–5; Sun., noon–5. Closed Mon., Jan. 1, July 4, Thanksgiving, Dec. 24–25.
Tours: Call (913) 864-4710 for information.

Wichita Art Museum

619 Stackman Dr., Wichita, Kan. 67203
(316) 268-4921

1993 Exhibitions

Jan. 17–Mar. 7
The World of Lois Mailou Jones
Jan. 24–Feb. 28
Vietnam Voyage: Paintings by Dong Phan
Jan. 31–Feb. 14
Annual Scholastic Art Exhibition
Feb. 28–Mar. 14
14th Annual Southcentral Kansas Very Special Arts Exhibition
Mar. 14–Apr. 11
1993 Kansas Watercolor Society Five-State Exhibition
Mar. 20–Apr. 18
Official Images: New Deal Photography
Apr. 25–June 20
Wendell Castle: Recent Work
July 11–Aug. 15
Passing Seasons: Paintings by Robert Sudlow
Oct. 3–Nov. 14
Roger Shimomura
The Return of the Yellow Peril: Paintings

Permanent Collection

American painting, graphics, sculpture, decorative arts, with an emphasis on painting from 1900 to 1950: American Impressionism, The Eight, early Modernism, Regionalism and American Scene. **Highlights:** Major works by Feke, Copley, Eakins, Ryder, Cassatt, Henri, Prendergast, Glackens, Burchfield, Hopper, Curry, Marin, Dove; paintings, drawings, sculptures by Charles M. Russell. **Architecture:** 1976 building by Edward Larrabee Barnes.

Admission: Free. Handicapped accessible.
Hours: Tues.–Sat., 10–5; Sun., noon–5. Closed Mon.
Tours: Call (316) 268-4921 for information.
Food & Drink: Museum restaurant open Tues.–Fri., 11:30–1:30; Sun., noon–2.

J. B. Speed Art Museum

2035 S. Third St., Louisville, Ky. 40201
(502) 636-2893

1993 Exhibitions

Jan. 12–Feb. 28
Breaking the Rules: Audrey Flack, A Retrospective 1950–1990
Chronicles the last four decades of Flack's career with 75 works, including photorealist paintings and large-scale sculpture. Catalogue.

Flashback, 1949–1950, Audrey Flack. From "Audrey Flack, A Retrospective 1950–1990." A traveling exhibition.

Permanent Collection

European and American paintings, sculptures, prints from antiquity to the present; American Indian and Asian art; 17th-century Dutch art; 18th-century French art; 20th-century sculpture, painting. **Highlights:** Elaborately carved oak-paneled English Renaissance room; sculpture garden; Brancusi, *Mlle. Pogany*; Rubens, *The Triumph of the Eucharist.* **Architecture:** 1927 building modeled after the Cleveland Museum of Art; 1954 and 1973 wings; 1983 addition by Geddes.

Admission: Free; parking, $2. Handicapped accessible.
Hours: Tues.–Sat., 10–4; Sun., noon–5. Closed Mon., holidays.
Tours: Call (502) 636-2893 for information.
Food & Drink: Café Musée open museum hours.

New Orleans Museum of Art

City Park, New Orleans, La. 70179-0123
(504) 488-2631

1993 Exhibitions

Thru Jan. 10
Art and Patronage: Ten Centuries of Islamic Art from Kuwait
Ceramics, gems, jewelry, manuscripts, metalwork, woodwork, and textiles. Catalogue.
Jan. 30–Mar. 30
Fritz Bultman Retrospective
Feb.
Bon Temps Rouler: Mardi Gras Photographs by Sydney Byrd

Feb.–Mar.
Between Home and Heaven: Contemporary American Landscape Photography
Catalogue.
Apr. 18–June 28
New Art for a New Building
Treasures of the Archdiocese of New Orleans: A Bicentennial Celebration

Permanent Collection

Kress collection of Renaissance, Baroque painting; French art including works by Degas, who visited New Orleans in 1871–72; Art of the Americas surveys the cultural heritage of North, Central, and South America. **Highlights:** Degas gallery, especially *Portrait of Estelle Muson Degas*; Federal- and Louisiana-style period rooms containing 18th- and 19th-century furniture and decorative arts; Fabergé Easter eggs from the Russian imperial collection and the jeweled Basket of Lilies of the Valley created for Empress Alexandra; Vigée-Lebrun, *Marie Antoinette, Queen of France*. **Architecture:** 1911 Beaux Arts structure by Marx in a 1,500-acre city park; 55,000-square-foot addition opens spring 1993.

Admission: Adults, $6; senior citizens, children under 18, $3. During renovation, adults, $3, and seniors and children under 18, $1.50; group rates available.
Hours: Tues.–Sun., 10–5. Closed Mon., holidays.
Tours: Call (504) 488-2631 for information.

Bowdoin College Museum of Art

Walker Art Building, Brunswick, Maine 04011
(207) 725-3275

1993 Exhibitions

Thru May 2
Book Illustration from the Permanent Collection
Artists include Haskell, Homer, Katz, and Kent.
Mar. 2–Apr. 18
Portraiture
Works on paper from the permanent collection.
Apr. 13–June 6
Henrietta Benson Homer
Watercolors by the artist, mother of Winslow Homer and a major influence on his art.
Apr. 20–June 6
Thomas Spande
Nine etchings based on Piranesi's compositions for *The Prisons*.

May–June
Paintings by Barbara Cooney Porter
Features the original paintings for the artist's book illustrations of *Island Boy*, *Hattie and the Wild Waves*, and *Miss Rumphius*.
Oct. 1993–May 1994
The Legacy of James Bowdoin III
Highlights include Bowdoin's bequest of American Colonial and Federal portraits, European drawings and paintings, and his library and mineralology collections.

Permanent Collection
Over 12,000 objects, including Assyrian, Greek, Roman antiquities; European and American paintings, prints, drawings, sculpture, decorative arts; Kress study collection; Molinari Collection of Medals and Plaquettes; Winslow Homer memorabilia; Far Eastern, African, New World, and Pacific art. **Architecture:** 1894 building by Charles Follen McKim of McKim, Mead and White; 1975 addition by Edward Larrabee Barnes.

Admission: Free. Handicapped accessible; call (207) 725-3275 in advance for assistance.
Hours: Tues.–Sat., 10–5; Sun., 2–5. Closed Mon., holidays.
Tours: Call (207) 725-3064 for reservations.

Portland Museum of Art

Seven Congress Sq., Portland, Maine 04101
(207) 775-6148

Confidences, 1875, Pierre Auguste Renoir. From "The Impressionists and Other Masters: Artists You Love." Portland Museum of Art.

1993 Exhibitions
Thru Mar. 28
Homburger Collection
Thru 1993
The Impressionists and Other Masters: Artists You Love
Works by Monet, Renoir, and other masters of the past two centuries.
May 1–July 11
Portsmouth Furniture: Masterworks from the New Hampshire Seacoast
Sixty pieces of furniture made during Portsmouth's "Golden Age" (1725–1825).
July 24–Oct. 17
Modernism Exhibition
Works by Matisse, Braque, and other successors of the Impressionists.
Nov. 3, 1993–Feb. 10, 1994
Maine Crafts Association

Permanent Collection
Eighteenth- and 19th-century European and American paintings, sculpture; works by Maine artists; Early American and Federal decorative arts, furniture. **Highlights:** Joan Whitney Payson Collection of Impressionist and Post-Impressionist art; Charles Shipman Payson Collection of paintings by Winslow Homer. **Architecture:** 1983 building by Henry N. Cobb of Pei, Cobb, Freed & Partners.

Admission: Adults, $3.50; senior citizens, students with ID, $2.50; children 6–18, $1. Sat., 10–noon, free. Handicapped accessible.
Hours: Tues.–Sat., 10–5; Thurs., 10–9; Sun., noon–5. Closed Mon.
Tours: Call (207) 775-6148 for information.

The Baltimore Museum of Art

Art Museum Dr., Baltimore, Md. 21218
(410) 396-7100 (recording)

1993 Exhibitions
Thru Jan. 3
Brice Marden: Prints 1961–1991
The only U.S. venue for this midcareer print retrospective. Catalogue.
Thru Jan. 17
Picture Perfect: Icons of Modernism from The Museum of Modern Art, New York
Presents seven paintings and 10 drawings by famous Modernist masters; works include van Gogh's *Starry Night*, Rousseau's *The Sleeping Gypsy*, and Cézanne's *The Bather*.
Thru Mar. 14
Friends and Neighbors: The Art of John Ahearn and Rigoberto Torres
Sculpture by the collaborators that depicts the people who live in their Bronx neighborhood.
Jan. 13–June 26
Chinese Children's Hats
Embroidered and appliquéd caps, collars, and shoes from private collections in Hong Kong.
Feb. 14–Apr. 25
Théâtre de la Mode
Recreation of a traveling exhibition of 170 mannequins dressed in the fashions of 1946, presented in sets designed by the leading French artists of the time. Catalogue.
Feb. 17–Apr. 18
Abstract Photography
Traces abstraction in photography through the 20th century.
Abstract Drawings
Twentieth-century works by artists including Kline, Marin, Pollock, and Schwitters.

I and the Village, 1911, Marc Chagall. From "Picture Perfect: Icons of Modernism from The Museum of Modern Art, New York." The Baltimore Museum of Art.

Mar. 17–May 30
Master Printmakers: Delacroix, Manet, Cassatt
Seventy-five rare and important prints by the 19th-century artists.
June 2–Aug. 22
Ansel Adams: The Early Years
In-depth examination of the first two decades of the photographer's artistic growth.
June 16–Aug. 15
Romare Bearden as Printmaker
First comprehensive exhibition of the artist's graphic works.
June 27–Sept. 26
Classical Taste in America 1800–1840
Presents over 225 paintings, sculpture, furniture, and other works that demonstrate America's captivation with the Classical or Grecian style.
Oct. 31, 1993–Jan. 9, 1994
The William S. Paley Collection
Paintings, drawings, and sculpture by Bonnard, Cézanne, Degas, Gauguin, Matisse, Toulouse-Lautrec, and others. Catalogue.
Nov. 17, 1993–Jan. 30, 1994
Northern Lights: Inuit Textile Art from the Canadian Arctic
Examples of contemporary embroidered and appliquéd wall hangings based on traditional clothing designs.

Permanent Collection

Paintings, sculptures, prints, photographs, drawings; period rooms from 19th-century Maryland houses; Asian, African, Pre-Columbian, Native American, Oceanic art. White Collection of Maryland silver; Cheney Miniature Rooms; Syrian mosaics from Antioch; sculpture gardens.
Highlights: Cone collection of Post-Impressionist works;

Cézanne, *Mont Sainte-Victoire Seen from the Bibemus Quarry*; van Gogh, *A Pair of Boots*; Matisse, *Large Reclining Nude and Purple Robe* and *Anemones*; Picasso, *Dr. Claribel Cone* and *La Coiffure*; Pollock, *Water Birds*; Raphael, *Emilia Pia da Montefeltre*; Rembrandt, *Titus*; Van Dyck, *Rinaldo and Armida*; West, *Self-Portrait.*
Architecture: 1929 building and 1937 addition by Pope; 1982 wing and 1986 addition by Bower Lewis Thrower; 1980 Wurtzburger Sculpture Garden by Bower Fradley Lewis Thrower and George Patton; 1988 Levi Sculpture Garden by Sasaki Associates; modern-art wing by Bower Lewis Thrower scheduled for late 1993 completion.

Admission: Adults, $5; full-time students, senior citizens, $3.50; children 4–18, $1.50; age 3 and under, members, free. Thurs., free. Handicapped accessible; wheelchairs available.
Hours: Wed.–Fri., 10–4; Sat.– Sun., 11–6. Closed Mon., Tues., Jan. 1, Good Friday, July 4, Thanksgiving, Dec. 25.
Tours: Call (410) 396-6320 for information.
Food & Drink: Museum Café open Tues.–Sun., 11:30–9:30. For reservations call (410) 235-3930.

The Walters Art Gallery

600 N. Charles St., Baltimore, Md. 21201
(410) 547-9000; 547-ARTS (recording)

1993 Exhibitions

Jan. 12–Apr. 11
The Art of Fine Binding in the Renaissance
Decorative bindings from the collection, including blind-stamped leather covers and gold-tooled and textile binding.

Jan. 17–Apr. 11
Renaissance Fantasy: Heemskerck's Abduction of Helen and the Pursuit of the Classical Ideal
Focus on painter Martin van Heemskerck's 1535 masterpiece, *Fantasy of the Ancient World with the Abduction of Helen.*

Mar. 14–June 13
Sisley, Master Impressionist
First major overview of the artist's career, illuminating three phases of his painting: the pre-Impressionist period (1865–70); his Impressionist years on the Seine and Thames (1870–80); and the "new horizons" explored in France and Wales (1880–90).

Apr. 13–July 11
Travel in Medieval Manuscripts
Illustrates medieval travel by land and sea through manuscripts and printed books.

July 13–Oct. 17
Henry Walters and Leon Gruel
Explores the relationship between rare-book collector Walters and Paris book dealer Gruel through documents, manuscripts, and bindings.

July 25–Sept. 12
Bronze in the Walters Art Gallery
Aug. 1–Sept. 12
Korean Ceramics in the Walters Art Gallery
Oct. 17, 1993–Jan. 9, 1994
African Zion: The Sacred Art of Ethiopia
Over 100 icons, manuscripts, and metalwork from Ethiopian and European collections presenting the cultural legacy of this civilization from the 4th to 18th centuries. Catalogue.
Oct. 19, 1993–Jan. 16, 1994
Medieval Writing and Calligraphy
Examples of fine writing from the Middle Ages from the Walters collection.
Jan. 18–Apr. 13, 1994
Manuscripts and Their Owners
Presents manuscripts from the collection that are visibly identified with the people for whom they were made.

Permanent Collection

Antiquities of Egypt and the ancient Near East; Asian, Greek, Etruscan, Roman art; Early Christian and Byzantine art; medieval art of Western Europe; Islamic art; illuminated manuscripts; 16th- to 19th-century paintings, sculptures, prints; Renaissance enamels, jewelry; Hackerman House (new adjacent museum of Chinese, Japanese, Southeast Asian, and Indian art). **Highlights:** Bellini, *Madonna and Child Enthroned with Saints*; Fabergé Easter eggs from the Russian Imperial collection; Géricault, *Riderless Racers at Home*; Manet, *At the Café*; Raphael, *Virgin of the Candelabra*; Van der Goes, *Portrait of an Unknown Man*. **Architecture:** 1904 Renaissance Revival building by Adams and Delano; courtyard modeled after Palazzo Balbi in Genoa, Italy; 1974 wing by Shepley, Bulfinch, Richardson, and Abbott. Hackerman House: 1850 mansion; 1991 renovation by Grieves, Worrall, Wright & O'Hatrich.

Admission: Adults, $4; senior citizens, $3; students with ID or age 18 and under, free. Wed., free. Handicapped accessible.
Hours: Tues.–Sun., 11–5. Closed Mon., holidays.
Tours: Wed., 12:30; Sun., 2. Call (410) 547-9000, ext. 232, Mon.–Fri., 9–5, for information.
Food & Drink: Pavilion at the Walters open Tues.–Sat., 11:30–4:30.

Isabella Stewart Gardner Museum

280 The Fenway, Boston, Mass. 02115
(617) 566-1401; 734-1359 (recording)

1993 Exhibitions

Rotating exhibitions from the permanent collection.

The Concert, Jan Vermeer. Isabella Stewart Gardner Museum.

Permanent Collection

Italian Renaissance paintings; Dutch, French, German, Spanish masterpieces; American paintings; rare books, manuscripts; decorative arts. Works permanently arranged as Mrs. Gardner specified. **Highlights:** Indoor sculpture and flower garden; Botticelli, *Madonna of the Eucharist*; Crivelli, *Saint George and the Dragon*; Giotto, *Presentation of the Child Jesus at the Temple*; Rembrandt, *Self-Portrait*; Sargent, *Isabella Stewart Gardner*; Titian, *The Rape of Europa.* **Architecture:** 1899–1902 Venetian-style building, created from 15th- and 16th-century fragments, by Sears.

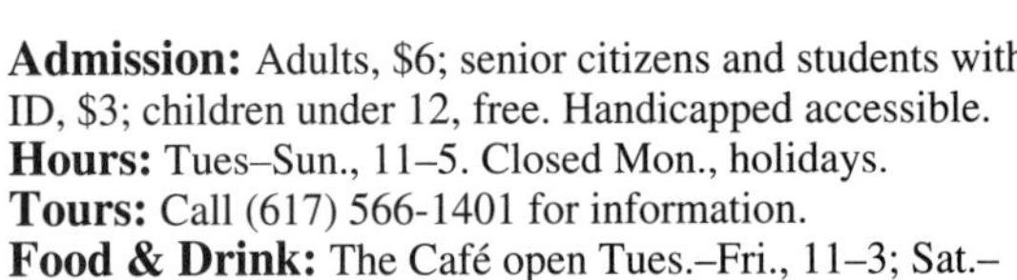

Admission: Adults, $6; senior citizens and students with ID, $3; children under 12, free. Handicapped accessible.
Hours: Tues–Sun., 11–5. Closed Mon., holidays.
Tours: Call (617) 566-1401 for information.
Food & Drink: The Café open Tues.–Fri., 11–3; Sat.–Sun., 11–4.

Museum of Fine Arts, Boston

465 Huntington Ave., Boston, Mass. 02115
(617) 267-9300

1993 Exhibitions

Thru Jan. 17
The Grand Tour: European and American Views of Italy
Features 17th–19th-century artists who traveled to Italy for education and inspiration; includes works by Claude, Canaletto, and Sargent.

Thru Jan. 31
Late 20th-Century Prints
European and American prints from the museum and Boston-area collections.

Thru Feb. 7
On Kawara: Date Paintings in 89 Cities
Retrospective of the Japanese-American artist with paintings from each of the 89 cities in which he has worked.

Thru Feb. 23
Leonardo da Vinci: The Anatomy of Man, Drawings from the Collection of Her Majesty Queen Elizabeth II
These 23 sheets contain 41 drawings from 1485 to 1519 incorporating hundreds of studies and commentaries. Catalogue.

Jan. 13–Mar. 28
Master European Paintings from The National Gallery of Ireland: Mantegna to Goya
Rarely seen works from the early Renaissance through the 18th century, including paintings by Titian, Velázquez, and David. Catalogue.
Mar. 13–May 9
Dutch and Flemish Seventeenth-Century Paintings: The Harold Samuel Collection
Landscapes, genre scenes, townscapes, still-lifes, and portraits are all represented; artists include Frans Hals, Jacob van Ruisdael, and Gerard ter Borch. Catalogue.
Apr. 28–Aug. 15
American Watercolors from the Museum of Fine Arts, Boston
American watercolors from the 1780s to the present.
Sept. 4–Nov. 28
Robert Cumming
Forty works in various media from the mid-1970s to the present, displaying the artist's gently skeptical vision of post-industrial society. Catalogue.

Ball with Hathor Head and Hollow Cylinder, mid-8th cent. B.C., Egypt/Sudan. From "Nubia: Ancient Kingdoms of Africa." Museum of Fine Arts, Boston.

Permanent Collection
Extensive holdings include Egyptian and Classical works; Asian and Islamic art including Chinese export porcelain; Peruvian and Coptic textiles, costumes; French and Flemish tapestries; European and American paintings, decorative arts; ship models; ancient musical instruments. **Highlights:** *Bust of Prince Ankh-haf*; *Minoan Snake Goddess*; *Greek Head of Aphrodite*; Cassatt, *Five o'clock Tea*; Chen Rong, *Nine Dragon Scroll*; Copley, *Mrs. Samuel Quincy*; Duccio, *Crucifixion*; Monet, *Haystack* series; O'Keeffe, *White Rose with Larkspur No. 2*; Picasso, *Rape of the Sabine Women*; Renoir, *Le Bal à Bougival*; Revere, *Liberty Bowl*; Sargent, *The Daughters of Edward D. Bois*; Turner, *The Slave Ship*; Velázquez, *Don Balthasar Carlos and His Dwarf*; Warhol, *Red Disaster.* **Architecture:** 1909 building by Guy Lowell; 1915 Evans Wing; 1928 White Wing by Stubbins; 1981 West Wing by I. M. Pei.

Admission: Adults, $7; senior citizens, college students, $6; ages 6–17, $3.50. Thurs. and Fri. evenings, adults, $6; seniors and students, $5; youths, $3; Wed. 4–closing, free. Handicapped accessible.
Hours: Tues.–Sun., 10–4:45; Wed., 10–9:45. West Wing only: Thurs.–Fri., 5–9:45. Closed Mon., Thanksgiving, Dec. 24–25.
Tours: Call (617) 267-9300 for information.
Food & Drink: Cafeteria open Tues., Sat.–Sun., 10–4; Wed.–Fri., 10–8. Fine Arts Restaurant open Tues., Sat.–Sun., 11:30–2:30; Wed.–Fri., 11:30–2:30 and 5:30–8:30. Galleria Café open Tues., Sat.–Sun., 10–4; Wed.–Fri., 10–9:30.

Harvard University Art Museums

The Arthur M. Sackler Museum
485 Broadway, Cambridge, Mass. 02138
(617) 495-9400

Buddha head, late 12th–early 13th cent., Thai or Cambodian. The Harvard University Art Museums.

1993 Exhibitions

Thru Jan. 31
The Arts of Korea
Features Korean paintings, sculpture, ceramics, and other decorative arts dating from the fifth to early 20th centuries.
Thru Feb. 14
Islam and China
A visual exploration that compares and contrasts Islamic and Chinese approaches to artistic design; features works from the museums' collections.
Feb. 27–Apr. 25
Infancy to Old Age: A Gallery of Indians
A collection of Indian paintings, drawings, and photographs.
May 22–continuing
Mark Rothko's Harvard Murals
Displays five monumental abstract murals given to Harvard by the artist 30 years ago; the works have not been exhibited since 1988 due to their fragile condition.

Permanent Collection

Renowned collections of ancient Chinese art, Japanese prints, Indian and Islamic paintings, Greek and classical sculpture, Roman coins; Oriental carpets. **Highlights:** Chinese jades, cave reliefs, bronzes; Japanese woodblock prints; Persian paintings, calligraphy. **Architecture:** 1985 building by James Stirling.

Tours: Tues.–Fri., 12. Call (617) 495-9400.

Busch-Reisinger Museum

29 Kirkland St., Cambridge, Mass. 02138
(617) 495-9400

1993 Exhibitions

Thru Jan. 10
Art and Image in the German Renaissance and Reformation
Includes works by Dürer, Altdorfer, and Holbein the Elder.
Apr. 17–June 13
The Work of Paul Klee: Singular and Universal
Traces the development of the artist's work, from his early etchings in 1902 to work from the year of his death in 1940.

Permanent Collection

Specializes in art of German-speaking Europe: 16th-century painting; late Medieval, Renaissance, Baroque sculpture; 18th-century porcelain from Germany, Austria, the Low Countries; 20th-century art. **Architecture:** 1921 building by

Bestelmeyer; 1991 building by Gwathmey, Siegel, and Associates.

Tours: Tues.–Fri., 12; call (617) 495-9400.

Fogg Art Museum

32 Quincy St., Cambridge, Mass. 02138
(617) 495-9400

1993 Exhibitions

Thru Mar. 7
The Harvard Society of Contemporary Art, 1929–1936
Explores the history of the society through original works of art and rare archival material, not shown since the society disbanded in 1936.

Jan. 16–Mar. 14
Print Connoisseurship
Analyzes the various components of the study of prints—their attribution, the definition of states and editions, discrimination of impression quality, and interpretation of condition.

Mar. 13–May 9
La Caricature: Wit, Humor, and Politics in French Caricature, 1830–1835
Explores the history and character of French caricature during the early years of the July Monarchy.

Apr. 3–June 13
A Noble Collection: The Spencer Albums of Old Master Prints
A selection from the collection of 3,400 Old Master prints.

May 15–July 11
Fragonard
Celebrates the recent acquisition of an important prepatory drawing for *The First Step*, a painting at the museum; includes 19 drawings and four paintings by the artist.

Permanent Collection

Masterpieces of Western painting, sculpture, graphic art. **Highlights:** Drawings by Michelangelo, Rembrandt; Fra Angelico, *Crucifixion*; van Gogh, *Self-Portrait*; Ingres, *Odalisque*; Monet, *Gare Saint-Lazare*; Picasso, *Mother and Child*; Poussin, *Infant Bacchus Entrusted to the Nymphs*; Renoir, *Seated Bather*. **Architecture:** 1927 Neo-Georgian exterior by Coolidge Bulfinch & Abbott; Italianate courtyard.

Tours: Tues.–Fri., 11. Call (617) 495-9400.

All Three Museums:

Admission: Adults, $4; senior citizens, students, $2.50; age 18 and under, free; Sat., 10–noon, free. Handicapped accessible.
Hours: Tues.–Sun., 10–5. Closed Mon., Jan. 1, July 4, Thanksgiving, Dec. 24–25.

MIT List Visual Arts Center

20 Ames St., Cambridge, Mass. 02139
(617) 253-4400

1993 Exhibitions

Thru Feb. 7
Corporal Politics
Artists Robert Gober, Annette Messager, Rona Pondick, Kiki Smith, and David Wojnarowicz explore the body fragment as both theme and content, demonstrating the dramatic degree of dissolution that has characterized recent art.

Permanent Collection

Works in all media, focusing on contemporary art, installed throughout the MIT campus. **Highlights:** Heizer, *Guennette* (long-term loan from the Metropolitan Museum of Art); bronzes by Lipchitz; Bartlett, *Overhill Road, Shawnee Mission*; Calder, *Big Sail*; two large reclining figures by Moore. **Architecture:** 1985 building by I. M. Pei in collaboration with artists Scott Burton, Kenneth Noland, Richard Fleishner.

Admission: Free. Handicapped accessible.
Hours: Mon.–Fri., noon–6; Sat.–Sun, 1–5.
Tours: Call (617) 253-4400 for information.

Smith College Museum of Art

Elm St. at Bedford Terr., Northampton, Mass. 01063
(413) 584-2760

1993 Exhibitions

Jan. 27–Mar. 19
Nineteenth-Century Photographs from the Collection
Feb.–mid-Mar.
An Installation by Pat Ward Williams
Site-specific installation addressing themes of the Columbus quincentenary.
An Installation to Celebrate the Fiftieth Anniversary of Rufino Tamayo's Nature and the Artist*: The Work of Art and the Observer*
The first showing of this fresco since 1979; includes prepatory drawings and other works by the artist.
Apr. 7–May 28
Mexican Prints and Drawings
Includes works by Tamayo, Rivera, and Orozco.
Apr.–summer
Early American Manuscript Illumination from the Ephrata Cloister
Richly illuminated works produced at the Ephrata Cloister, a Pietist communal society in 18th-century Pennsylvania.

Apr.–May
Jaune Quick-to-See Smith
Works by the artist that draw on storytelling, music, and dance from her Native American heritage.

Dodo and her Brother, 1908–1920, Ernst Kirchner. Smith College Museum of Art.

Permanent Collection

Emphasis on 18th- to 20th-century French and American works in all media. **Highlights:** Late Roman head of Emperor Gallienus; Bouts, *Portrait of a Young Man*; Courbet, *La Toilette de la Mariée*; Degas, *Jephthah's Daughter*; Eakins, *Mrs. Edith Mahon*; Elmer, *Mourning Picture*; Kirchner, *Dodo and her Brother*; Lehmbruck, *Torso of the Pensive Woman*; Picasso, *Table, Guitar, and Bottle*; Rembrandt, *The Three Crosses*; Rodin, *Walking Man*; Sheeler, *Rolling Power*; Terbrugghen, *Old Man Writing by Candlelight.* **Architecture:** 1973 building by John Andrews/ Anderson/Baldwin.

Admission: Free. Handicapped accessible.
Hours: Academic year: Tues.–Sat., 12–5; Sun., 2–5. Closed Mon. Closed Jan., June; call for July–Aug. hours.
Tours: Group tours can be arranged by reservation during the academic year. Call (413) 585-2760 for information.

Rose Art Museum

Brandeis University, Waltham, Mass. 02254-9110
(617) 736-4207

1993 Exhibitions

Thru Jan. 17
Jackie Ferrara Sculpture: A Retrospective
Traces the career of this formalist sculptor from early '70s stack-wood pieces to recent tabletop sculpture. About 50 pieces, including maquettes, drawings, and photographs. Catalogue.
Feb. 6–Mar. 14
The Lois Foster Exhibition of Boston Area Artists: Contemporary African American Art
Mar. 27–May 2
Contemporary Art from the Permanent Collection
May 16–July 31
Manny Farber
The 16th Annual Patrons and Friends Exhibition of Contemporary Art
Features the artist's large, shaped, paint-on-paper abstractions. Catalogue.

Permanent Collection

Major contemporary art assemblage in New England.

Admission: Free. No handicapped access.
Hours: Tues.–Sun., 1–5, Thurs., 1–9.
Tours: Call for information.

Davis Museum and Cultural Center

(Formerly the Wellesley College Museum)
Wellesley College, Wellesley, Mass. 02181
(617) 283-2051

1993 Exhibitions

NOTE: New museum opens Oct. 15, 1993.
Oct. 15–Nov. 28
Flemish Drawings in the Age of Rubens
First American survey of Flemish Baroque draftsmanship in the 17th century includes 20 works by Rubens and drawings by Jam Beckhorst and lesser-known artists.
The Costa Rican Trophy Heads: Representations of Identity
Trophy heads presented in relation to Central American ideas about identity and the body.
Amerika
Multipartite installation by German sculptor-filmmaker Rebecca Horn.

Permanent Collection

5,000 paintings, sculptures, and works on paper spanning 3,000 years of the history of art. **Architecture:** 1993 building by Jose Rafael Moneo.

Admission: Free. Handicapped accessible.
Hours: Mon.–Sat., 10–5; Sun, 2–5.
Tours: Call (617) 283-2051.
Food & Drink: Call (617) 283-2051 for café hours.

Sterling and Francine Clark Art Institute

225 South St., Williamstown, Mass. 01267
(413) 458-9545

1993 Exhibitions

Thru Mar. 28
American Art at the Clark
Features works by Homer and Sargent.
Alfred Stevens and Modernism
About 15 works by one of the major chroniclers of Parisian life at the end of the 19th century.
Apr. 17–June 13
The Graphic Art of Les XX and the Belgian Avant-Garde
Demonstrates the importance of Belgian graphic arts to such movements as Neo-Impressionism, Symbolism, Art Nouveau, and Arts & Crafts; artists include James Ensor and Félicien Rops.

Saco Bay, 1896, Winslow Homer. From "American Art at the Clark." Sterling and Francine Clark Art Institute.

July 3–Sept. 12
Rookwood Pottery: The Glorious Gamble
Spans the "glory years" of Rookwood's decorating history from the early 1880s to the 1940s. Catalogue.
May 14–July 10, 1994
English Silver: Masterpieces by Omar Ramsden from the Campbell Collection
Handcrafted silver and metal pieces by the English Arts and Crafts artist.

Permanent Collection

Old Master paintings, prints, drawings by della Francesca, Gossaert, Memling, Rembrandt, Tiepolo; distinguished holdings of French 19th-century Impressionist and academic painting and sculpture; work by Barbizon artists Corot, Millet, Troyon; English silver; American works by Cassatt, Homer, Remington, Sargent. **Highlights:** Degas, *Dancing Lesson*; Homer, *Saco Bay, Prout's Neck*; Renoir, *Sleeping Girl with Cat*; Turner, *Rockets and Blue Lights*; Fragonard, *Portrait of a Man (The Warrior)*. **Architecture:** 1955 building by Daniel Perry; 1973 building by Pietro Belluschi and The Architects Collaborative; 1963 service building with 1986 addition.

Admission: Free. Handicapped accessible.
Hours: Tues.–Sun., 10–5. Closed Mon., Jan. 1, Thanksgiving, Dec. 25.
Tours: July–Aug.: Tues.–Sun., 3.

Road to the Village, 1910–13, Maurice Prendergast. From "Maurice Prendergast: Highlights from WCMA's Collection." Williams College Museum of Art.

Williams College Museum of Art

Main St., Williamstown, Mass. 01267
(413) 597-2429

1993 Exhibitions

Thru Jan. 31
The Prendergasts and the History of Art
Thru Mar. 28
ARTWORKS: Vivienne Koorland
Jan. 16–Mar. 21
Williams College Studio Art Facility Group Exhibition
Jan. 27–June 27
Maurice Prendergast: Highlights from WCMA's Collection
Feb. 13–June 27
Hot, Dry Men, Cold, Wet Women: The Theory of Humours and Depictions of Men and Women in Western European Art of the 1600s
June 12–Nov. 28
Third Williams Alumni Loan Exhibition
May 15–June 6
Annual Student Show
July–Dec.
Across the Dark Water: Indian Paintings from the Bequest of Mrs. Horace W. Frost in the Permanent Collection
Aug.–Dec.
Charles Prendergast: Highlights from the WCMA's Collection

Permanent Collection

Late 18th- to 19th-century American art by Copley, Eakins, Harding, Harnett, Hunt, Inness, Peto, Stuart; early Modern works by Demuth, Feininger, Hopper, Marin, O'Keeffe, Prendergast, Wood; contemporary works by de Kooning, Avery, Hofmann, Holzer, Motherwell, Rauschenberg, Warhol; South Asian art including Indian 10th- to 18th-century sculpture, 17th- to 19th-century Mughal paintings. **Highlights:** American Modernist painting and sculpture; Cambodian and Indian sculptures; Charles and Maurice Prendergast; Warhol, *Self-Portrait.* **Architecture:** 1846 Classical Revival building by Tefft; 1983 and 1986 additions by Centerbrook Architects and Planners.

Admission: Free. Handicapped accessible.
Hours: Mon.–Sat., 10–5; Sun., 1–5. Closed Jan. 1, Thanksgiving, Dec. 25.
Tours: Call (413) 597-2429 for information.

Worcester Art Museum

55 Salisbury St., Worcester, Mass. 01609-3196
(508) 799-4406

1993 Exhibitions

Thru Jan. 17
Clinton Hill: Paperworks and Constructions
The artist's brightly colored constructions of handmade paper, plastic, and wood.
Thru Feb. 28
**Ottocento: Romanticism and Revolution in Nineteenth-Century Italian Painting*
First major exhibition to present an overview of 19th-century Italian painting; features works by Appiani, Fatori, Boldini, and Segantini. Catalogue.
Feb. 9–Apr. 25
Master Printmakers: Piranesi's Dream of Ancient Rome
The artist's monumental etchings, which present a fantastic vision of Rome and transformed the historical image of the ancient civilization.
Feb. 25–May 30
Insights: Erik Levine
Contemporary large-scale sculpture, composed of wooden armatures covered with plywood skin.
Apr. 15–July 3
The Caribbean and Latin American World 500 Years Later: Photographs by Ann Parker
Works reflecting the artist's commitment to creating pictures of native peoples who face extinction in the modern world.
May 18–Aug. 15
Master Printmakers: Goya, Moralist amid Chaos
Features prints by the preeminent Spanish artist.
Aug. 31–Nov. 7
Master Printmakers: The Poetic Vision of Odilon Redon
Works by the 19th-century artist, who used printmaking to explore the dramatic possibilities of black and white.
Sept. 19–Dec. 5
Judith Leyster: A Dutch Master of the Golden Age
Exhibition that marks the 100th anniversary of the artist's rediscovery in 1893; an alleged pupil of Frans Hals, she is now a celebrated woman painter. Catalogue.
Oct. 7, 1993–Jan. 16, 1994
Insights: A Distant View

Permanent Collection

Encompasses 50 centuries of art from East to West, antiquity to the present: Indian, Persian, Japanese, Chinese art; 17th-century Dutch paintings; American 17th- to 19th-century paintings; contemporary art. **Highlights:** Anonymous, *Captain John Freake*; Benson, *Portrait of Three Daughters*; Copley, *John Bours*; Hokusai, *The Great Wave at Kanagawa*; Kandinsky, *Untitled*; Massys, *Rest on the Flight into Egypt*; del Sarto, *Saint John the Baptist.* Renaissance court with 10 mosaics from Antioch dating from the second to sixth centuries; Bancroft collection of u*kiyo-e* prints. **Architecture:** 1898 Neoclassical building by Stephen C. Earle; 1933 addition by William T. Aldrich; 1970 Higgins Wing by the Architects Collaborative; 1983 Hiatt Wing by Irwin A. Regent.

Admission: Adults, $4; senior citizens, college students with ID, $2.50; members, children age 18 and under, free. Handicapped accessible.
Hours: Tues.–Fri., 11–4; Thurs, 11–8, Sat., 10–5; Sun., 1–5. Closed Mon., Jan. 1, Easter, July 4, Thanksgiving, Dec. 25.
Tours: Sun., 3; Thurs., 7:30. For group tours call (508) 799-4406, ext. 269 four weeks in advance.
Food & Drink: Museum Café open Tues.–Sat., 11:30–2 for lunch, 2–3 for beverages, desserts; Sun., noon–4 for brunch, desserts, teas; Thurs., 5–8 for dinner. Call (508) 799-4406, ext. 255 for information.

Portrait of General Desaix, after 1800, Andrea Appiani. From "Ottocento: Romanticism and Revolution." A traveling exhibition. AFA.

The Detroit Institute of Arts

5200 Woodward Ave., Detroit, Mich. 48202
(313) 833-7900 (general information); 833-2323 (ticket office)

1993 Exhibitions

Thru Apr. 8
American Drawings and Watercolors: Selections from the Permanent Collection
Jan. 3–Mar. 21
Arnold Newman's Americans
Jan. 27–Apr. 30
Photographs from the Permanent Collection
May 1–June 27
Master Drawings from the Permanent Collection
May 12–July 3
A Privileged Eye: The Photographs of Carl Van Vechten
Between 1932 and 1964, Van Vechten photographed major figures in arts and letters. This show features 76 prints.
June 21–Aug. 29
Songs of My People
The regional traditions and lifestyles of African Americans as recorded on film by 50 black photojournalists in summer 1990. Catalogue.
Sept. 11–Nov. 14
A Private View: Small Paintings in the Manoogian Collection
Masterpieces include informal portraits by Sargent, genre scenes by Millet, and still-lifes by Harnett. Catalogue.
Oct. 17, 1993–Feb. 6, 1994
Art of the American Indian Frontier, 1800–1900: The Chandler/Pohrt Collection
Illustrates the close relationship between cultural and artistic changes in 19th-century Native American history. Catalogue.

Feather headdress, c. 1890, and man's shirt, c. 1860, Crow, Native American. From "Art of the American Indian Frontier, 1800–1900: The Chandler/Pohrt Collection." A traveling exhibition.

Permanent Collection

Extensive holdings of African and Native American arts; European and American painting from the Middle Ages to the present; decorative arts; graphic arts; theater arts; textiles; Asian and Near Eastern art; 20th-century decorative arts, design; period rooms. **Highlights:** Brueghel, *Wedding Dance*; Caravaggio, *Conversion of the Magdalen*; Degas, *Violinist and Young Woman*; Van Eyck, *Saint Jerome in His Study*; Picasso, *Bather by the Sea*; Rembrandt, *The Visitation*; van Gogh, *Self-Portrait*; Whistler, *Arrangement in Gray: Portrait of the Painter* and *Nocturne in Black and Gold: The Falling Rocket*; German Expressionist paintings by Kirchner, Klee, Nolde; courtyard with Rivera's *Detroit Industry* fresco. **Architecture:** 1927 Italian Renaissance–style building by Cret and Zantzinger, Borie and Medary; 1966 south wing; 1971 north wing.

Admission: Donation required. Suggested donation: adults, $4; children, students, $1. Handicapped accessible.
Hours: Wed.–Sun., 11–4. Closed Mon.–Tues., holidays.
Tours: Wed.–Sat., 1; Sun., 1, 2:30. For group-tour reservations call (313) 833-7978.
Food & Drink: Kresge Café open Wed.–Sun., 11–3.

Grand Rapids Art Museum

155 Division North, Grand Rapids, Mich. 49503
(616) 459-4677

1993 Exhibitions
Thru Jan. 5
Through the Path of Echoes: Contemporary Art in Mexico
Works by 17 artists place contemporary Mexican art in the center of international avant-garde aesthetics, while demonstrating its strong ties to the past.
Thru Jan. 17
Other Images: Other Realities
Mexican photography since 1930.
Thru Feb. 7
José Narezo
Recent paintings and sculpture by the Grand Rapids artist.
Jan. 22–Mar. 14
Antique Soup Tureens from the Campbell Museum
Eighteenth-century soup tureens from the Campbell Museum collection.
Feb. 5–Sept. 12
A Body of Work
Figurative works from the permanent collection.
Feb. 19–Apr. 11
Misha Gordin: Photographs
Mar. 26–May 9
The Art of the Frame
Apr. 24–May 15
Seats on Show
June 18–Oct. 3
I Too Know What I Like

Harvest, Karl Schmidt-Rotluff. Grand Rapids Art Museum.

July 2–Aug. 22
The Work of Tyree Guyton
Sept. 10–Oct. 24
David Greenwood Retrospective
Oct. 1–Dec. 5
African-American Work from Michigan Collections
Nov. 11, 1993–Jan. 16, 1994
Contemporary Quilts from West Michigan
Nov. 19, 1993–Jan. 9, 1994
The Definitive Contemporary American Quilt

Permanent Collection

Old Master prints, drawings; American and European paintings, furniture, photographs, sculpture, decorative arts. **Highlights:** Chase, *The Opera Cloak*; Schmidt-Rottluff, *Harvest*; Pechstein, *Reflections*; Diebenkorn, *Ingleside*; Hartigan, *Riviera*; Calder, *Red Rudder in the Air*; prints by Vlaminck, Miró, Braque, Matisse, Moore, Picasso; Baker Study Collection of European furniture from the Renaissance to the 20th century; English, French, Italian, Asian furniture from the late 18th century; furniture by Eames. **Architecture:** 1910 building by James Knox Taylor.

Admission: Adults, $2; senior citizens, full-time students, 50¢; children 5 and under, members, free. Handicapped accessible.
Hours: Tues., Sun., noon–4; Wed., Fri., Sat., 10–4; Thurs., 10–9.
Tours: Call (616) 459-4677 three weeks in advance.

The Minneapolis Institute of Arts

2400 Third Ave. South, Minneapolis, Minn. 55404
(612) 870-3131; 870-3200 (recording)

1993 Exhibitions

Thru Jan. 31
Nightmare at Helmsley Palace
Artist Judith Yourman's multimedia exhibition examining the Leona Helmsley persona and her recent trial.
Thru Feb. 21
19th-Century Topographical Photographs
Photographs documenting the Middle East, Italy, Japan, Western United States, and Minneapolis before postcards and snapshots came into existence.
Thru June 6
Blue and White Porcelain
Features 50 international examples of underglaze porcelain dating from 13th-century China to the industrialized world of the 18th century.

Thru July 11
A Renaissance Masterpiece: Portrait of Six Tuscan Poets *by Giorgio Vasari*
Examines an important 16th-century Italian painting from the institute's collection.

Feb. 6–Apr. 4
Painting with Light: The Photographic Aspect in the Work of E.M. Lilien
The artist's photographs, etchings, and drawings of Ottoman-Palestine executed between 1906 and 1918. Catalogue.

Feb. 20–July 18
The Printing Revival in America: Bruce Rogers and Frederic Goudy
Thirty books by the artists designed between 1895 and 1940.

Mar. 13–June 27
The Panoramic Photographs of Gus Foster
Recent color images, primarily landscapes from the Southwestern United States.

Mar. 21–June 20
Images of a Queen's Power: Royal Tapestries of France
Ten tapestries from the celebrated *Stories of Queen Artemisia* series, woven in 17th-century Paris and formerly in the collection of the Barberini princes of Rome. Catalogue.

Apr. 23–July 3
American Masters: Selections from the Collection of Richard Lewis Hillstrom
American modernist prints, drawings, watercolors, and oil paintings; features works by George Bellows, Robert Henri, John Henry Twachtman, and others. Catalogue.

July 18–Sept. 12
Two Lives: Georgia O'Keeffe and Alfred Stieglitz—A Conversation in Paintings and Photographs
Tracks the visual and intellectual correspondences in the work of the two artists, who were artistic collaborators as well as husband and wife. Catalogue.

July 18–Oct. 10
Alfred Stieglitz's Camera Notes
Ninety-one photogravures from the formative stage of Stieglitz's career as an editor-photographer.

Permanent Collection

African and Asian art; European and American paintings, prints, drawings, sculptures, photographs, decorative art; period rooms; American textiles. **Highlights:** Chinese bronzes, jades, silks; Greco-Roman Doryphoros; American and British silver; works by Poussin, Rembrandt, van Gogh, Degas, Goya, Bonnard; prints, drawings by Goya, Rembrandt, Watteau, Blake, Ingres, Toulouse-Lautrec, Johns; photography by Stieglitz, Steichen, Adams; sculpture by Picasso, Brancusi, Calder; nine original period rooms. **Architecture:** 1915 Neoclassical building by McKim, Mead, & White; 1974 wing by Kenzo Tange.

Admission: Free.
Hours: Tues.–Sat., 10–5; Thurs., 10–9; Sun., noon–5. Closed Mon., July 4, Thanksgiving, Dec. 25.
Tours: Tues.–Sun., 2; Thurs., 7; Sat.–Sun., 1. American Sign Language interpretation first Sun. of month. Call (612) 870-3140 for group tours.
Food & Drink: Studio Restaurant open Tues.–Sun., 11:30–2:30.

Walker Art Center

Vineland Place, Minneapolis, Minn. 55403
(612) 375-7600

1993 Exhibitions

Thru Feb. 14
Claes Oldenburg: In the Studio
Showcases a number of little-known and unique works borrowed from the artist's own studio.

Thru Apr. 4
Viewpoints: Malcolm X: Man, Ideal, Icon
A multimedia exhibition featuring historical information, newly commissioned art works, and music videos documenting the life of Malcolm X.

Feb. 14–June 6
In the Spirit of Fluxus
Five hundred objects of Fluxus art, ranging from performance pieces and experimental films to artist's books and posters. Catalogue.

Mar. 7–May 2
James Rosenquist: Time Dust/The Complete Graphics
Survey of the artist's graphic work, from his Pop images of the 1960s to recent handmade paper and collage prints. Catalogue.

July 10–Oct. 3
Jeff Koons
Comprehensive presentation featuring 65 mixed-media sculpture and wall pieces by the controversial contemporary artist. Catalogue.

Michael Jackson and Bubbles, 1988, Jeff Koons. From "Jeff Koons." A traveling exhibition.

Permanent Collection

Primarily 20th-century art of all major movements; over 11-acre outdoor sculpture garden containing works by Modernists and contemporaries. **Highlights:** Johns, *Green Angel*; Marc, *The Large Blue Horses*; works by Rothko; Warhol, *16 Jackies*; Polke, *Mrs. Autumn and Her Two Daughters*; Minneapolis Sculpture Garden: 40 works by established 20th-century masters and by leading contemporaries. **Architecture:** 1971 building, 1983 addition, and 1988 Minneapolis Sculpture Garden by Barnes.

Admission: Adults, $3; students, children 12–18, groups of 10 or more, $2 per person; senior citizens, members, children under 12, free. Thurs., first Sat. of each month, members, free. Handicapped accessible.
Hours: Tues.–Sat., 10–8; Sun., 11–5. Closed Mon., major holidays.
Tours: Thurs., Sat.–Sun., 2. For group-tour reservations call (612) 375-7609.
Food & Drink: Gallery 8 Restaurant open Tues.–Sun., 11:30–3.

Minnesota Museum of Art

Landmark Center Galleries, Fifth at Market; Jemne Building Galleries, St. Peter at Kellogg, St. Paul, Minn. 55102
(612) 292-4355

1993 Exhibitions

Thru May 2
Garden of Delights: Nature in Asian Art
East Asian screen and scroll paintings, textiles, ceramics, and lacquer and metal objects that portray scenes of nature.
Thru May 9
The Still-Life in American Art
Oil paintings, works on paper, and photographs by American artists from the 19th and 20th centuries.
Jan. 24–Mar. 28
SPIRITS: Selections from the Collection of Geoffrey Holder and Carmen de Lavallade
Works include African sculpture, Haitian painting and sculpture, Mexican masks, and North American folk and visionary art.
Apr. 18–June 6
Twentieth Century American Crafts: An Era of Change
Surveys the work of innovators in contemporary craft, including both renowned and regional artists.
May–Oct.
Animals
Celebrates the theme of animals in art.

June 13–Aug. 22
As Seen by Both Sides: American and Vietnamese Artists Look at the War
Works by 20 American and 20 Vietnamese artists that trace how both countries have portrayed the war in Vietnam.
Sept. 10–Nov. 7
Charles Burchfield
Retrospective of the artist's career, including his drawings, paintings, and watercolors.
Nov. 21, 1993–Jan. 16, 1994
Breaking Boundaries: American Puppetry in the 1980s
Features state-of-the-art American puppetry.
Dec. 12, 1993–Feb. 27, 1994
Seeing Straight: The f.64 Revolution in Photography
Eighty works by group members including Ansel Adams, Imogen Cunningham, and Edward Weston, who searched for "observable essence" through their sharp-focus images.

Permanent Collection
Features American, Asian, African, Oceanic art. **Highlights:** Jemne Building: American and non-Western Art; Landmark Center: contemporary American art.

Admission: Free.
Hours: Tues.–Fri., 10:30–4:30; Thurs. 10:30–7:30; Sat.–Sun., 1–4:30; (the Jemne Building: Sun., 11:30–4:30). Closed Mon., major holidays.
Tours: Call (619) 292-4369 for information.
Food & Drink: The DECO Restaurant open museum hours.

The Nelson-Atkins Museum of Art

4525 Oak St., Kansas City, Mo. 64111
(816) 561-4000; (816) 751-1ART (recording)

1993 Exhibitions
Thru Jan. 10
A Privileged Eye: The Photography of Carl Van Vechten
Between 1932 and 1964, Van Vechten photographed major figures in arts and letters. This show features 76 prints.
Thru Feb. 7
Rookwood Pottery: The Glorious Gamble
Spans the "glory years" of Rookwood's decorating history from the early 1880s to the 1940s. Catalogue.
Jan. 24–Mar. 7
Oliphant's Presidents: Twenty-five Years of Caricature
Ninety works by editorial cartoonist Pat Oliphant.
Mar. 28–May 9
Changing Realities: Two Decades of Soviet Photography

Apr. 17–June 6
Master European Drawings from Polish Collections: Fifteenth Through Eighteenth Centuries
More than 100 drawings, selected from the Old Master collections of 10 Polish museums. Catalogue.
Three Centuries of Roman Drawings from the Villa Farnesina
Documents the development of drawing in Rome from the 16th to18th centuries; includes works by Bernini, da Cortona, and Maratta. Catalogue.
May 23–July 25
Graphic Masterworks from the Permanent Collection
July 16–Sept. 5
Common Ground/Uncommon Vision: The Michael and Julie Hall Collection of American Folk Art
More than 150 objects, ranging from an 18th-century weather vane to works by Rev. Howard Finster. Catalogue.
Aug. 8–Sept. 19
Paris 1938: Photographs by Fritz Henle
Oct. 3–Nov. 14
The Intimate Collaboration: Prints from Teaberry Press
Oct. 10–Nov. 28
Gods, Guardians, and Lovers: Temple Sculptures from North India, 700–1200 A.D.

Permanent Collection

European and American paintings, sculptures, prints, decorative arts; American, Indian, Oceanic, Pre-Columbian art; renowned collection of Asian art. **Highlights:** Largest permanent U.S. display of Bentons; Bingham, *Canvassing for a Vote*; Caravaggio, *Saint John the Baptist*; Guercino, *Saint Luke Displaying a Painting of the Virgin*; de Kooning, *Woman IV*; Moore sculpture garden; Poussin, *The Triumph of Bacchus*; Rembrandt, *Youth with a Black Cap*; Renoir, *The Large Bather.* **Architecture:** 1933 Neoclassical building by Wight and Wight.

Admission: Adults, $4; students, children 6–18, $1; children under 6, free. Sat., permanent collection free. Handicapped accessible.
Hours: Tues.–Thurs., 10–4; Fri., 10–9; Sat., 10–5; Sun., 1–5. Closed Mon., Jan. 1, July 4, Thanksgiving, Dec. 24–25.
Tours: Tues.–Sat., 10:30, 11, 1, 2; Fri., 7; Sun., 1:30, 2, 2:30, 3. Call (816) 751-1238.
Food & Drink: Rozzelle Court Restaurant open Tues.–Thurs., 10–3; Fri., 10–8 (closed 4–5); Sat., 10–3:30; Sun., 1–3:30.

The Saint Louis Art Museum

One Fine Arts Drive, Forest Park, St. Louis, Mo. 63110
(314) 721-0072

1993 Exhibitions

Thru Jan. 3
Photography in Contemporary German Art 1960-1990
An overview of various nontraditional approaches to photography explored by German artists including Joseph Beuys, Anselm Kiefer, and Gerhard Richter. Accompanied by several publications.

Thru Feb. 7
Art and Artisans of Renaissance Nuremburg
Objects produced during the Renaissance in Nuremberg, Germany's artistic center of the time.
Contemporary Inuit Drawings from Arctic Canada
Provides viewers with a window into past and present Canadian Eskimo culture.

Thru Feb. 16
Currents 52: Frank Gehry: New Bentwood Furniture Designs
A series of lightweight chairs resembling woven baskets, noteworthy for the artist's technological innovations.

Thru Feb. 28
Hear My Quilt: 150 Years of African-American Quilt Making
Reflects the roles played by African-American quilt makers and their social, political, and economic conditions.

Feb. 2–Apr. 18
Visions of the People: A Pictorial History of Plains Indian Life
Over 300 objects, including clothing, tipi covers and liners, drums, shields, paintings, and Ghost Dance materials.

Feb. 19–Apr. 25
Matisse: Image into Sign
Demonstrates the artist's move from realistic imagery to a pictorial language based on signs drawn from memory and imagination.

Feb. 23–May 31
First Light: Prints by James Turrell
Twenty aquatints by the artist exploring lights as an artistic medium.

May 28–July 25
Susan Rothenberg: Paintings and Drawings
A retrospective tracing the career of this American imagist painter from her early horse images to recent autobiographical, expressionist paintings. Catalogue.

June 15–Sept. 12
Bob Kolbrener Retrospective
Twenty-five years of Western photography by the St. Louis artist.

Sept. 28, 1993–Jan. 2, 1994
Moneta Sleet
Works by the celebrated photojournalist, including images of the Civil Rights Movement in the 1960s.
Dec. 17, 1993–Feb. 13, 1994
The Dorothy and George Saxe Collection: A Passion for Studio Crafts
One of the most comprehensive craft collections in the United States; includes glass, ceramics, wood, and textiles.

Permanent Collection
Encompasses art of many periods, styles, and cultures: African, Asian, Oceanic, American Indian, Pre-Columbian art; European Old Master paintings, drawings; American art from Colonial times to the present; French Impressionism, Post-Impressionism, German Expressionism; 20th-century European art; decorative arts, including six period rooms.
Highlights: Chagall, *Temptation*; Fantin-Latour, *The Two Sisters*; Van Goyen, *Skating on the Ice near Dordrecht*; Smith, *Cubi XIV*; Vasari, *Judith and Holofernes*; Stella, *Marriage of Reason and Squalor*; Kiefer, *Breaking of the Vessels*; world's largest Max Beckmann collection.
Architecture: 1904 building by Gilbert for World's Fair; 1977 renovation by Hardy Holzman Pfeiffer Associates; 1980 South Wing by Howard, Needles, Tammen, and Bergendorff; 1988 West Wing renovation by SMP/Smith-Entzeroth.

Admission: Free. Entrance fee for special exhibitions; Tues., free. Members, free. Handicapped accessible; wheelchairs available.
Hours: Tues., 1:30–8:30; Wed.–Sun., 10–5. Closed Mon., Jan. 1, Thanksgiving, Dec. 25.
Tours: Thirty-minute tour, Wed.–Fri., 1:30; 60-minute tour, Sat.–Sun., 1:30.
Food & Drink: Museum Café open for coffee, lunch, light fare; Tues., dinner; Sun., brunch.

Yellowstone Art Center

410 N. 27th St., Billings, Mont. 59101
(406) 256-6804

1993 Exhibitions
Jan. 22–Feb. 28
Selections from the Permanent Collection
Jan. 24–Mar. 6
25th Annual Art Auction Exhibition
Works by over 100 contemporary artists, including Rudy Autio, Deborah Butterfield, and Jaune Quick-to-See Smith.
Mar. 5–May 30
The Virginia Snook Collection
Includes works by cowboy artist and author Will James.

Thorn Hacker
Features work by the Oregon architect, who will design an expanded art facility for the center.
Tom Rippon: Ceramic Sculpture
June 4–Aug. 29
50th Anniversary Crow Sun Dance, Photographs by Michael Crummett
Color and black-and-white prints documenting the Crow Sun Dance.
L. A. Huffman Photographs
Images of late–19th-century Montana by the frontier photographer.
Animals
Works from the collection that portray wild and domestic animals.
Nov. 5–Dec. 31
Old Master Prints

Permanent Collection

Over 2,400 objects, including paintings, drawings, prints, sculpture, ceramics, photography, and fiber works; highlights contemporary art and regional artists.
Architecture: Turn-of-the-century building; 1964 renovation into exhibition space. Former Yellowstone County Jail renovated to house exhibitions and classes.

Admission: Free. First floor is handicapped accessible.
Hours: Tues.–Sat., 11–5; Thurs., 11–8; Sun., noon–5. Summer hours: daily, 10–5.
Tours: Sun. afternoons: gallery talks; call (406) 256-6804 for group-tour reservations at least one week in advance.

Sheldon Memorial Art Gallery

University of Nebraska–Lincoln, 12th and R sts., Lincoln, Nebr. 68588
(402) 472-2461

1993 Exhibitions

Thru Jan. 13
Akari: Sculpted Light by Isamu Noguchi
A selection of the artist's Japanese paper and steel-wire sculptures.
Thru Jan. 30
The Modern Eye: A Painting by Hugo Robus
Features one of the Modernist artist's early paintings, *Bathers* of 1917.
Thru Feb. 21
Chromolithography: The Democratic Art
Chromolithographic works from the museum's permanent collection.

Room in New York, 1932, Edward Hopper. Sheldon Memorial Art Gallery.

Jan. 15–Mar. 14
No Laughing Matter
Works by 13 artists who use humor to address social, political, and cultural subject matter; artists include Jonathan Borofsky and the Guerilla Girls.

Feb. 1–Apr. 1
Ansel Adams: American Wilderness
The artist's vintage photographs of the American landscape.

Feb. 23–Apr. 24
Louis H. Sullivan: Unison with Nature
The artists's architectural features, including chimney caps, door panels, and plates, viewed as works of art.

Mar. 18–May 30
Department of Art & Art History Studio Faculty Biennial

Apr.–July
Sheldon Solo: Cameron Shaw and Craig Roper
Two-man exhibition of works by Shaw, a found-object artist, and Roper, a photographer.

Apr. 4–June 18
Chicanismo: Photographs by Louis Bernal
Fifty of the artist's photographs that address what he defines as "personal religious and family experiences as a Chicano."

June–July
Charles Rain
Comprehensive look at work by the 20th-century painter.

July 12–Sept.
Brancusi Photographs
Vintage photographs by the artist, famous for his sculptural work.

Aug. 30–Oct. 25
Milton Glaser
Features 180 works, from magazine and book designs to posters and limited-edition prints.

Nov. 13, 1993–Jan. 23, 1994
Duncan Phillips Collects: Augustus Vincent Tack
First retrospective of the artist's work, which ranged from impressionism in his early years to spiritual abstraction. Catalogue.

Permanent Collection
Prominent holdings of 19th-century landscape and still-life, American Impressionism, early Modernism, geometric abstraction, Abstract Expressionism, Pop, Minimalism, and contemporary art; sculpture garden features 20th-century works by artists including Lachaise, Lipchitz, and Serra.
Architecture: 1963 Italian travertine marble building by Philip Johnson.

Admission: Donation suggested. Handicapped accessible.
Hours: Tues.–Sat., 10–5; Thurs.–Sat. eves., 7–9; Sun., 2–9.
Tours: Call (402) 472-2462 for reservations.

Joslyn Art Museum

2200 Dodge St., Omaha, Nebr. 68102
(402) 342-3300

1993 Exhibitions
Thru Jan. 31
Midlands Invitational 1992: Installations
Jan. 21–July 3
Beauty in the Beasts: The Art of the Animalier
Feb. 13–Apr. 25
Jacob Lawrence: The Frederick Douglass and Harriet Tubman Series of Narrative Paintings
African-American artist Lawrence's 1938–1940 paintings portraying the lives of abolitionists and the artist's concern with the human struggle.
May 22–July 25
Visions of the People: A Pictorial History of Plains Indian Life
Over 300 objects, including clothing, tipi covers and liners, drums, shields, paintings, and Ghost Dance materials.
June 3–Aug. 8
Contemporary Photography Exhibition
June 10–Aug. 22
Gyorgy Kepes: Photographs (1930–1988)
Aug. 14–Sept. 26
Red Grooms: Ruckus Rodeo
The artist's room-sized "sculpto-pictorama," based on the annual Southwestern Exposition and Stock Show, on view for the first time in 10 years.
Aug. 19–Oct. 24
Karl Bodmer: Eastern Views
Oct. 16–Nov. 28
Toulouse-Lautrec: The Baldwin M. Baldwin Collection
Nov. 4, 1993–Jan. 9, 1994
Selections 5: Recent Works from the Polaroid Collection
Dec. 11, 1993–Jan. 30, 1994
**Facing the Past: 19th-Century Portraits from the Collection of the Pennsylvania Academy of the Fine Arts*
Eighty paintings by such artists as Stuart, Sully, Eakins, Beaux, and Chase.

Mother and Child, c. 1897, George de Forest Brush. From "Facing the Past: 19th-Century Portraits from the Collection of the Pennsylvania Academy of the Fine Arts." A traveling exhibition. AFA.

Permanent Collection
Works from antiquity to the present. Major holdings of 19th- and 20th-century European and American art; Native American art; works by artist-explorers Bodmer, Catlin, Miller, Remington documenting the movement to the American West. **Highlights:** Degas, *Little Dancer, Fourteen Years Old*; Pollock, *Galaxy*; Renoir, *Young Girls at the Piano*; Segal, *Times Square at Night*; Titian, *Man with a Falcon*; sculpture garden; Monet, *Small Farm at Bordighera*; Storz Fountain Court. **Architecture:** 1931 Art Deco building by John and Alan McDonald.

Admission: Adults, $3; senior citizens, children 6–12, $1.50. Children under 6 and Sat., 10–noon, free. Group rates available. Handicapped accessible.
Hours: Tues.–Sat., 10–5; Thurs., 10–9; Sun., 1–5. Closed Mon., holidays.
Tours: Wed., 1; Sat., 11. For groups, call (402) 342-3300 two weeks in advance.
Food & Drink: Gallery Buffet open Tues.–Sat., 11:30–2; Sun., 1–3.

Hood Museum of Art

Dartmouth College, Hanover, N.H. 03755
(603) 646-2808

1993 Exhibitions
Thru Mar. 14
Twentieth-Century Works from the Permanent Collection
Jan. 9–Mar. 14
Utagawa Hiroshige: The Tokaido Road Series
About 50 woodcut block prints by the 19th-century Japanese printmaker.
Mar. 27–June 20
Fumio Yoshimura: A Retrospective
Sculptures and drawings by the Dartmouth professor.

Apr. 10–June 20
Under Changing Skies: Landscapes by Frederic E. Church
Sixty-five drawings and oil sketches by the renowned 19th-century American artist.
June 30–Sept. 26
To Imagine and to See: Photographs of the Crow Indians by Edward S. Curtis and Richard Throssel
Images by two photographers who chronicled daily life on the Crow reservation at the turn of the century.
Sept. 26–Nov. 28
Tales of Japan: Three Centuries of Japanese Painting from the Chester Beatty Library, Dublin
Painted hand scrolls and albums from the 16th to 19th centuries illustrating famous Japanese stories and historical events.

Permanent Collection
Represents nearly every area of art history and ethnography; strengths include African and Native American art, early American silver, 19th- and 20th-century American painting, European prints, and modern art. **Highlights:** Assyrian reliefs; Panathenaic Prize amphora by the Berlin painter; Orozco murals; Claude, *Landscape*; Eakins, *Portrait of John Joseph Borie*; Picasso, *Guitar on the Table*; recent acquisition of 1,000 works of Oceanic art. **Architecture:** 1985 building by Moore and Floyd of Centerbrook Architects.

Admission: Free. Handicapped accessible.
Hours: Tues.–Fri., 11–5; Sat.–Sun., 9:30–5. Closed Mon., holidays.
Tours: Sat.–Sun., 2. For group tours call (603) 646-2808.
Food & Drink: Courtyard Café open during museum hours.

The Montclair Art Museum
3 S. Mountain Ave., Montclair, N.J. 07042
(201) 746-5555

1993 Exhibitions
Thru Jan. 10
Three Hispanic-American Masters
Works by sculptor Roberto Estopinan, painter Dario Suro, and multimedia artist Juan Sanchez.
Thru Jan. 24
The Rubens of 14th St.: Reginald Marsh
Paintings, drawings, watercolors, and prints.
Jan. 31–Apr. 4
Hans Weingaertner: A Retrospective
About 40 works by the New Jersey artist.
Jan. 31–Apr. 18
Bearden, Lawrence and Woodruff
Works by the African-American artists.

Feb. 14–Apr. 25
Bookplates from the Permanent Collection
Highlights bookplates created by book owners, noted artists, illustrators, and engravers.
Feb. 28–June 6
Henri and the Ash Can School
Works by Robert Henri and others from the museum's collection.
Apr. 10–Aug. 22
The Beach Collection
An exhibition of Currier & Ives prints, including genre scenes and still-lifes.
Apr. 18–June 6
Walter and Emilie Greenough
About 20 works by the Montclair Art Colony artists.
Apr. 25–Aug. 29
The Crayon*: An End of an Era*
Begun in 1855, *The Crayon* was the earliest journal of art criticism; connects the periodical with artworks of the time.
May 9–July 11
Gustavo Ojeda: Drawings
20 drawings from the museum's collection and the estate of the late Hispanic-American landscapist.

Permanent Collection

American paintings, sculptures, works on paper, costumes; Native American art. **Highlights:** 18th-century paintings by Copley, West, Peale, Stuart, Sully, Smibert; 19th-century landscapes by Cole, Durand, Kensett, Church, Moran, Bierstadt, Inness; other 19th-century paintings by Allston, Morse, Cassatt, Eakins, Sargent; 20th-century paintings by Sloan, Glackens, Henri, the Soyer brothers, Gorky, Motherwell, Albers; Henry Reed Collection of paintings and documents of Morgan Russell. **Architecture:** 1914 Neoclassical building by Albert B. Ross.

Admission: Suggested donation: adults, $4; senior citizens, students over 18 with ID, $2; children under 18, members, free. Handicapped accessible.
Hours: Tues.–Wed., Fri.–Sat., 10–5; Sun., first and third Thurs. of the month, 2–5; second and fourth Thurs. of the month, 2–9. Closed Mon., major holidays.
Tours: Tues.–Wed., Fri., 10–4; Thurs, 2–4. Call (201) 746-5555 three weeks in advance for reservations.

The Newark Museum

49 Washington St., Newark, N.J. 07101
(201) 596-6550

1993 Exhibitions

Thru Jan. 3
Dragon Threads: Court Costumes of the Celestial Kingdom
Over 100 court costumes, headdresses, and jewelry from Imperial China.
John Hein, Furniture
Oriental-influenced cabinets by the Trenton-based craftsman.
Thru Jan. 21
Trenton Artists' Workshop Association
Thru Feb. 28
⋆ *Alone in a Crowd: Prints of the 1930s and 1940s by African American Artists from the Collection of Reba and Dave Williams*
Jan. 13–Mar. 21
William Manfredi: Silversmith
Jan. 30–Feb. 28
Through Sisters' Eyes: Children's Books Illustrated by African-American Women Artists
Feb. 4–Mar. 28
New Jersey Arts Annual: Fine Arts
Mar. 17–June 20
Sumptuous Surrounds: Silver Overlay
Focus on the unique process of depositing sterling silver on ceramic and glass vessels, developed in Newark in the 1880s.
Mar. 31–May 30
Lore Lindenfeld: Fiber Graphics
Works which combine elements of collage with needlework and applique.
Mar. 31, 1993–1994
Furniture from the Decorative Arts Collection
Traces changes in furniture forms and production between 1850 and 1900.
Apr. 3, 1993–continuing
E Pluribus Unum: The Search for 'A More Perfect Union'
Apr. 10–May 9
Contrasts: 40 Years of Change and Continuity in Puerto Rico, Photographs of Jack Delano
The photographer's view of Puerto Rican society in the 1940s, contrasted with his vision of similar events, people, and places in the 1980s.
Puerto Rican Senior Citizen Art Expo
Apr. 29–Sept. 5
Twenty-Five Years of Collecting: The Director's Anniversary, 1968–1993

Voters Puppets, 1929, Henry Glintenkamp. From "American Prints in Black and White, 1900–1950: Selections from the Collection of Reba and Dave Williams." A traveling exhibition. AFA.

May 15–Sept. 5
Art of the Philippines
Clothing, hats, bags, pipes, jewelry, and other works from the northern and southern Philippines.
June 9–Aug. 8
Twentieth-Century Handmade Silver
Works from 1910 to 1987 by craftsmen as well as shops such as Jensen, Tiffany, and Kalo.

Permanent Collection

Nineteenth- and 20th-century American painting, sculpture; renowned collection of Tibetan art; American decorative arts; folk art; numismatics; Native American art; classical antiquities. **Architecture:** 1926 building by Jarvis Hunt; 1989 award-winning renovation by Michael Graves combining four separate buildings.

Admission: Free. Handicapped accessible.
Hours: Wed.–Sun., noon–5. Closed Mon.–Tues.
Tours: Daily. For group-tour information, call (201) 596-6615.
Food & Drink: Museum Café open Wed.–Sun., noon–3:30.

Museum of New Mexico

Museum of Fine Arts
West Palace Ave. on the Plaza, Santa Fe, N.M. 87501
(505) 827-4455

1993 Exhibitions

Thru 1993
Art of New Mexico: The Early Years
Survey of New Mexico art history from 1900 to 1945; artists include early Taos painters, Santa Fe painters, and artists who visited or lived in New Mexico.
Thru Jan. 10
Alcove Show: Gandert, Gonzales, Montoya, Vigil
Thru Feb. 7
Art of New Mexico: 75th Anniversary Exhibition
Photography, painting, sculpture, and works on paper from the permanent collection.
Jan. 23–July 11
Alcove Show: Fine Crafts/New Mexico Artists
Mar. 6–May 23
New Mexico '93: Fine Arts, Fine Crafts, A Juried Exhibition
Apr. 17–Sept. 12
Maynard Dixon
Forty paintings that illustrate the artist's modernist approach to the desert landscape.
June 26–Oct. 10
FSA Photography in New Mexico

July 24–Dec. 5
Alcove Show
Sept. 25, 1993–Mar. 13, 1994
Gustave Baumann: Master Printmaker
Nov. 11, 1993–Jan. 30, 1994
Landscape in Photography
Dec. 18, 1993–Apr. 1994
New Acquisitions

Museum of International Folk Art
706 Camino Lejo, Santa Fe, N.M. 87501
(505) 827-6350

1993 Exhibitions
Thru Apr. 25
Folk Art of Brazil's Northeast
Thru Sept. 12
Turkish Traditional Art Today
Jan. 31–July 5
De Tal Palo, Tal Astilla/(As the Log, So the Splinter)
June 6, 1993–Apr. 1994
Mud, Mirror, and Thread: Adornment in Rural India
July 24, 1993–Jan. 2, 1994
The Art of the Santera
Dec. 5, 1993–Mar. 27, 1994
Swedish Folk Art: Tradition and Change

Museum of Indian Arts and Culture
710 Camino Lejo, Santa Fe, N.M. 87501
(505) 827-6344

The Palace of Governors
West Palace Ave. on the Plaza, Santa Fe, N.M. 87501
(505) 827-6483

Permanent Collection
Twentieth-century American art, primarily by artists working in the Southwest including O'Keeffe; photography, sculpture; extensive holdings of American Indian art, including work by Taos and Santa Fe masters.
Architecture: 1917 building patterned after New Mexico mission churches.

Admission: Adults, $3.50; two-day pass to all four museums, $6; children under 16, free; Wed., senior citizens admitted free; Sun., $1 for New Mexico residents.
Hours: Daily, 10–5.
Tours: Call (505) 827-4455 for information.

The Albany Institute of History & Art

125 Washington Ave., Albany, N.Y. 12210
(518) 463-4478

1993 Exhibitions

Thru Feb. 14
In Medusa's Gaze: Still-Life Painting in Upstate New York Collections
Explores the development of still-life painting from its 17th-century inception through the 20th century; includes works by Rousseau, Léger, and Picasso.

Mar. 6–June 6
Please Post: Broadsides from the McKinney Library
A look back in time through advertisements of yesterday.

June 25–Aug. 29
1993 Exhibition by Artists of the Mohawk-Hudson Region

Sept. 11–Nov. 7
Thomas Cole: Drawn to Nature
Works by the founding artist of the Hudson River School.

Permanent Collection

Hudson River School landscape paintings; early Dutch limner portraits; Albany-made silver; 18th- and 19th-century New York furniture, sculpture, pewter, ceramics; 19th-century cast-iron stoves; work by contemporary regional artists; Egyptian Gallery; paintings by Walter Launt Palmer; artifacts and documents from the New York Central Railroad Company; period room depicting 18th-century Dutch colonial *groote kamer*; sculpture by Erastus Dow Palmer; textiles, costumes, and societal artifacts. **Architecture:** 1907 American Renaissance building.

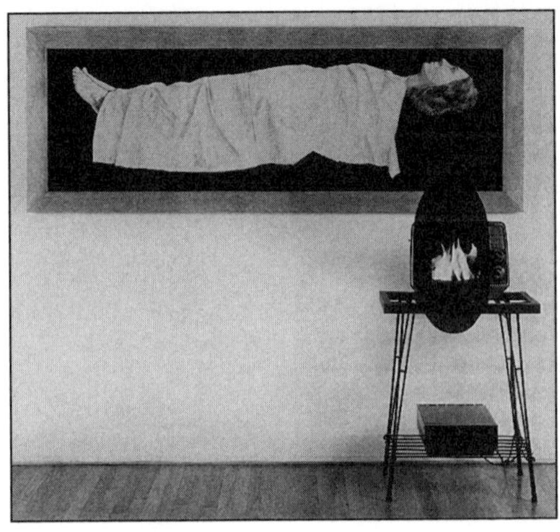

Untitled, 1989, Adrienne Klein. Albany Institute of History & Art.

Admission: Free; contribution suggested. Handicapped accessible.
Hours: Tues.–Fri., 10–5; Sat.–Sun., noon–5. Closed Mon.
Tours: Group tours: adults, $4; seniors and students, $2; reservations required 2 to 4 weeks in advance. Call (518) 463-4478.
Food & Drink: Luncheon Gallery open Tues.–Fri., 11:30–1:30.

Albright-Knox Art Gallery

1285 Elmwood Ave., Buffalo, N.Y. 14222
(716) 882-8700

1993 Exhibitions

Thru Jan. 3
Susan Rothenberg: Drawings and Paintings
A retrospective tracing the career of this American imagist painter, from her early horse images to recent autobiographical, expressionist paintings. Catalogue.

Jan. 16–Mar. 7
Clyfford Still: The Buffalo & San Francisco Collections
Brings together two collections of the abstract painter's work; features masterpieces from 1936 to 1963. Catalogue.

Mar. 20–May 2
In Medusa's Gaze: Still-Life Painting in Upstate New York Collections
Explores the development of still-life painting from its 17th-century inception through the 20th century; includes works by Rousseau, Léger, and Picasso.

May 15–June 13
In WNY 1993
Biennial invitational of work by western New York artists.

June 26–Aug. 29
This Sporting Life, 1878–1991
Survey of sports photography, featuring nearly 200 works by such artists as Adams, Avedon, and Eakins as well as photojournalists.

Sept. 12–Oct. 31
Jess: A Grand Collage, 1953–1993
First major retrospective of paintings and collages by the reclusive artist. Catalogue.

Nov. 12, 1993–Jan. 2, 1994
Common Ground/Uncommon Vision: The Michael and Julie Hall Collection of American Folk Art
More than 150 objects, ranging from an 18th-century weather vane to works by Rev. Howard Finster. Catalogue.

Permanent Collection

Sculpture from 3,000 B.C. to the present; 18th-century English and 19th-century French and American painting; noted holdings of Modern art. **Highlights:** Gauguin, *Spirit of the Dead Watching* and *Yellow Christ*; Hogarth, *The Lady's Last Stake*; Kiefer, *The Milky Way*; Lichtenstein, *Picture and Pitcher*; Matisse, *La Musique*; Moore, *Reclining Figure*; Pollock, *Convergence*; Samaras, *Mirrored Room*; Segal, *Cinema*. **Architecture:** 1905 Greek Revival building by Green; 1962 addition with sculpture court by Gordon Bunshaft of Skidmore, Owings, and Merrill.

Admission: Adults, $4; senior citizens and students, $3; children 12 and under, members, free. Handicapped accessible.
Hours: Tues.–Sat., 11–5; Sun., noon–5. Closed Mon., Jan. 1, Thanksgiving, Dec. 25.
Tours: Wed.–Thurs., 12:15; Sat.–Sun., 1:30. For group reservations call (716) 882-8700, ext. 226.
Food & Drink: Garden Restaurant open Tues.–Sat., 11:30–3:45; Sun., noon–3.

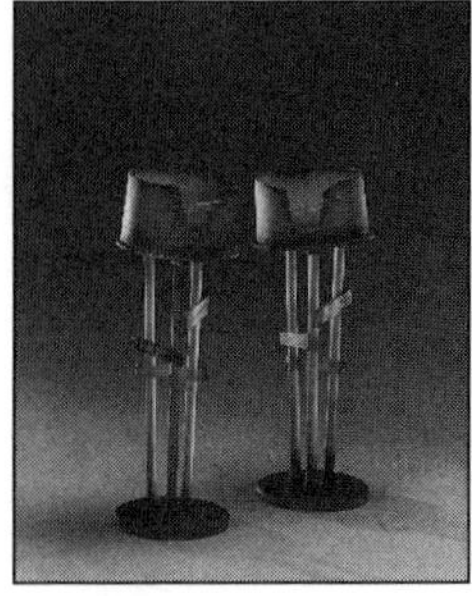

Water Towers, 1982, Jay Musler. From "Glasses for Drinking." The Corning Museum of Glass.

The Corning Museum of Glass

One Museum Way, Corning, N.Y. 14830-2253
(607) 937-5371

1993 Exhibitions

Apr. 24–Oct. 17
Glasses For Drinking
A survey of drinking vessels from Roman times to the present.

Permanent Collection

Glass objects from 35 centuries, with specialized collections of ancient Roman; 9th- and 10th-century Islamic; late 15th- to 19th-century Venetian; mid 19th-century French; English; Chinese; Art Nouveau; Art Deco; contemporary glass. **Architecture:** 1980 building by Gunnar Birkerts.

Admission: Corning Glass Center (including the museum): adults, $6; senior citizens, $5; youth, $4; families, $14. Handicapped accessible.
Hours: Daily, 9–5. Closed Jan. 1, Thanksgiving, Dec. 24–25.
Tours: Call (607) 937-5371 for information.
Food & Drink: Snack Bar open 9–5; café open summer and fall, 11–3.

Herbert F. Johnson Museum of Art

Cornell University, Ithaca, N.Y. 14853-4001
(607) 255-6464

1993 Exhibitions

Jan. 19–Mar. 21
The Patricia and Phillip Frost Collection: American Abstraction 1930–1945
Seventy-five paintings, collages, and sculpture by members of the American Abstract Artists group including Josef Albers, Irene Rice Pereira, and László Moholy-Nagy.
Jan. 23–Mar. 7
Changing Reality: Recent Soviet Photograhy
Ninety black-and-white photographs from the 1970s and 1980s by 15 Soviet photographers.
Mar.–Apr.
Council of the Creative and Performing Arts Awards Exhibition
May 1–June 25
Gardens: Real and Imagined
Focuses on the work of 13 contemporary artists, including Joyce Kozloff, Miriam Schapiro, and Mitch Epstein, who use the garden as a metaphor.
June
Richard Heinrich Reunion Exhibition
Sculpture and works on paper by the Cornell graduate.
Sept.–Oct.
Jack Squier Retrospective Exhibition
Works by the Cornell art professor and sculptor.

Permanent Collection

Paintings, sculptures, prints, drawings, photographs, crafts, textiles from 30 centuries and six continents with strengths in Asian, American, and graphic arts. **Highlights:** Daubigny, *Fields in the Month of June*; Durand, View of th*e Hudson Valley*; Giacometti, *Walking Man II*; Leoni, *Portrait of Angela Gratiani*; Russell, *Synchrony No. 5*; Stieglitz, *The Steerage*; Tiffany blue vase. **Architecture:** 1973 building by I. M. Pei.

Admission: Free. Handicapped accessible.
Hours: Tues.–Sun., 10–5. Closed Mon., holidays.
Tours: Call (607) 255-6464.

Storm King Art Center

Old Pleasant Hill Rd., Mountainville, N.Y. 10953
(914) 534-3190; 534-3115 (recording)

1993 Exhibitions

Apr. 1–Nov. 30
Four Outdoor Sculptures by Ursula von Rydingsvard
May 17–Oct. 31
Works by Siah Armajani
Selections from the Permanent Collection: Indoor Works

Permanent Collection

A 400-acre sculpture park and museum in the Hudson River Valley collecting and exhibiting post-1945 sculpture.
Highlights: Two new site-specific works by Serra: *Schunnemunk Fork*; Armajani, *Gazebo for Two Anarchists: Gabriella Antolini and Alberto Antolini;* 13 sculptures by David Smith; Aycock, *Three-Fold Manifestation II*; Calder, *The Arch*; Nevelson, *High Mountain*; Noguchi, *Momo Taro*; Snelson, *Free Ride Home*; di Suvero, *Mon Père, Mon Père.*
Architecture: 1935 French Norman–style building by Maxwell Kimball.

Admission: Adults, $5; senior citizens and students, $3; members and children under 5, free. Handicapped accessible.
Hours: Apr. 1–Nov. 30: daily, 11–5:30. Special evening hours June 18–20 and Sept. 17–19. Closed Dec. 1–Mar. 31.
Tours: Daily, 2; call (914) 534-3190 for group-tour reservations and discounted admission.
Food & Drink: Extensively landscaped picnic area; outdoor café open Sat.–Sun., noon–3:30.

Ene Due Rabe, 1990, Ursula von Rydingsvard. From "Four Outdoor Sculptures by Ursula von Rydingsvard." Storm King Art Center.

American Craft Museum

40 W. 53rd St., New York, N.Y. 10019
(212) 956-3535

Lamp, c. 1905, Elizabeth Burton. From "The Nation at Home—1900–1920." American Craft Museum.

1993 Exhibitions

Thru Mar. 28
John McQueen: The Language of Containment
Midcareer survey of the influential basket artist.
Nancy Crow: Work in Transition
Over 35 new, large-scale quilts by the leading quiltmaker.
Apr. 8–July 4
New Glass
Glass installations by five artists.
July 15–Sept. 5
Paul Soldner: A Retrospective
First retrospective of work by this artist, responsible for the popularity of contemporary raku ceramics.
July 15–Oct. 10
Beatrice Wood: A Retrospective
Works including the artist's Dada drawings and satirical ceramic sculpture.
Otto Natzler: A Retrospective
A survey of the ceramicist's career.
Oct. 21, 1993–Feb. 27, 1994
The Nation at Home: 1900–1920
First of eight exhibitions on the history of 20th-century American craft; features work in ceramics, glass, fiber, metal, and wood.

Permanent Collection

Documents the history and development of 20th-century craft in America; significant objects in all contemporary media—clay, enamel, fiber, glass, leather, metal, mosaic, paper, plastic, wood—and an outstanding jewelry collection. The collection is unique in its concentration on contemporary craft objects created since World War II. **Highlights:** More than 200 ceramic pieces; artists include Arneson, Grotell, Voulkos in ceramics; Hicks, Tawney, Zeisler in fiber; Chihuly, Labino, Littleton in glass; Choo in metal; Nakashima, Maloof, Castle in wood. **Architecture:** 1986 building by Fox & Fowle Architects.

Admission: Adults, $4.50; students and senior citizens, $2; members, children under 12, free. Handicapped accessible.
Hours: Tues., 10–8; Wed.–Sun., 10–5. Closed Mon., major holidays.
Tours: Call (212) 956-3535 for information.

The Brooklyn Museum

200 Eastern Pkwy., Brooklyn, N.Y. 11236
(718) 638-5000

1993 Exhibitions

Thru Jan. 10
Max Weber: The Cubist Decade, 1910–20
About 70 Cubist still-lifes, figure studies, and New York scenes by the artist, who was instrumental in bringing Modernist ideas to the United States.

Thru Jan. 24
Frédéric Bazille: Prophet of Impressionism
Sixty works by the little-known but pivotal 19th-century French painter. Catalogue.

Thru May 2
James Turrell
Museum lobby installation using light and space as media.

Feb.–May
Consuelo Kanaga: A Retrospective
First major retrospective for this pioneer (1894–1977) in social photography, who captured the beauty of African Americans through still-lifes, urban and rural views, and portraiture. Catalogue.

Spring 1994
Louise Bourgeois/Venice Biennale Exhibition

Permanent Collection

Represents virtually the entire history of art, ranging from one of the world's foremost Egyptian collections to comprehensive holdings of American painting and sculpture; collections are multicultural and include a balance of works outside the European tradition; significant holdings of Greek, Roman, ancient Middle Eastern and Islamic art; Asian, Pre-Columbian, African, Oceanic art; European

Frances with a Flower, 1928, Consuelo Kanaga. From "Consuelo Kanaga: An American Photographer." A traveling exhibition.

painting, sculpture; decorative arts; prints, drawings; American period rooms. **Highlights:** Assyrian reliefs; Egyptian female figure, 3500 B.C; Rodin Sculpture Gallery; Monet, *Doge's Palace*; Eakins, *William Rush Carving the Allegorical Figure of the Schuylkill.* **Architecture:** 1893 Beaux Arts building by McKim, Mead & White; 1992 renovation.

Admission: Donation suggested: adults, $4; senior citizens, $1.50; students with ID, $2; children under 12 accompanied by adult, free. Handicapped accessible.
Hours: Wed.–Sun., 10–5. Closed Mon.–Tues., Jan. 1, Thanksgiving, Dec. 25.
Tours: Call (718) 638-5000, ext. 221.
Food & Drink: Museum Café open Wed.–Sun., 10–4.

Cooper-Hewitt, National Museum of Design

Smithsonian Institution, 2 E. 91st St., New York, N.Y. 10128
(212) 860-6868

1993 Exhibitions

Thru Mar. 7
The Power of Maps
About 300 old and new maps, atlases, and globes show the history of maps, tools and techniques of mapmakers, and ways maps are used for change.
Thru Apr. 4
Revolution, Life, and Labor: Soviet Porcelains 1918–1985
Illustrates the close link between politics and design; features porcelains by Malevich, Chashnik, and Danko.
Thru Apr. 6
From Background to Foreground: Looking at an 18th-Century Wallpaper
An arabesque-design wallpaper, printed by Jean-Baptiste Reveillon during the 1780s, studied in a historical and aesthetic context.
Apr. 6–July 25
Czech Cubism: Architecture and Design 1910–1925
Features drawings and examples of furniture, ceramics, and metalwork.
Sept. 28, 1993–Jan. 23, 1994
Packaging the New: Donald Deskey and Modern Design in America
Over 150 appliances, furnishings, packaging, and recreational equipment by the industrial designer. Catalogue.

Permanent Collection

Covers 3,000 years of design history in cultures around the world. Major holdings include drawings, prints, textiles, furniture, metalwork, ceramics, glass, woodwork, wall coverings. **Highlights:** Egyptian, Islamic, Mediterranean, and Near Eastern textiles from the third to the 15th centuries; large group of Homer drawings; 19th-century jewelry by Castellani and Giuliano; glass desk by Bourgeois; chromium steel and canvas chair by Breuer. **Architecture:** 1901 Carnegie mansion by Babb, Cook, and Willard.

Admission: Adults, $3; senior citizens, students under 12, $1.50. Tues., 5–9, free. Handicapped accessible.
Hours: Tues., 10–9; Wed.–Sat., 10–5; Sun., noon–5. Closed Mon., Jan. 1, Thanksgiving, Dec. 25.
Tours: Call (212) 860-6871.

The Frick Collection

1 E. 70th St., New York, N.Y. 10021
(212) 288-0700

1993 Exhibitions

Jan. 27, 1993–Apr. 10, 1994
The Currency of Fame: The Renaissance Portrait Medal
Significant European medals from c. 1400 to 1600. Catalogue.
Sept. 13–Nov. 7
Dutch Eighteenth-Century Watercolors from the Rijksmuseum Printroom, Amsterdam

Permanent Collection

Includes works by Goya, Ingres, Rembrandt, Renoir, Titian, Van Dyck; Renaissance sculptures; Renaissance and French 18th-century furniture; Sèvres porcelains; Limoges enamels. **Highlights:** Bellini, *Saint Francis in Ecstasy*; della Francesca, *Saint Simon the Apostle*; Van Eyck, *Virgin with Child, with Saints and Donor*; Holbein, *Sir Thomas More* and *Thomas Cromwell*; Rembrandt, *Self-Portrait*; Stuart, *George Washington*. **Architecture:** 1913–1914 Frick residence by Thomas Hastings; 1931–1935 changes and additions by John Russell Pope; 1977 extension and garden.

Admission: Adults, $3; senior citizens, students, $1.50; children under 16 must be accompanied by adult; children under 10 not admitted. Handicapped accessible; wheelchairs available, call for reservation.
Hours: Tues.–Sat., 10–6; Sun., 1–6. Closed Mon., Jan. 1, July 4, Thanksgiving, Dec. 24–25.
Tours: Group visits by appointment only. Call (212) 288-0700 for information.

Catharina Hooft and her Nurse, 1619–1620, Franz Hals. From "The Dawn of the Golden Age." A traveling exhibition.

Study for Drawing No. 4, 1955, Stuart Davis. From "The Drawings of Stuart Davis: The Amazing Continuity." An AFA traveling exhibition.

Hollyhock Window, 1885, John LaFarge. The Saint Louis Art Museum.

Library, Phillips Exeter Academy, 1965–72, Louis Kahn. From "Louis I. Kahn: In the Realm of Architecture." A traveling exhibition.

Portrait d'Alphonse Tisse, 1869. Frederic Bazille. From "Frederic Bazille: Prophet of Impressionism." A traveling exhibition.

Philistines, 1982, Jean-Michel Basquiat. From "Jean Michel Basquiat." A traveling exhibition.

The Assination of St. Peter Martyr, 15th century, Giovanni Bellini and assistants. Courtauld Institute Galleries, London.

Ein moderne Maler, 1966, Georg Baselitz. Berlinische Galerie, Berlin.

Personage of Butterfly Wings, 1963, Jean Dubuffet. From " Jean Dubuffet 1943–1963: Paintings, Sculptures, Assemblages." Hirshhorn Museum.

President Elect, 1960–61, James Rosenquist. From "Hand-Painted Pop: American Art in Transition, 1952–62." A traveling exhibition.

From the *Cremation Shrine Series, #8, Prague*, April 1990, Benis Von Zur Muehlen. New Orleans Museum of Art.

Woman with Crow, 1904, Pablo Picasso. Toledo Museum of Art.

Parisians Enjoying the Parc Monceau, Claude Monet. From "Corot to Cézanne: 19th-Century French Paintings from the Metropolitan Museum of Art." A traveling exhibition.

My Shanty, Lake George, 1922, Georgia O'Keeffe. From "Two Lives: Georgia O'Keeffe and Alfred Stieglitz—A Conversation in Paintings and Photographs." A traveling exhibition.

From *Harmonia Macrocosmica,* 1708, Andreas Cellarius. From "The Power of Maps." A traveling exhibition.

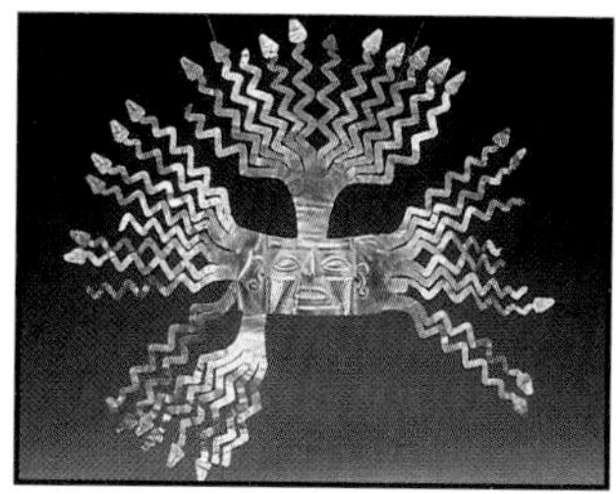

Sun Mask (Diadem), A.D. 200–400, La Tolita, Ecuador. From "The Ancient Americas: Art from Sacred Landscapes." A traveling exhibition.

In the Mirror, 1902, Giacomo Balla. From "Ottocento: Romanticism and Revolution in 19th-Century Italian Painting." An AFA traveling exhibition.

Ruckus Rodeo, 1975–1976, Red Grooms. A traveling exhibition.

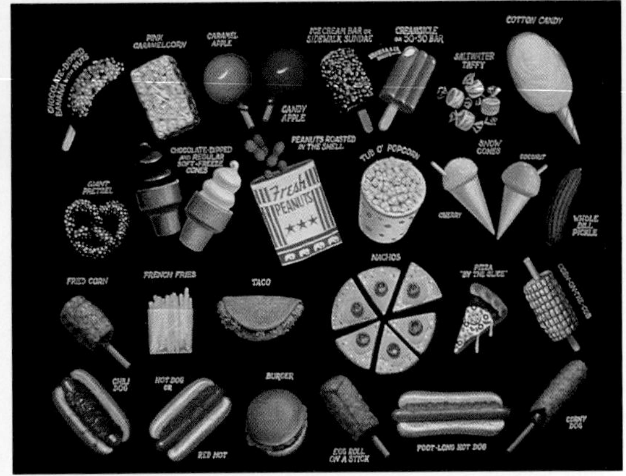

Carnival and Boardwalk Food, 1991, Julie Bozzi. From "Julie Bozzi: American Food." A traveling exhibition.

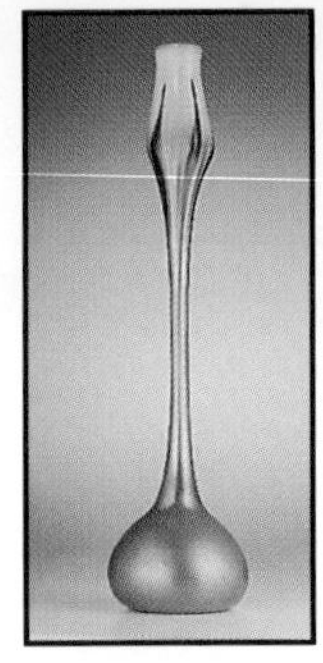

Egyptian onion flower-form vase, c.1900–1905, Louis Comfort Tiffany. From "The Nation at Home: 1900–1920." American Craft Museum.

La Pia De'Tolomei, 1880, Dante Gabriel Rossetti. From "The Art of Seeing: John Ruskin and the Victorian Eye." A traveling exhibition.

Migration of the Negro panel no. 45, Jacob Lawrence. From "Jacob Lawrence's *Migration of the Negro*." A traveling exhibition.

The Card Players, 1890–1892, Paul Cézanne. From "Great French Paintings from the Barnes Foundation: Impressionist, Post-Impressionist, and Early Modern." A traveling exhibition.

Sun and Wind, 1914, Frederick Frieseke. From "Masterworks of American Impressionism from the Pfeil Collection." A traveling exhibition.

The Solomon R. Guggenheim Museum

1071 Fifth Ave., New York, N.Y. 10128
(212) 423-3500 (recording)

1993 Exhibitions

Thru Jan.

Osmosis: Haim Steinbach and Ettore Spalletti
A series that brings together pairs of artists to create works designed specifically for the museum's unique spaces; this installment features collaborative work by Israeli-born Steinbach and Italian artist Spalletti.

Lothar Baumgarten
The German artist will inscribe the names of the native societies of the Americas on the entire 100-foot-tall spiral of the museum's rotunda. Accompanied by a book of essays.

Feb.–Apr.

Osmosis: Wim Wenders and Laurie Anderson
This installment in the collaborative series features site-specific work by German film director Wenders and performance artist Anderson.

Feb.–May

Picasso and the Age of Iron
Traces the development of the art of assemblage and the force of forged iron through works by Alexander Calder, Alberto Giacometti, Julio Gonzalez, Pablo Picasso, and David Smith from the 1920s to 1940s. Catalogue.

May–Aug.

Rebecca Horn
Retrospective of the contemporary German sculptor, filmmaker, and performance artist's work. Catalogue.

Roy Lichtenstein
An in-depth survey of the works of one of the most influential artists of the American Pop Art movement and entire postwar era. Catalogue.

Sept.–Dec.

Total Risk, Freedom, Discipline: Abstraction in the Twentieth Century
A chronological exhibition of the century-long movement of pure non-objectivity, including works by Brancusi, Delaunay, de Kooning, Flavin, and others. Catalogue.

Permanent Collection

Nineteenth- and 20th-century works including contemporary and avant-garde paintings; paintings by Appel, Bacon, Bonnard, Cézanne, Chagall, Davis, Dubuffet, Gris, Kokoschka, Louis, Marc, Miró, Modigliani, Mondrian, Pollock, Rousseau, Seurat, Soulages, Villon; sculptures by Archipenko, Arp, Brancusi, Pevsner, Smith. **Highlights:** Cézanne, *Man with Crossed Arms*; Gris, *Still Life*; noted collection of works by Kandinsky, Klee; Louis, Saraband; Mondrian, *Composition*; Picasso, *Mandolin and Guitar*;

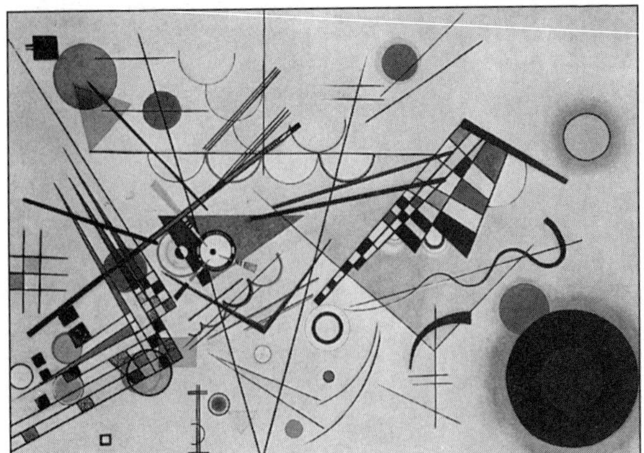

Composition 8, 1923, Wassily Kandinsky. Solomon R. Guggenheim Museum.

Pissarro, *The Hermitage at Pontoise*. **Architecture:** 1959 building by Frank Lloyd Wright; 1992 wing by Gwathmey Siegel & Associates.

Admission: Adults, $7; seniors, students with ID, $4; accompanied children under 12, members, free; Tues. 5–8, pay what you wish. Handicapped accessible.
Hours: Mon.–Wed., Fri.–Sun., 10–8. Thurs., closed.
Tours: Call (212) 435-3500 for information; group tours require reservations three weeks in advance.
Food & Drink: Mon.–Wed., Fri.–Sun., 8–9; Thurs, 8–3.

Branch: Guggenheim Museum SoHo

575 Broadway (at Prince St.), New York, N.Y. 10012
(212) 423-3500 (recording)

1993 Exhibitions

Thru Jan. 17
Marc Chagall: The Moscow Jewish Theatre Murals
Seven restored murals on canvas, created in 1920 for the State Jewish Kamerny Theatre in Moscow and viewed outside the Soviet Union for the first time in 1991. Catalogue.
Robert Rauschenberg: The Early 1950s
Showcases 100 works including Abstract Impressionist paintings, imagist collages, assemblages of found objects, and early conceptual pieces. Catalogue.
Jan.–May
Photography in Contemporary German Art 1960–1990
An overview of various nontraditional approaches to photography explored by German artists including Joseph Beuys, Anselm Kiefer, and Gerhard Richter. Accompanied by several publications.

Dec. 1993–Feb. 1994
Robert Morris
A retrospective of the artist's career, from his Minimalist and conceptual work to his investigations of materials such as felt and mirrors. Catalogue.

Admission: Adults, $5; seniors, students with ID, $3; children under 12 and members, free.
Hours: Sun., Mon., Wed., 11–6; Thurs.–Sat., 11–10. Closed Tues.

IBM Gallery of Science and Art

590 Madison Ave., New York, N.Y. 10022
(212) 745-6100

1993 Exhibitions

Thru Jan. 23
Josef Hoffmann Designs: Selections from the Austrian Museum of Applied Arts (MAK), Vienna
Works in almost every area of design by the Austrian designer, a founder of the Wiener Werkstatte and one of the most influential designers of the 20th century.
Feb. 9–Apr. 10
Highlights from the Butler Institute of American Art, Youngstown
Works from the first structure designed specifically to house American art; famous paintings include Homer's *Snap the Whip* and Hopper's *Pennsylvania Coal Town.*
Free Within Ourselves: African-American Art from the National Museum of American Art
Showcases works from one of the premier collections of African-American art.
Apr. 27–June 26
Master European Paintings from the National Gallery of Ireland: Mantegna to Goya
Rarely seen works from the early Renaissance through the 18th century, including paintings by Titian, Velázquez, and David. Catalogue.

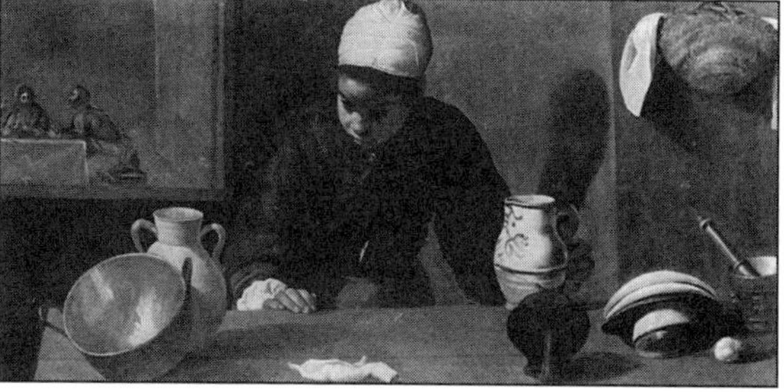

Kitchen Maid with the Supper at Emmaus, c. 1618–19, Diégo Velázquez. From "Master European Paintings from The National Gallery of Ireland: Mantegna to Goya." A traveling exhibition.

Apr. 27–June 26
Two Lives: Georgia O'Keeffe and Alfred Stieglitz—A Conversation in Paintings and Photographs
Tracks the visual and intellectual correspondences in the work of the two artists, who were artistic collaborators as well as husband and wife. Catalogue.
July 13–Sept. 11
Twentieth-Century Works from the University of Iowa Museum of Art
Focuses on European and American modern masterworks, including Max Beckmann's *Carnival Triptych* and Motherwell's *Elegy to the Spanish Republic.*
Highlights from the Vassar College Art Collection
Works ranging from Greek, Roman, and Etruscan antiquities to Western paintings from the Renaissance to the 20th century.

Permanent Collection
No permanent collection. **Architecture:** Housed in lower level of IBM Corporation's New York offices, designed by Edward Larrabee Barnes in 1983.

Admission: Free. Handicapped accessible.
Hours: Tues.–Sat., 11–6. Closed Mon.
Tours: Call (212) 745-5214 for guided tours.

International Center of Photography

Uptown
1130 Fifth Ave. (at 94th St.), New York, N.Y. 10028

Midtown
1133 Ave. of the Americas (at 43rd St.), New York, N.Y. 10036
(212) 860-1778

1993 Exhibitions
Thru Jan. 24 (Midtown)
Karsh: American Legends
Eighty large-format images from the past two years by the Armenian-born artist.
Ernst Haas: In Black and White
Thru Jan. 31 (Uptown)
From Sea to Shining Sea: A Portrait of America—Photographs by Hiroji Kubota
A Selection of Recent Acquisitions
Jan. 29–Apr. 18 (Midtown)
The Concerns of Roman Vishniac: Man, Nature, and Science
Feb. 5–Mar. 28 (Uptown)
Joyce Tenneson
Apr. 2–June 27 (Uptown)
Intimate Visions: The Photographs of Dorothy Norman

Apr. 23–July 18 (Midtown)
Commodity Image: Contemporary Artists and Cultural Values
Sept. 24, 1993–Feb. 6, 1994 (Midtown)
Iterations: The New Digital Imaging

Permanent Collection

More than 12,500 prints, including works by Abbott, Capa, Eisenstadt, Rodgers; archives include original audio- and videotape recordings and cameras. **Architecture:** 1915 Neo-Georgian building by Delano & Aldrich.

Admission: Adults, $4; students, senior citizens, $2.50. Handicapped accessible.
Hours: Tues., 11–8; Wed.–Sun., 11–6. Closed Mon.
Tours: By appointment; call (212) 860-1789.

The Jewish Museum

1109 Fifth Ave., New York, N.Y.
(212) 399-3344

1993 Exhibitions

NOTE: Reopens March 1993.
Mar.–continuing
Contemporary Art Exhibition Representing the Work of Eight Artists
Artists represented are Eleanor Antin, Christian Boltanski, Clegg & Guttman, Moshe Gershuni, Ilya Kabakov, Nancy Spero, Barbara Steinman, and Lawrence Weiner.
Exhibition on the Jewish Experience Covering 4,000 Years of Art, Culture, and History
Over 800 works in various media that tell the story of the Jewish experience across centuries and continents.

Rendering of the expanded Jewish Museum, reopening March 1993.

Permanent Collection

Over 24,000 artworks and artifacts covering 4,000 years of Jewish culture. Paintings, graphics, sculptures inspired by the Jewish experience; Jewish ceremonial art; archaeological artifacts; objects from Central European homes and synagogues brought to the museum after the Holocaust; Israeli art; contemporary art; National Jewish Archive of Broadcasting. **Highlights:** Ancient Israeli ossuary; Rembrandt, *The Triumph of Mordecai*; paintings by Chagall, Epstein; sculpture by George Segal. **Architecture:** 1908 Warburg mansion by Gilbert; 1959 sculpture court; 1963 List Building; 1993 renovation and expansion by Roche, Dinkeloo & Associates.

Admission: Call (212) 399-3344 for information. Handicapped accessible.
Hours: Call (212) 399-3344 for information.
Tours: Call (212) 399-3344 for reservations.
Food & Drink: Call (212) 399-3344 for cafe hours.

The Metropolitan Museum of Art

Fifth Ave. at 82nd St., New York, N.Y. 10028
(212) 879-5500; 535-7710 (recording)

1993 Exhibitions

Thru Jan. 10

The Century of Tung Ch'i-Ch'ang

First major retrospective of the 17th-century Chinese painter and calligrapher, with many works never before published or on view. Catalogue.

Thru Jan. 17

Arthur B. Davies at The Metropolitan Museum of Art

Highlights of the museum's collection of works on paper by Davies, featuring a selection of landscape drawings.

Masterworks from Lille: Old Master Paintings and Drawings from the Musée des Beaux Arts, Lille

An alternative view of French painting and drawing during the 18th and 19th centuries; includes works by David, Delacroix, Courbet, and others from the Musée des Beaux-Arts, Lille, France.

Thru Jan. 24

Alexander Jackson Davis

First major exhibition to examine the career of the great Romantic of American 19th-century architecture, commemorating the centennial of his death. Catalogue.

Thru Mar. 7

The Royal City of Susa: Ancient Near Eastern Treasures from the Louvre Museum

Selected works from the Iranian city of Susa, ranging in date from 5000 to 500 B.C., on loan from the Louvre. Recovered in the 19th and 20th centuries from tombs, temples, and palaces, the works reveal ties between the settlement and many ancient Near Eastern cultures. Catalogue.

Thru July 4
Loma Negra: A Lord Governor's Tomb
Pre-Columbian gold, silver, and copper metalwork, including nose and ear ornaments, necklaces, headdresses, and masks from the Black Hills find of the late 1950s in northern Peru.

Thru 1993
Islands and Ancestors: Indigenous Styles of Southeast Asia
About 60 tribal sculptures from Borneo, Sumatra, Sulawesi, and Austronesian-speaking peoples of Vietnam and the Philippines; most are on long-term loan from the Barbier-Mueller Museum, Geneva.

Mid-Feb.–Aug.
Louis Comfort Tiffany at The Metropolitan Museum of Art
Highlights of the museum's collection of works by the artist, including blown glass and design drawings; selection to be changed after the first three months.

Feb. 26–May 2
Honoré Daumier
First major exhibition devoted to the artist's drawings, featuring about 100 works in charcoal, crayon, and watercolor; also features examples of his paintings, prints, and sculpture. Catalogue.

Statuette of a Woman Wearing a Peplos, c. 460 B.C. From "The Greek Miracle: Classical Sculpture from the Dawn of Democracy, The Fifth Century B.C." A traveling exhibition.

Mar. 9–June 6
Havemeyer Collection
About 350 works from the historic collection, spanning several museum departments. Features works by such 19th-century artists as Courbet, Manet, and Cézanne. Catalogue.

Mar. 10–May 9
Imperial Painting from the Ming Dynasty: The Zhe School
About 100 paintings, mostly on silk, from a professional school of the Ming Dynasty (1368-1644), emphasizing a revival of Sung Dynasty styles. Catalogue.

Mar. 23–July 5
Photographs from the Gilman Paper Company Collection
Traces 19th-century developments in England, France, and the United States through masterpieces in every genre. Catalogue.

Mar. 11–May 23
The Greek Miracle: Classical Sculpture from the Dawn of Democracy, The Fifth Century B.C.
Some of the finest examples of original sculpture from an age that transformed the history of Western art.

Spring 1993
Chinese Lore for Japanese Spaces
Large-scale paintings selected to demonstrate the transformation of Chinese figure painting into the Japanese mode developed by Kano school painters for official rooms during the 16th and 17th centuries.

Permanent Collection

One of the largest and most comprehensive museums in the world, covering in depth every culture and period. **Highlights:** Babylonian Striding Lions; Temple of Dendur; grand drawing room in American wing; Astor Court Chinese rock garden; Song dynasty Tribute Horses; Cantor Roof Garden sculpture (May 1–Oct. 30); Brown collection of musical instruments; Louis XIV bedroom; Bingham, *Fur Traders Descending the Missouri*; Brueghel the Elder, *The Harvesters*; Church, *Heart of the Andes*; Degas, *Dance Class*; Van Eyck, *Crucifixion*; El Greco, *View of Toledo*; Leutze, *Washington Crossing the Delaware*; Matisse, *Nasturtiums* and *Dance*; *Picasso, Gertrude Stein*; Rembrandt, *Aristotle Contemplating the Bust of Homer*; Velázquez, *Juan de Pareja*; Vermeer, *Young Woman with a Water Jug*. **Architecture:** 1880 building by Vaux and Mould; 1902 central pavilion by Hunt; 1913 wings by McKim, Mead, and White; 1975 Lehman Wing, 1979 Sackler Wing, 1980 American Wing, 1982 Rockefeller Wing by Roche, Dinkeloo, & Associates; 1987 Lila Acheson Wallace Wing for 20th-century art.

Admission: Donation suggested: adults, $6; senior citizens, students, $3; members, children under 12 accompanied by adult, free. Entrance fee for selected exhibitions. Handicapped accessible.
Hours: Tues.–Thurs., Sun., 9:30–5:15; Fri.–Sat., 9:30–8:45. Closed Mon., Jan. 1, Thanksgiving, Dec. 25. Certain galleries are operating on an alternating schedule; call (212) 570-3791 for information.
Tours: Daily; call museum for information.
Food & Drink: Cafeteria open Tues.–Thur., Sun., 9:30–4:30; Fri.–Sat., 9:30–8:30. Café open Tues.–Thurs., Sun., 11:30–4:30; Fri.–Sat., 11:30–9; Great Hall Balcony Bar open Fri.–Sat., 4–8:30; with music, 5–8; Restaurant open Tues.–Thurs., Sun., 11:30–3; Fri.–Sat., 11:30–10 (last reservation 8:30); Patrons and Sponsor Members Dining Room open noon–2:30 weekdays; for reservations call (212) 570-3786.
Branch: The Cloisters, Fort Tryon Park, New York, N.Y. 10040, (212) 923-3700.

Portrait of Guillaume Guillon Lethière, 1815, Jean Ingres. From "The French Drawing: Masterpieces from the Collection of the Pierpont Morgan Library." A traveling exhibition.

The Pierpont Morgan Library

29 E. 36th St., New York, N.Y. 10016
(212) 685-0008

1993 Exhibitions
Continuing
Art Objects and Bindings from the Permanent Collection
Treasures from Permanent Collections
Thru Jan. 10
A Christmas Carol
Thru Apr. 4
The Bernard H. Breslauer Collection of Manuscript Illuminations
Miniatures by such notable 15th- and 16th-century masters as Simon Bening, Jean Bourdichon, and Lorenzo Monaco highlight over 100 examples of European manuscript painting. Catalogue.
Printers and Miniaturists: Illuminated Books from Venice
Thru Apr. 18
Thomas Jefferson: 250th Anniversary of His Birth
Features materials from the library's autograph manuscript collection.
Apr. 13–Aug. 15
Henry James: 150th Anniversary of his Birth
Americana
Apr. 21–Aug. 15
A Great Legacy: Morgan Collections, 1913–1943
Sept. 15, 1993–Jan. 2, 1994
The French Drawing: Masterpieces from the Collection of the Pierpont Morgan Library
Spans five centuries of French draftsmanship; includes works by Poussin, Watteau, Delacroix, and Ingres. Catalogue.

Permanent Collection

Medieval and Renaissance illuminated manuscripts; printed books; bindings from the fifth to the 20th century; European drawings; autograph manuscripts; early children's books; original music manuscripts; ancient Near Eastern seals; Gilbert and Sullivan archive; Chinese, Egyptian, Roman art. **Highlights:** Three Gutenberg Bibles; Carolingian covers of Lindau Gospels; drawings by Mantegna, Dürer, Rubens, Rembrandt, Degas; paintings by Memling, Perugino, and Francia; autograph manuscripts including Milton's *Paradise Lost*, Dickens' *A Christmas Carol*; original manuscript of Saint-Exupéry's *The Little Prince*. **Architecture:** 1906 Neoclassical building by Charles F. McKim; 1928 west wing; 1852 Victorian brownstone The Morgan House; 1991 Garden Court by Voorsanger & Associates.

Admission: Suggested contribution: adults, $5; students, senior citizens, $3. Handicapped accessible.
Hours: Tues.–Sat., 10:30–5; Sun., 1–5. Closed Mon., holidays.
Tours: Library: Tues., Thurs., 2:30 and by appointment. Exhibitions: Wed., Fri., 2:30 and by appointment. Call (212) 685-0008, ext. 347 for appointments.
Food & Drink: Cafe serving lunch and tea; open museum hours.

The Museum of Modern Art

11 W. 53rd St., New York, N.Y. 10019
(212) 708-9400

1993 Exhibitions

Thru Jan. 12

Henri Matisse: A Retrospective
A comprehensive survey of 450 works—including paintings, drawings, prints, sculptures, and cut-outs—by this modern master. Catalogue. Admission fee.

New Photography 8
Presents recent work by eight artists: Dieter Appelt, Ellen Brooks, Darrel Ellis, Dennis Farber, Robert Flynt, Mary Miss, Gundula Schulze, and Toshio Shibata.

Thru Feb. 16

The Artist and the Book in Twentieth-Century Italy
Over 125 books created by Italian artists from the early 20th century through today; artists include de Chirico and Severini. Catalogue.

Feb. 21–May 4

Thinking is Form: The Drawings of Joseph Beuys
A range of Beuys' drawings—from highly finished renderings to sketches on the backs of envelopes—that attest to his conception of drawing as a reservoir of ideas. Catalogue.

Mar. 4–July 6
Reading Prints
Explores the use of language as a pictorial element in 20th-century printed art; includes works by LeWitt, Ruscha, and Twombly.
Mar. 12–May 2
Max Ernst: Dada and the Dawn of Surrealism
An exploration of the artist as a Dadaist, through collages, prints, paintings, and relief sculpture. Catalogue.
Mar. 25–May 18
Santiago Calatrava
The Spanish artist and architect's works that combine engineering, architecture, and sculpture.
Apr. 15–July 6
John Heartfield: Photomontages
Over 100 works from 1930 to 1939 by the German artist.
June–Aug.
The David Rockefeller Collection: Gifts to The Museum of Modern Art
Masterpieces include *View of Charing Cross Bridge*, Derain, and *Interior with Girl Reading*, Matisse.
June 5–Sept. 7
Latin American Artists of the Twentieth Century
In-depth examination of Latin American Modernism, encompassing over 300 works by 70 artists.
Sept. 22, 1993–Jan. 4, 1994
Robert Ryman
Retrospective of the career of the Minimalist artist, from 1955 to the present.
Fall
O. M. A. at MOMA: Rem Koolhaas and the Place of Public Architecture
Features five urban projects by the Office of Metropolitan Architecture (O.M.A.), Rotterdam, founded by Koolhaas in 1980.
Oct. 13, 1993–Jan. 18, 1994
Joan Miró: A Retrospective
Full-scale retrospective, spanning the entire range of Miró's creative activity from 1915 through late 1970; over 325 works including paintings, drawings, sculptures, and ceramics.
Feb. 20–May 10, 1994
Frank Lloyd Wright: A Retrospective
Most comprehensive survey of the architect's work to date. Includes 425 original drawings, many shown for the first time; 40 scale models, many specially commissioned for this exhibition; and a selection of decorative arts and furnishings. Catalogue.

Permanent Collection
Masterpieces of modern art by nearly every major artist of this century: paintings, sculptures, prints, drawings, illustrated books, architectural designs, photographs, films.

Highlights: Boccioni, *The City Rises*; Cézanne, *The Bather*; Chagall, *I and the Village*; van Gogh, *Portrait of Joseph Roulin* and *Starry Night*; Hopper, *House by the Railroad*; Matisse, *The Blue Window*, nine-panel *The Swimming Pool*; Mondrian, *Broadway Boogie-Woogie*; Monet, *Poplars at Giverny* and *Water Lilies*; Picasso, *Les Demoiselles d'Avignon* and *Three Musicians*; Rauschenberg, *Bed*; Rousseau, *The Sleeping Gypsy*; sculpture garden. **Architecture:** 1939 building by Goodwin and Stone; 1984 expansion and renovation by Pelli and Gruen.

Admission: Adults, $7; senior citizens, students with ID, $4; members, children under 16 accompanied by adult, free. Thurs., 5–9, donation suggested. Handicapped accessible; wheelchairs available.
Hours: Fri.–Tues., 11–6; Thurs., 11–9. Closed Wed., Dec. 25.
Tours: Mon.–Fri., 12:30, 3; Thurs., 5:30, 7.
Food & Drink: Garden Café open Thurs., 11–8; Fri.–Tues., 11–4:30.

National Academy of Design

1083 Fifth Ave. (at 89th St.), New York, N.Y. 10128
(212) 369-4880

1993 Exhibitions

Thru Jan. 10
Helene Schjerfbeck: Finland's Modernist Rediscovered
Thru winter
The Artist's Eye: Philip Pearlstein Selects Paintings from the Permanent Collection
Feb.–Mar.
The 168th Annual Exhibition
Apr.–May
Women Artists from the Collections of the National Academy of Design
May–July
Italian Old Master Drawings from the Horvitz Collection

Permanent Collection

The National Academy of Design is a museum, organization of artists, and art school founded in 1826, presenting painting, sculpture, prints, drawings, architecture. **Highlights:** Library, archives; American figurative art from 1826 to the present, including works by Church, Eakins, Homer, Sargent, Saint-Gaudens. **Architecture:** 1913 Beaux Arts townhouse; 1942 renovation by William A. Delano.

Admission: Adults, $3.50; students, senior citizens, children under 16, $2; Academy Friends, free. Fri., 5–8, free; Wed., art students with ID, free.
Hours: Wed.–Sun., noon–5; Fri, noon–8. Closed Mon.
Tours: Call (212) 369-4880 for information.

The New Museum of Contemporary Art

583 Broadway, New York, N.Y. 10012
(212) 219-1222; (212) 219-1355 (recording)

1993 Exhibitions

Jan. 17–Apr. 11
In Transit
Addresses the contexts that have displaced and relocated people, including Native Americans and African Americans, in American urban and rural environments. Catalogue.
May 7–Aug. 15
The Final Frontier
Examines developments in space exploration and scientific inquiries into the cosmos in relation to a changing understanding of the world's boundaries.
Sept. 10–Nov. 28
Trade Routes
Framed by references to the mercantile routes through which the New World of 15th and 16th centuries was charted, the exhibition emphasizes the enabling role of new technologies and patterns of exchange on cultural production.
Dec. 11, 1993–Mar. 27, 1994
Marie-Jo Lafontaine
The first major museum show of work by the Belgian artist.

Permanent Collection

To maintain a constant focus on recent art, the "semi-permanent" collection consists of works retained for a 10-year period: paintings, sculptures, prints, drawings, photographs, videotapes. **Architecture:** 1896 Astor building by Cleverdon and Putzel.

Admission: Donation suggested: adults, $3.50; senior citizens, artists, students, $2.50; children under 12, free.
Hours: Wed.–Thurs., Sun., noon–6; Fri.–Sat., noon–8. Closed Mon.–Tues., some holidays; call (212) 219-1355 for information.

The New-York Historical Society

170 Central Park W. at 77th St., New York, N.Y. 10024
(212) 873-3400

1993 Exhibitions

Spring–summer
The World of Thomas Jefferson
Celebrates the 250th birthday of Jefferson through portrait paintings, sculpture, prints, and other works. Shown at the Equitable Center gallery, 787 Seventh Ave. at 52nd St.
Sept.–Dec.
Dreams and Shadows: Thomas H. Hotchkiss in 19th-Century Italy
First retrospective of this member of the Hudson River School, who painted extensively in Italy.
Sept. 1993–continuing
Highlights from the Collections of the N-YHS
Sept. 28, 1993–Jan. 2, 1994
"Visiting Nurse": The Life of Lillian Wald
Artifacts and documents commemorating the centennial of the Visiting Nurse Service.
Dec. 1993–Feb. 1994
Early New York Printing from the Library of the N-YHS

Permanent Collection

Founded in 1804, the society is the oldest museum in the state, with collections of 17th-, 18th-, and 19th-century American fine and decorative arts; renowned holdings of Hudson River landscape painting and Colonial portraits; architectural drawings and manuscripts spanning the 19th–20th centuries; collections of silver, porcelain, furniture, toys. **Highlights:** Largest collection of Tiffany lamps and glass; all 431 extant original watercolors for *Birds of America*, Audubon; recreated painting galleries of 19th-century art patron; office contents of Cass Gilbert and McKim, Mead, and White. **Architecture:** 1909 Greek Revival building by York & Sawyer; New York City historic landmark.

Admission: Adults, $4.50; students, senior citizens, $3; children under 12, $1. Members free. Tues., discretionary admission.
Hours: Tues.– Wed., Fri., Sun., 11–5; Thurs., 11–8. Mon., Sat., closed.
Tours: Gallery talks daily, 1. Group tours: Tues.–Fri., Sun., 11–3; call (212) 873-3400 ext. 261 for reservations.

The Studio Museum in Harlem

144 W. 125th St., New York, N.Y. 10027
(212) 864-4500

1993 Exhibitions
Thru Apr. 11
Wifredo Lam and His Contemporaries
Focuses on the influences of Afro-Cuban culture, contemporary Cuban artists, the New York School, and the CoBrA group on Lam's works from 1938 to 1952. Catalogue.
May 2–Aug. 22
Artists Respond: The "New World" Question
Nine artists approach the quincentenary of Columbus's voyages to America through installations and performances.

Permanent Collection
Art of the African Diaspora, including works by African, Caribbean, African-American, and Latino artists; James Van Der Zee archives of 1920s–1940s photographs of Harlem.
Architecture: 19th-century building; 1982 renovation by Max Bond; sculpture garden.

Admission: Adults, $3; senior citizens, children under 12, $1; members, free. Handicapped accessible.
Hours: Wed.–Fri., 10–5; Sat.–Sun., 1–6. Closed Mon.–Tues.
Tours: Gallery group tours: Tues.–Fri., 10–4; Sat., 1–5. Reservations required; call (212) 864-4500, ext. 230.

Whitney Museum of American Art

945 Madison Ave., New York, N.Y. 10021
(212) 570-3676 (information)

1993 Exhibitions
Thru Jan. 31
Agnes Martin
A major retrospective of the career of one of America's leading contemporary reductivist painters.
Thru Feb. 14
Jean Michel Basquiat
First U.S. exhibition to survey the work of this 20th-century artist.
The Geometric Tradition in 20th-Century American Art
Examines the development of geometric abstraction in American painting and sculpture.

Telephone, 1916, Andy Warhol. From "Hand-Painted Pop: American Art in Transition, 1955–62." A traveling exhibition.

Mar. 5–June 13
1993 Biennial Exhibition
Sixty-seventh invitational survey of American art produced during the past two years.
June 24–Sept. 5
Permanent Collection
July 9–Oct. 17
In the Spririt of Fluxus
Five hundred objects of Fluxus art, ranging from performance pieces and experimental films to artist's books and posters. Catalogue.
July 16–Oct. 3
Hand-Painted Pop: American Art in Transition, 1955–62
Examines the evolution of Pop Art from stylistic techniques used by first-generation Abstract Expressionists of the New York School; artists include Jim Dine, Jasper Johns, and Cy Twombly. Catalogue.
Sept. 15–Nov. 29
Vija Celmins: Mid-Career Retrospective
More than 65 works by the American artist, from the 1960s through the present. Catalogue.

Permanent Collection

Comprehensive holdings of 20th-century American art; includes works by Calder, Dove, de Kooning, Lichtenstein, Nevelson, Pollock, Rothko, Stella, Warhol. **Highlights:** Bellows, *Dempsey and Firpo*; Calder, *Circus*; Hartley, *Painting, Number 5*; Henri, *Gertrude Vanderbilt Whitney*; Hopper, *Early Sunday Morning*; Johns, *Three Flags*; Lachaise, *Standing Woman*. **Architecture:** 1966 building by Marcel Breuer.

Admission: Adults, $6; senior citizens, students with ID, $4; children under 12 accompanied by adult, free. Thurs., 6–8, free. Handicapped accessible; wheelchairs available.
Hours: Wed., Fri.–Sun., 11–6; Thurs., 1–8. Closed Mon., Tues., national holidays.
Tours: Wed.–Fri., various times; Sat.–Sun., 2, 3:30. Call (212) 606-0395 for group visits.
Food & Drink: Sarabeth's at the Whitney open Tues., noon–5; Wed., Fri., 11–5:30; Thurs., 12:30–7:30; Sat., Sun., 10–5.
Branches: Champion in Fairfield County, One Champion Plaza, Stamford, Conn., (203) 358-7630. Philip Morris, 120 Park Ave., New York, N.Y., (212) 878-2550.

Neuberger Museum

SUNY Purchase, 735 Anderson Hill Rd., Purchase, N.Y. 10577
(914) 251-6133

1993 Exhibitions

Continuing
Object and Intellect: African Art from the Permanent Collection
A selection of ceremonial headdresses, masks, religious, and non-religious sculptures.

Thru Jan. 3
Sette and Segura Publishing Company: A Decade of Print Publishing
Retrospective exhibition of fine-art prints created at Sette and Segura; artists include William Wegman, Keith Haring, and Suzanne Caporael.

Thru Jan. 24
Rebecca Medel: Transcendental Fiber Constructs
Room-size, knotted-linen installation in the museum's South Gallery.

Thru Mar. 14
Threnody
Commissioned abstract wall panels by Cleve Gray.

Thru Mar. 28
Ancient Art from the Permanent Collection
Examples of classical Greek pottery from the 6th to 4th centuries B.C.

Jan. 17–Mar. 21
Sylvia Plimack Mangold: Works on Paper 1970–1990

Apr. 4–June 27
Melvin Edwards Sculpture: A 30-Year Retrospective 1963–1993
Over 80 works in steel by the African-American artist. Catalogue.

Study for *Banister Painting*, 1971, Sylvia Plimack Mangold. From "Sylvia Plimack Mangold: Works on Paper, 1970–1990." Neuberger Museum of Art.

Permanent Collection
Twentieth-century American and European paintings, sculpture, photographs, prints, drawings; 19th–20th-century African art; ancient art. **Highlights:** Works by Avery, Frankenthaler, Diebenkorn, Hopper, Prendergast, Lawrence, O'Keeffe, de Kooning, Moore, Calder, Pollock. **Architecture:** 1974 building by Philip Johnson.

Admission: Adults, $4; seniors, students with ID, $2; children under 12 and museum friends, free. First Sat. of each month, free. Handicapped accessible.
Hours: Tues.–Fri., 10–4; Sat.–Sun., 11–5. Closed Mon. and major holidays.
Tours: Informal gallery talks: Sept.–June, Tues.–Fri., 1; Sun., 2, 3. No reservations. Group tours: Tues.–Fri., 10–3; Sat., 11–4. Fee. For groups of 10 to 50, call (914) 251-6110 three weeks in advance.

Memorial Art Gallery of the University of Rochester

500 University Ave., Rochester, N.Y. 14607
(716) 473-7720

1993 Exhibitions
Thru Feb. 7
**Light, Air, and Color: American Impressionist Paintings from the Collection of the Pennsylvania Academy of the Fine Arts*
These 56 paintings by Childe Hassam, Cecilia Beaux, Robert Vonnoh, and others demonstrate the academy's role in introducing impressionism to the United States. Catalogue.
Mar. 6–Apr. 25
Traditional Masterpieces from Zaire: Royal Kuba Art
Ceremonial textiles, masks, hats, clothing, and ritual objects of the Kuba kings of central Zaire.
May 15–June 20
1993 Rochester-Finger Lakes Exhibition
July 11–Aug. 29
Iterations: The New Digital Imaging
Explores the new forms emerging from the union of camera and computer, and the impact of digital technology on the art world and popular culture.
Oct. 9–Dec. 5
Sites of Recollection: Four Altars and a Rap Opera
Five installations by artists that draw on their histories as Korean, Jewish, Native, African, and Hispanic Americans.

Permanent Collection

Work from relics of antiquity to contemporary movements; focus on medieval art, 17th-century European art; 19th- and early 20th-century French and American paintings, American folk art, European and American prints and drawings; ethnographic room with African, Oceanic and ancient American art; Asian room. **Highlights:** Rembrandt, *Portrait of a Young Man in an Armchair*; Van Dyck, *Portrait of an Italian Nobleman*; Monet, *Waterloo Bridge*; Braque, *Still Life with Pipe*; works by Cassatt, Homer, Cole, Nevelson, Frankenthaler. **Architecture:** 1913 Italian Renaissance building by Foster, Gade and Graham; 1927 addition by McKim, Mead and White; 1987 sculpture pavilion by Handler, Grosso.

Admission: Adults, $4; college students with ID, senior citizens, $2.50; children 6–18, $1; children 5 and under, members, University of Rochester students, free; Tues., 5–9, free. Handicapped accessible.
Hours: Tues., 12:30–9; Wed.–Fri., 10–4; Sat.–Sun., noon–5. Closed Mon., major holidays.
Tours: Tues., 7:30; Fri., 11; Sun., 2. Call (716) 473-6380 to arrange group tours.

Interior, Memorial Art Gallery of the University of Rochester.

Food & Drink: Gallery café open Tues.–Sat. for lunch and dinner, Sun. for brunch. Closed Mon. Call (716) 473-6380 for reservations.

Mint Museum of Art

2730 Randolph Rd., Charlotte, N.C. 28207
(704) 337-2000; 333-MINT (recording)

Boy in Dublet, c. 1600–10, Paulus Jansz Moreelse. Mint Museum of Art.

1993 Exhibitions

Thru Jan. 31
The Silhouette Selection: Recent Celebrity Photography 1979–1991
Portraits of such celebrities as Robert De Niro and Madonna by 14 premier photographers, including Annie Leibovitz, Herb Ritts, and Bruce Weber.

Thru May 29
Fortuny Costumes
A selection of garments by the Spanish-born designer, illustrating an aesthetic founded on ancient, antique, and decorative arts.

Jan. 23–Mar. 21
Native American Tradition: North American Indian Collection of the Lowe Art Museum
A presentation of American Indian textiles and utilitarian and art objects. Catalogue.

Mar. 20–May 16
Processing the Image: Prints
An examination of various printmaking techniques featuring works from the museum collection.

Apr. 10–June 6
1992–93 North Carolina Arts Council Fellowships

June 26–Aug. 29
Carolina Collects
Examines traditional fine arts held in private North and South Carolina collections.

Sept. 25–Jan. 2, 1994
River of Gold: Pre-Columbian Treasures from Sitio Conte
Over 125 pieces of Pre-Columbian goldwork from this region of central Panama.

Nov. 20, 1993–Mar. 13, 1994
Classical Taste in America 1800–1840
Presents over 225 paintings, sculpture, furniture, and other works that demonstrate America's captivation with the Classical or Grecian style.

Permanent Collection

Pre-Columbian, African art; European painting; American works by Cole, Inness, Prendergast, Stuart; regional crafts; American pottery; historic artifacts of North Carolina's Piedmont region; gold coins. **Highlights:** Dalton collection of works by Constable, Eakins, Homer, Remington, Wyeth; Delhom Gallery of pottery and porcelain from ancient times to 18th century; Ghirlandaio, *Madonna and Child with Four*

Saints; West, *Agriculture Aided by Arts and Commerce.* **Architecture:** 1835 Federal-style building by Strickland; 1967 Delhom Gallery by Odell & Associates; 1985 Dalton Wing by Clark, Tibble, Harris, and Li.

Admission: Adults, $4; senior citizens, $3; seniors, $2; children 12 and under, members, free. Tues., 5–10, second Sunday of each month, free. Handicapped accessible.
Hours: Tues., 10–10; Wed.–Sat., 10–5; Sun., 1–6. Closed Mon., Jan. 1, Dec. 25.
Tours: Daily, 2; or call (704) 337-2000 for reservations.

North Carolina Museum of Art

2110 Blue Ridge Rd., Raleigh, N.C. 27607
(919) 833-1935

1993 Exhibitions

Thru Feb. 28
Perspectives of Conceptualism: The New Russian Avant-Garde
Over 20 of the leading artists of "Moscow Conceptualism," only a few of whom are known outside of Russia.
Thru July 3
From the Ground Up: Experiencing Architecture
Exhibition will show visitors how to look at buildings by focusing on site, function, structure, and aesthectics.
Feb. 6–June 20
A Selection from The Birds of America *by John James Audubon*
A rare copy of the four-volume folio published from 1827 to 1838 by Audubon, the noted ornithologist and artist.
May 1–Aug. 1
The Naked Soul: Polish Fin-de-Siècle Painting from the National Museum, Poznan
Forty-six paintings by 21 Polish artists active at the turn of the century represent the search for a national cultural identity.
Oct. 2–Dec. 5
1993 North Carolina Artists Exhibition

St. Catherine, c. 1505–10, Tilmann Riemenschneider. North Carolina Museum of Art.

Permanent Collection

European and American paintings, sculpture; 20th-century paintings, sculpture; African, Oceanic, Pre-Columbian ceremonial art; ancient Greek, Roman, Egyptian art; Judiaca. **Highlights:** Collections of European paintings from 1300 to 1800, American 19th-century paintings. **Architecture:** 1983 International Style by Edward Durell Stone & Assoc., and Holloway-Reeves.

Admission: Free. Handicapped accessible.
Hours: Tues.–Sat., 9–5; Fri., 9–9; Sun., 11–6. Closed Mon.

Tours: Daily, 1:30; call (919) 833-1935 for group reservations.
Food & Drink: Museum Cafe open weekdays, 11:30–2:30; weekends, 11–3; Fri. dinner, 5:30–8:45.

Reynolda House Museum of American Art

Box 11765, Reynolda Rd., Winston-Salem, N.C. 27116
(919) 725-5325

1993 Exhibitions

Thru Aug.
Georgia O'Keeffe's Clamshell
Continuing
Breaking the Code: William Sidney Mount, The Card Players

Permanent Collection

Works by American artists including Eakins, Prendergast, Wyeth, Lawrence, Close, Motherwell, Johns, Dine, Nevelson. **Highlights:** Wood, *Spring Turning*; Bierstadt, *Sierra Nevada*; Church, *The Andes of Ecuador*; O'Keeffe, *Pool in the Woods, Lake George*. **Architecture:** 1912–17 house by Charles Barton Keen; 1934 addition; 1991 renovation.

Admission: Adults, $6; senior citizens, $5; children, students, $3. Handicapped accessible.
Hours: Tues.–Sat., 9:30–4:30; Sun., 1:30–4:30.
Tours: Call or write for group-tour reservations.

Southeastern Center for Contemporary Art

750 Marguerite Dr., Winston-Salem, N.C. 27106
(919) 725-1904

1993 Exhibitions

Feb. 6–Apr. 18
The Nearest Edge of the World: Art and Cuba Now
Work by members of the youngest generation of artists now working in Cuba.
Oliver Wasow
The artist's photographic collages of advertisements, postcards, and magazine pictures.
Feb. 13–Apr. 18
Fauna
Painters and photographers explore the connection, dependence, and similarities of animals and humankind.

Apr. 10–July 18
David Hanson
May 8–July 18
Destruction/Reclamation: Art and the Environment in the Nineties
Focus on nine artist-activists whose work deals with damaged ecosystems and ways to reclaim land; combination of site-specific installations and plans for future work. Catalogue.
June 11–Sept. 5
David Dunlap
The documentary artist's personal, historical, and political commentary on contemporary life.
July 31–Sept. 30
David Wilson
Presents the artist's work in drawing, sculpture, and installation.
Garnett Puett
Features works that are a combination of the artist's hand and the activity of working bees.
Sept. 24–Dec. 12
North Carolina Glass
Celebrates the major impact of the studio glass movement associated with the Penland School of Crafts, N.C.
Oct. 23, 1993–Jan. 2, 1994
National Crafts Invitational
Oct. 30–Jan. 16
Color
Attempts to present the black experience as seen by persons of color, specifically photographers; artists include Lorna Simpson and Carrie Mae Weems. Catalogue.

Permanent Collection

No permanent collection. **Architecture:** 1929 house by Peabody, Wilson & Brown; 1978 addition by Jim White of Newman, Calloway, Johnson, Van Etten and Winfree; 1990 addition by Newman & Jones.

Admission: Adults, $3; seniors, $2; students, members, children under 12, free. Handicapped accessible.
Hours: Tues.–Sat., 10–5; Sun., 2–5. Closed Mon.
Tours: Reservations required; contact the education department for information.

Cincinnati Art Museum

Eden Park, Cincinnati, Ohio 45202
(513) 721-5204

1993 Exhibitions

NOTE: Renovated galleries reopen Jan. 15, 1993.
Jan. 15–Apr. 11
Six Centuries of Master Prints: Treasures from the Herbert Greer French Collection
Survey of the significant print collection, featuring artists from Rembrandt and Pollaiuolo to Degas and Goya. Catalogue.
Jan. 15–Apr. 18
Photographic Treasures from the Cincinnati Art Museum
Features works from the permanent collection.
Mar. 13–June 6
Rookwood Pottery: The Glorious Gamble
Spans the "glory years" of Rookwood's decorating history from the early 1880s to the 1940s. Catalogue.
May 23–Sept. 5
With Grace and Favour: Fashion from the Victorian and Edwardian Eras
Represents all aspects of the fashionable woman's wardrobe from 1837 to 1910, including wedding gowns and evening wear. Catalogue.

Permanent Collection

Greek, Roman, Etruscan art; Near and Far Eastern art; African, Pre-Columbian, South Pacific art; North American Indian art; medieval sculpture; decorative arts; ancient musical instruments; American paintings by Cassatt, Church, Cole, Copley, Sargent; 20th-century art; Cincinnati artists.
Highlights: Near Eastern collection (both ancient and Islamic); Corot, *Mantes*; Gainsborough, *Portrait of Mrs. Philip Thicknesse*; Sargent, *Italian Girl with Fan*; Titian, *Philip II of Spain*; Wood, *Daughters of the Revolution.*
Architecture: 1886 Romanesque building by James MacLaughlin; early 1890s Greek Revival addition by Daniel Burnham; 1930 Beaux Arts wings by Garber & Woodward; 1937 addition by Rendings, Panzer & Martin; 1965 International Style addition by Potter, Tyler, Martin & Roth; 1993 renovation by Glazier Associates.

Admission: Adults, $5; senior citizens, students, $4; children under 18, free. Groups, $4 each. Sat., free. Handicapped accessible.
Hours: Tues.–Sat., 10–5, Sun., 11–5. Closed Mon., holidays.
Tours: Groups of 10–60: Tues.–Sat., 10–3. Call (513) 721-5204 for reservations at least three weeks in advance.
Food & Drink: Terrace Court Restaurant open Tues.–Fri., 11:30–2:30; Sat., 11:30–3:30; Sun. noon–4; dinner Wed., 5–7:30.

The Taft Museum

316 Pike St., Cincinnati, Ohio 45202
(513) 241-0343

1993 Exhibitions

Thru Jan. 10
Italian Old Master Drawings from the Collection of Jeffrey E. Horvitz
Includes drawings by Guercino, Tiepolo, Canaletto, and others. Catalogue.
Feb. 3–Apr. 25
Tell Me a Story
Works in clay and glass that depict both personal and universal narratives. Catalogue.
May 21–Aug. 15
19th- and 20th-Century Folk Art from the Collection of Isabelle and Bates Lowry
First public exhibition of the collection of fine arts, quilts, toys, and other objects produced mainly by Appalachian itinerant artists. Catalogue.

Permanent Collection

The collections of Charles Phelps and Anna Simon Taft, featuring French Renaissance enamels, Chinese ceramics, and European Old Master paintings, opened to the public in 1932. **Highlights:** Murals by Robert Scott Duncanson; Limoges painted enamel; the Monvaerni triptych; paintings by Rembrandt, Hals, Corot, Gainsborough, Reynolds, and Turner. **Architecture:** 1820 Federal mansion.

Admission: Suggested donation: adults, $3; seniors, $2; students, $1. Handicapped accessible.
Hours: Mon.–Sat., 10–5; Sun., holidays, 12–5.
Tours: Weekdays, 10–5; call (513) 241-0343.

The Cobbler's Apprentice, 1877, Frank Duveneck. Taft Museum.

The Cleveland Museum of Art

11150 East Blvd., Cleveland, Ohio 44106
(216) 421-7340

1993 Exhibitions

Thru Jan. 3
Contemporary American Photographs
Artists include Joel Meyerowitz, William Eggleston, and Duane Michals.

Thru Feb. 7
Flor Garduño: Photographs of Central and South America
A glimpse of traditional pre-Hispanic practices still thriving in remote areas of Central and South America.

Thru Mar. 7
Fans–East & West
Traces the history of fans through Chinese, Japanese, and European examples.

Jan. 27–Mar. 28
Small Works in Fiber: The Collection of Mildred Constantine
Miniature textiles by leading fiber artists.

Feb. 3–Apr. 11
The Lure of Italy: American Artists and the Italian Experience 1760–1914
Examines the influence of Italian art from antiquity to contemporary times on American 18th- and 19th-century artists. Catalogue.

Feb. 9–Apr. 11
Arms & Armor
Explores armor components and weapon types and their place in the Middle Ages and Renaissance through examples, illuminations, and engravings.
Hendrik Goltzius and the Netherlandish Chiaroscuro Woodcut
Illustrates the history of the medium in the Netherlands before Goltzius and includes all 37 of Goltzius' chiaroscuro woodcuts; only U.S. venue. Catalogue.

Feb. 10–Apr. 11
Selected Acquisitions

May 26–Sept. 5
The May Show: Juried Exhibition

July 13–Sept. 5
The Graphic Art of Les XX and the Belgian Avant-Garde
Demonstrates the importance of Belgian graphic arts to such movements as Neo-Impressionism, Symbolism, Art Nouveau, and Arts & Crafts; artists include James Ensor and Félicien Rops.

Permanent Collection

Comprehensive holdings of art from antiquity to the present. Important Asian and Medieval Western collections; European and American paintings, sculpture, decorative arts, prints, drawings, photographs; European and Islamic textiles. **Highlights:** Chinese paintings from the Song, Ming, Qing dynasties; Warring States Period *Cranes and Serpents*; Cambodian Krishna Govardhana; the Guelph Treasure (medieval German liturgical objects in precious metal, enamel, ivory); alabaster mourners from tomb of Philip the Bold; 18th-century French decorative arts, including silver tureen by Meissonnier; sculpture garden; Caravaggio, *Crucifixion of Saint Andrew*; Kline, *Accent Grave*; Monet, *Water Lilies*; Picasso, *La Vie*; Rubens, *Portrait of his Wife, Isabella Brant*; Ryder, *Death on a Pale Horse*; Turner, *Burning of the Houses of Parliament*; Zurbarán, *Holy House of Nazareth*; Mount, *The Power of Music*. **Architecture:** 1916 Neoclassical building by Hubbell and Benes; 1958 wing and addition by Hays and Ruth; 1971 addition by Breuer and Smith; 1984 addition by Dalton, van Dyck, Johnson & Partners.

Admission: Free. Handicapped accessible.
Hours: Tues.–Fri., 10–5:45; Wed., 10–9:45; Sat., 9–4:45; Sun., 1–5:45. Closed Mon., Jan. 1, July 4, Thanksgiving, Dec. 25.
Tours: Call (216) 421-7340 during museum hours.
Food & Drink: Museum Café open Tues.–Fri., 10–4:30; Sat., 10–4:15; Sun., 1–4:45.

Columbus Museum of Art

480 E. Broad St., Columbus, Ohio 43215
(614) 221-6801; 221-4848 (recording)

1993 Exhibitions

Jan. 24–May 16
Elijah Pierce, Woodcarver
Retrospective exhibition celebrating the centennial of the Columbus folk artist; 173 carvings on display.

Mar. 14–Apr. 25
Emmet Gowin: Photographs
More than 120 photographs from the 25-year career of the artist, who focuses on issues involving the "changing earth." Catalogue.

Sept. 5, 1993–Feb. 28, 1994
People, Places, and Things: An African-American Perspective
Featured African-American artists include Larry Collins, William Hawkins, and Aminah Robinson.

Sept. 15, 1993–mid-Feb. 1994
New Photography Acquisitions: Selections from the Ross Collection
Significant examples of portrait, documentary, landscape, and art photography, including works by Alfred Stieglitz and Ansel Adams.

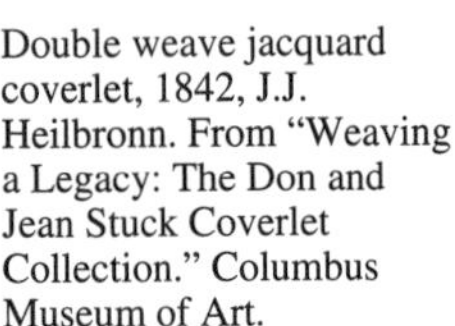
Double weave jacquard coverlet, 1842, J.J. Heilbronn. From "Weaving a Legacy: The Don and Jean Stuck Coverlet Collection." Columbus Museum of Art.

Oct. 3, 1993–Jan. 16, 1994
Weaving a Legacy: The Don and Jean Stuck Coverlet Collection
Features 85 of the collection's 19th-century American "figured and fancy" woven coverlets. Catalogue.

Permanent Collection

European and American collections from 1850 to 1945, including Impressionist, Post-Impressionist, German Expressionist, Cubist, Fauvist works; 16th- and 17th-century Dutch and Flemish painting; Pre-Columbian and South Pacific art; Oriental ceramics. Galleries arranged chronologically, focusing on artistic movements in different countries from the Renaissance to the Modern era. **Highlights:** Monet, *View of Bennecourt*; Degas, *Houses at the Foot of a Cliff* and *Dancer at Rest*; Renoir, *Christine Lerolle Embroidering*; a group of 11 works by Klee; Bellows paintings, lithographs; Boucher, *Earth*; Ingres, *Raphael and the Fornarina*; O'Keeffe, *Autumn Leaves*; Rubens, *Christ Triumphant over Sin and Death*; 350 coverlets by Ohio and Midwest artists; sculpture by Archipenko, Maillol, Manzù, Moore. **Architecture:** 1931 Italian Renaissance building; 1974 addition.

Admission: Donation suggested; special exhibit admission varies. Group rates available. Handicapped accessible.
Hours: Tues.–Fri., 11–4; Sat., 10–5; Sun., 11–5. Closed Mon., Jan. 1, July 4, Thanksgiving, Dec. 25.
Tours: Fri., noon; Sun., 2. For group tour reservations call (614) 221-6801 four weeks in advance.
Food & Drink: The Palette Café open Tues.–Fri., 11:30–1:30; Sat., Sun., noon–2.

The Dayton Art Institute

P.O. Box 941, Forest and Riverview aves., Dayton, Ohio 45405-0941
(513) 223-5277

1993 Exhibitions

Thru Jan. 31
Theme and Improvisation: Kandinsky and the American Avant-Garde, 1912–1950
Traces the influence of this father of pure abstraction on American artists.
Jan. 26–June 27
Japanese Space
Feb. 13–Mar. 28
Tales of Japan: Three Centuries of Japanese Painting from the Chester Beatty Library, Dublin
Painted hand scrolls and albums from the 16th to 19th centuries illustrating famous Japanese stories and historical events.
Apr. 16–June 13
African-American Artists of Ohio: The 1993 Ohio Selection
July 15–Nov. 30
Elmer Webster Collection
Dec. 18, 1993–Jan. 29, 1994
**I Dream a World: Portraits of Black Women who Changed America*
Seventy-five portraits by Pulitzer Prize–winning photographer Brian Lanker of Maya Angelou, Shirley Chisholm, Odetta, Rosa Parks, Sarah Vaughan, and others. Catalogue.

Branch: Museum of Contemporary Art at Wright State University

1993 Exhibitions

Thru Jan. 22
Peter Eisenmann and Frank Gehry
Focuses on two projects presented at the International Fifth Architectural Biennale in Venice, Italy, in 1991.
Mar. 21–May 8
Sites of Recollection: Four Altars and a Rap Opera
Five installations by artists that draw on their histories as Korean, Jewish, Native, African, and Hispanic Americans.

Permanent Collection

American, European, Asian, Oceanic, African art; Art of Our Time (contemporary art); ancient art. **Highlights:** Greco-Roman *Aphrodite Pudica*; Hopper, *High Noon*; Monet, *Water Lilies*; Rubens, *Two Study Heads of an Old Man*; Warhol, *Russell Means*; Preti, *St. Catherine of Alexandria*; Experiencenter, where visitors experience art by seeing and doing. **Architecture:** 1930 Italianate building by Edward B. Green modeled after a 16th-century villa; 1982 Propylaeum (entry) by Levin Porter Smith Inc.

Admission: Adults, $3; senior citizens, students with ID, $2; members, children under 18, free. First Sat. of month, free. Handicapped accessible.
Hours: Tues.–Sun., noon–5. Closed Mon., Dec. 25.
Tours: Call (513) 223-5277 for information. Tours free with admission, with the exception of "Tea & Tour" and lunch tours. Tours are available for the visually or hearing impaired.

The Toledo Museum of Art

2445 Monroe St., Box 1013, Toledo, Ohio 43697
(419) 255-8000

1993 Exhibitions

Feb. 7–Mar. 14
From the Ground Out: Toledo's Frank Gehry Building
Feb. 7–Apr. 18
Noah's Raven: A Video Installation by Mary Lucier
Multichannel video installation including images videotaped in Alaska, the Amazon rain forest, and Midwestern sites.
Mar. 14–May 2
Max Beckmann Prints from the Collection of The Museum of Modern Art
One-third of the artist's graphic works is represented, capturing dramatic high points in 20th-century art.
Mar. 21–May 2
The University of Toledo B.F.A. Exhibition I
May 9–June 27
The University of Toledo B.F.A. Exhibition II
June 13–July 3
Toledo Area Artists 75th Annual Exhibition
Athena Society 90th Anniversary Exhibition
Sept. 12–Nov. 14
The Saxe Contemporary Studio Craft Collection
Contemporary craft objects in glass, ceramics, fiber, metal, and wood.

Winged Deity, 885–860 B.C., Assyrian. The Toledo Museum of Art.

Permanent Collection
Traces the history of art from ancient Egypt to the present: European and American paintings, sculpture; extensive glass collection; graphic arts; photographs; tapestries; decorative arts. **Highlights:** Chase, *The Open Air Breakfast;* Cole, *The Architect's Dream*; El Greco, *Agony in the Garden*; Rembrandt, *Man in a Fur-lined Coat*; Rubens, *The Crowning of Saint Catherine.* **Architecture:** 1912 Neoclassical building by Edward Green; 1992 addition by Frank O. Gehry.

Admission: Donation suggested. Entrance fee for selected exhibitions. Handicapped accessible; wheelchairs, strollers available.
Hours: Tues.–Sat., 10–4; Sun., 1–5. Closed Mon., holidays.
Tours: Call (419) 255-8000 for information.
Food & Drink: Museum Café open Tues.–Sat., 10–2, Sun., 1–4; closed Aug.

The Philbrook Museum of Art

2727 S. Rockford Rd., Tulsa, Okla. 74114
(918) 749-7941

1993 Exhibitions
Thru Feb. 14
Objects and Drawings from the Sanford M. and Diane Besser Collection
Twentieth-century works on paper and craft objects by such artists as Everett Shinn, Romare Bearden, and John Sloan.
Apr. 4–May 30
Paul Manship: Changing Taste in America
Sculpture, drawings, and photographs by the American artist.
July 4–Aug. 22
Baroque Gold and Jewelry from The Hungarian National Museum
Seventeenth- and 18th-century gems and jewelry, silver, and ecclesiastical treasures from one of the largest such collections.
Sept. 12–Nov. 7
From Elizabeth I to Elizabeth II: 400 Years of Drawings from the National Portrait Gallery, London
One hundred drawings, watercolors, and portrait miniatures, including works by Hilliard, Gainsborough, and Constable.
Dec. 19, 1993–Feb. 14, 1994
Glass from Ancient Craft to Contemporary Art: 1962–1992 and Beyond
Surveys the development of glass as a medium for aesthetic expression; features 86 works by 60 international artists.

Self-Portrait, c. 1779, Henry Fuseli. From "From Elizabeth I to Elizabeth II: 400 Years of Portrait Drawings from the National Portrait Gallery, London." A traveling exhibition.

Permanent Collection
Collections include Italian painting, sculpture; Native American basketry, pottery, paintings; African sculpture; 18th- and 19th-century European paintings; 19th- and 20th-century American art. **Architecture:** 1927 Villa Philbrook by Edward Buehler Delk; 1990 wing by Urban Design Group in association with Michael Lustig.

Admission: Adults, $3; senior citizens, groups of 10 or more, $1.50 per person; members, free. Handicapped accessible.
Hours: Tues.–Sat., 10–5; Thurs., 10–8; Sun., 1–5. Closed Mon.
Tours: Call (918) 748-5309, preferably two weeks in advance.
Food & Drink: Philbrook Restaurant open museum hours.

Portland Art Museum

(formerly the Oregon Art Institute)
1219 S.W. Park Ave., Portland, Oreg. 97205
(503) 226-2811

1993 Exhibitions
Thru Feb. 7
History of Oregon Photography
Collection of early images of Oregon towns and landscapes by settlers and photographers.
Mar. 2–May 2
PDX and the State of Collecting
Explores the art of being a "serious" collector of both traditional arts and unusual collections.
Mar. 23–May 15
Carl Morris—A Retrospective
Works by the contemporary modernist painter and Oregonian.
Oct. 20–Dec. 30
The Floating World Revisited
Focus on the late 18th-century Japanese classic period of *ukiyo-e*, including screens, scrolls, decorative arts, and prints.

Permanent Collection
19th- and 20th-century works; Northwest Native American art; Kress collection of Renaissance and Baroque paintings; Cameroon sculptures; Elizabeth Cole Butler collection of Native American art. **Highlights:** Pre-Han *Standing Horse*; Brancusi, *Muse*; Monet, *Water Lilies*; Renoir, *Two Girls Reading*; Tlingit *Wolf Hat*. **Architecture:** 1932 building by Belluschi; 1989 renovation.

Admission: Adults, $4; senior citizens, students, $2; children 6–12, $1; children under 6, free. First Thurs. of month, 4–9, free for all; every Thurs., free for senior citizens. Handicapped accessible.
Hours: Tues.–Sat., 11–5; Sun., 1–5; first Thurs. of month, 11–9. June–Aug.: Thurs., 11–9. Closed Mon.
Tours: Call (503) 226-2811 for information.
Food & Drink: Restaurant open 11–2.

Brandywine River Museum

Brandywine Conservancy, Route 1, Chadds Ford, Pa. 19317
(215) 388-2700

1993 Exhibitions
Thru Jan. 10
A Brandywine Christmas
An O-gauge model train display, antique dolls, holiday trees.
Jan. 20–Apr. 18
Expressions of Place: The Art of William Stanley Haseltine
An examination of the career of this 19th-century landscape painer, whose work was tied to Luminism and evinced a concern for the "scientific truth." Catalogue.
May 29–May 31
22nd Annual American Antiques Show

Torn in Transit, c. 1890, John Haberle. Brandywine River Museum.

June 5–Sept. 6
Grainger McKoy
Woodcarvings by the contemporary American artist.
Sept. 11–Nov. 7
Fall Harvest Market
Sept. 11–Nov. 21
Highlights from the Butler Institute of American Art, Youngstown
Works from the first structure designed specifically to house American art; famous paintings include Homer's *Snap the Whip* and Hopper's *Pennsylvania Coal Town.*
Nov. 26, 1993–Jan. 8, 1994
A Brandywine Christmas

Permanent Collection
American art with special emphasis on the art of Brandywine region. Nineteenth- and 20th-century landscapes by Cropsey, Doughty, Moran, Trost Richards; 19th-century trompe l'oeil works by Cope, Harnett, Peto; illustrations by Darley, Pyle, Parrish, Gibson, Dunn. **Highlights:** Paintings by three generations of Wyeths; Andrew Wyeth gallery. **Architecture:** 1864 grist mill renovated in 1971 by James Grieves; 1984 addition by Grieves.

Admission: Adults, $5; senior citizens, $2.50; students with ID, children, 6–12, $2.50; members, children under 6, free. Handicapped accessible.
Hours: Daily, 9:30–4:30; Dec. 26–30, 9:30–8. Closed Dec. 25.
Tours: Available by reservation for groups of 15 or more. Call (215) 388-2700, ext. 166.
Food & Drink: Restaurant open daily, 11–3; Jan.–Feb., open Wed.–Sun.

Institute of Contemporary Art

University of Pennsylvania, 34th & Sansom sts.,
Philadelphia, Pa. 19104
(215) 898-7108

1993 Exhibitions
Thru Jan. 17
Vija Celmins: Mid-Career Retrospective
More than 65 works by the American artist, from the 1960s through the present. Catalogue.
Feb.–Apr.
Architecture as Elemental Shelter: Recent Thoughts and Work of Venturi, Scott Brown and Associates
Work by the architectural theoreticians, whose slogan "less is a bore" sounded the end of minimal modern architecture.

Feb. 18–Apr. 25
Investigations 1993
African-American artist Homer Jackson will create a theatrical installation with several other artists.
May 13–July 18
Penn Collects
Contemporary art from the museum collection.
Fall
James Turrell
Carrie Mae Weems
Photographs and installations reveal the artist's use of photographic imagery and text to comment on issues of identity, race, gender, and class. Catalogue.
Marlene Dumas

Permanent Collection

No permanent collection. **Architecture:** 1991 building by Adele Naude Santos, and Jacob/Wyper Architects.

Admission: Adults, $3; artists, senior citizens, students over 12, $1; children under 12, free. Tues., free. Handicapped accessible.
Hours: Tues.–Sun., 10–5; Wed., 10–7. Closed Mon.
Tours: Call (215) 898-7108 for information.

Pennsylvania Academy of the Fine Arts

118 N. Broad St., Philadelphia, Pa. 19102
(215) 972-7600

1993 Exhibitions

Thru Jan. 31
Louise Fishman, Paintings: 1986–1992
Features eight small-scale works by the contemporary abstract painter.

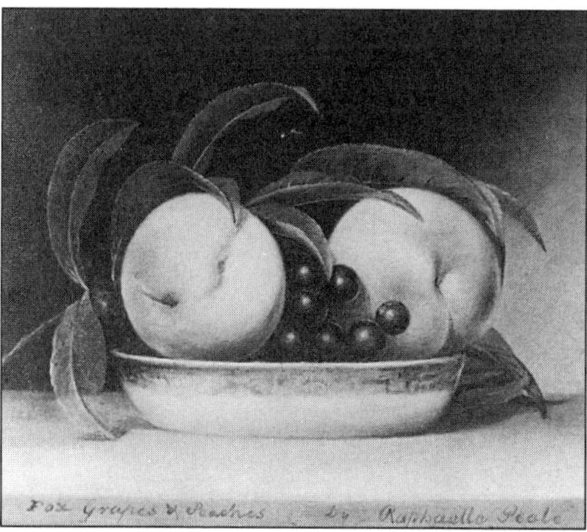

Fox Grapes and Peaches, 1815, Raphaelle Peale. From "Masterworks of American Art: 1750–1950." Pennsylvania Academy of the Fine Arts.

Thru Apr. 11
**Facing the Past: 19th-Century Portraits from the Collection of the Pennsylvania Academy of the Fine Arts*
Eighty paintings by such artists as Stuart, Sully, Eakins, Beaux, and Chase.
Masterworks of American Art: 1750–1950
Eighty-four of the museum's most famous paintings and sculptures, including works by Hopper, Sheeler, and O'Keeffe.

Permanent Collection

Paintings, sculptures, works on paper spanning more than three centuries of American art. **Highlights:** Diebenkorn, *Interior with Doorway*; Eakins, *Portrait of Walt Whitman*; Graves, *Hay Fever*; Henri, *Ruth St. Denis in the Peacock Dance*; Hicks, *The Peaceable Kingdom*; Homer, *Fox Hunt*; Peale, *The Artist in His Museum*; Pippin, *John Brown Going to His Hanging*; Rush, *Self-Portrait*; West, *Death on the Pale Horse; Wyeth, Young America.* **Architecture:** 1876 High Victorian Gothic–style building by Furness and Hewitt; 1976 restoration by Myers; designated a national historic landmark.

Admission: Adults, $5; senior citizens, $3; students, $2; members, children under 5, free. Sat., 10–1, free. Handicapped accessible.
Hours: Tues.–Sat., 10–5; Sun., 11–5. Closed Mon., holidays.
Tours: Tues.–Sun., 12:30, 2. Call (215) 972-7608.

Philadelphia Museum of Art

26th St. & Benjamin Franklin Pkwy., Philadelphia, Pa. 19130
(215) 763-8100

1993 Exhibitions

Thru Feb. 14
Beauty and Violence: Japanese Prints by Yoshitoshi, 1839–1892
Bold images by the foremost printmaker of the Meiji period that document the changes in Japan after its opening to Western trade in 1854.
Mar. 7–June 6
The Impressionist and the City: Late Series Paintings by Pissarro
Eighty of the artist's paintings from his urban series, united for the first time.
Apr.–May
Man at Work: The Photographs of Sebastião Selgado
Works by the renowned photographer that portray the dignity of the laborer.

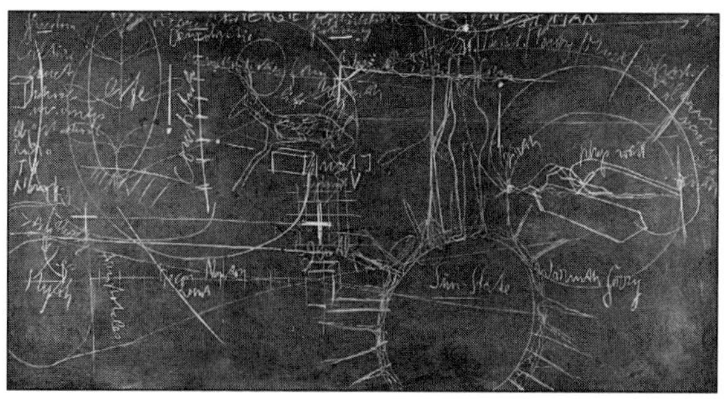

Energie Plan for the Westman, 1974, Joseph Beuys. From "Thinking is Form: The Drawings of Joseph Beuys." A traveling exhibition.

Sept. 19, 1993–Jan. 2, 1994
Thinking is Form: The Drawings of Joseph Beuys
A range of Beuys' drawings—from highly finished renderings to sketches on the backs of envelopes—that attest to his conception of drawing as a reservoir of ideas. Catalogue.

Permanent Collection

Significant works from many periods, styles, cultures in diverse media. Architectural installations and period rooms include a 12th-century French Romanesque facade and portal; 16th-century carved granite Hindu temple hall; Japanese tea house and temple; 17th-century Dutch domestic interior; Robert Adams' drawing room from Lansdowne House. Modern sculpture with major Brancusi collection; German folk art; Kretzschmar von Kienbusch collection of arms and armor. **Highlights:** Cézanne, *Large Bathers*; Duchamp, *Nude Descending a Staircase*; Van Eyck, *Saint Francis Receiving the Stigmata*; van Gogh, *Sunflowers*; Picasso, *The Three Musicians*; Poussin, *Birth of Venus*; Renoir, *The Bathers*; Rubens, *Prometheus Bound*; Saint-Gaudens, *Diana*; Van der Weyden, *Crucifixion with the Virgin and Saint John.* **Architecture:** 1928 replica of a Grecian temple by Abele, Borie, Trumbauer, and Zantzinger; 1940 Oriental Wing.

Admission: Adults, $6; senior citizens, students with ID, children, $3. Sun., 10–1, free. Handicapped accessible; wheelchairs available.
Hours: Tues.–Sun., 10–5; Wed., 10–8:45. Closed Mon., holidays.
Tours: Tues.–Sun., hourly, 11–3. Call (215) 787-5498 for information.
Food & Drink: Restaurant open Tues.–Sun., 11:45–2:15. Cafeteria open Tues.–Fri., 10–3:30; Sat.–Sun., 11–3:45.
Branches: The Rodin Museum, 22nd St. & Benjamin Franklin Pkwy., Philadelphia, Pa. 19104, (215) 763-8100. Fleisher Art Memorial, 719 Catharine St., Philadelphia, Pa. 19147, (215) 787-5477. Fairmount Park Houses, Cedar Grove and Mt. Pleasant, (215) 787-5449.

The University Museum of Archaeology and Anthropology

University of Pennsylvania, 33rd & Spruce sts., Philadelphia, Pa. 19104
(215) 898-4000

1993 Exhibitions

Thru Oct. 3
Ancient Nubia: Egypt's Rival in Africa
Traces a 3,500-year history (from c. 3100 B.C. to 400 A.D.) with statues, pottery, vessels, and adornments.

Thru May 1994
The Gift of Birds: Featherwork of Native South American Peoples
Feathered objects with special emphasis on works from the Waiwai, Cashinahua, and Bororo peoples.

Jan. 10–Apr. 4
Terra Maya
Photographs by archaeologist Peter D. Harrison capture the tropical rain forest environment of the Maya region and its religion, housing, and subsistence.

Apr. 10–May 29
Tutavoh: Learning the Hopi Way
Contemporary cibachrome photographs, archival prints from late 19th- and 20th-century negatives, and contemporary Hopi artifacts illustrate continuity and change in the Hopi tradition.

Sept. 11–Dec. 31
Symbolic Heat: Gender, Health, and Worship among the Tamils of South India and Sri Lanka
Documentary photographs and accompanying text consider how an intergrated system of religious and medical beliefs affects the lives of the Tamil Hindus.

Permanent Collection

More than 30 galleries feature materials from ancient Egypt, Mesopotamia, Mesoamerica, Asia, the Greco-Roman world; artifacts from native people of North and South America, Africa, Polynesia. **Highlights:** Jewelry from the Royal Tombs of Ur, Egyptian and Peruvian mummies, Benin bronzes from Nigeria, histories in stone of the ancient Maya. **Architecture:** 1899 Italianate building by William Eyre, Jr., Cope & Stewardson, Frank Miles, Day & Brother; 1915 Harrison rotunda—the largest free-standing dome in the United States—added.

Admission: Adults, $4; students, senior citizens, $2; children 6 and under, free. Handicapped accessible.

Hours: Tues.–Sat., 10–4:30; Sun., 1–5. Closed Mon., holidays; closed Sun., Memorial Day to Labor Day.
Tours: Mid-Sept.–mid-May, Sat.–Sun., 1:15. Call (215) 898-4015 for group-tour information.
Food & Drink: The Museum Cafe open Mon.–Fri., 8:30–3:30; Sat., 10–4; Sun., 1–4.

The Carnegie Museum of Art

4400 Forbes Ave., Pittsburgh, Pa. 15213
(412) 622-3131

1993 Exhibitions

Thru Jan. 10
Africa Explores: 20th Century African Art
African artists who confront and reinterpret Western images in light of their own culture; features 133 works from 15 countries. Catalogue.
Space Without Art
Jan. 22–Mar. 21
Cicognani Kalla Architects
Feb. 6–Apr. 18
Gary Hill: Sites Recited
Sept. 11–Nov. 7
Frank Gehry: New Bentwood Furniture Designs
A series of lightweight chairs resembling woven baskets, noteworthy for the artist's technological innovations.
Nov. 6, 1993–Jan. 16, 1994
Duncan Phillips Collects: Paris Between the Wars
Highlights include the Modernist painting of Bonnard, Braque, Derain, and Soutine. From the Phillips Collection, Washington, D.C.

Permanent Collection

French Impressionist and Post-Impressionist paintings; 19th- and 20th-century American art; contemporary American and European paintings, sculpture; American, English, Continental furniture, silver, ceramics; Asian and African art; monumental architectural casts. **Highlights:** Baumgarten, *The Tongue of the Cherokee*; Serra, *Carnegie*; Kiefer, *Midgard*; Bonnard, *Nude in Bathtub*; Homer, *The Wreck*; de Kooning, *Woman VI*; Monet, *Water Lilies*; Christain Herter, Herter Brothers, *Side Chair*; de Saint-Germain, *Long Case Clock*; Meissen, *Covered Beaker*; film and video program; sculpture court. **Architecture:** 1896–1907 Beaux Arts Carnegie building by Longfellow, Alden and Harlow; 1974 Bauhaus-style Sarah Scaife Galleries by Edward Larrabee Barnes.

Admission: Adults, $5; senior citizens, $4; students, children 3–18, $3; members, free. Handicapped accessible; wheelchairs available.
Hours: Tues.–Sat., 10–5; Sun., 1–5. Mon., 10–5, July 6–Aug. 31 only.
Tours: Call (412) 622-3289.
Food & Drink: Museum Café open Oct.–Apr., Tues.–Sat., 11–2; Sun., noon–2. May–Sept., Tues.–Fri., 11:30–2; closed weekends. Cafeteria open Tues.–Sat., 10–4; Sun., 1–4.

The Frick Art Museum

7227 Reynolds St., Pittsburgh, Pa. 15208
(412) 371-0600

1993 Exhibitions

Thru Feb. 14
Dutch and Flemish Seventeenth-Century Paintings: The Harold Samuel Collection
Landscapes, genre scenes, townscapes, still-lifes, and portraits are all represented; artists include Frans Hals, Jacob van Ruisdael, and Gerard ter Borch. Catalogue.
Mar. 12–Apr. 23
**Ottocento: Romanticism and Revolution in Nineteenth-Century Italian Painting*
First major exhibition to present an overview of 19th-century Italian painting; features works by Appiani, Fatori, Boldini, and Segantini. Catalogue.
May 15–July 15
Renaissance and Baroque Bronzes from the Permanent Collection
Catalogue.
Sept. 4–Oct. 24
Three Centuries of Drawings from the Villa Farnesina, Rome
Documents the development of drawing in Rome from the 16th to18th centuries; includes works by Bernini, da Cortona, and Maratta. Catalogue.
Nov. 20–Jan. 2, 1994
Ninenteenth-Century German, Austrian, and Hungarian Drawings from Budapest
Catalogue.

Permanent Collection

Rare 14th- and 15th-century Florentine and Sienese paintings by Duccio, Sassetta, Giovanni de Paolo; portrait by Rubens; landscape by Boucher, devotional altarpiece by Jean Bellegambe; 16th-century tapestries; Chinese porcelains; Renaissance bronzes; terracotta bust by Houdon; 18th-century French salon room; 17th-century English country-house room. **Architecture:** 1970 Renaissance-style building by Pratt, Schafer, and Slowik.

Admission: Free. Handicapped accessible.
Hours: Tues.–Sat., 10–5:30; Sun., noon–6.
Tours: Sat.–Sun., 2. Call (412) 371-0600 to arrange group tours.

Museum of Art, Rhode Island School of Design

224 Benefit St., Providence, R.I. 02903
(401) 454-6500

1993 Exhibitions

Thru Jan. 17
Folk Textiles of Japan
Thru Jan. 24
German Expressionism
Native Arts of North America
Thru June 26
Nineteenth-Century American Painting and Furniture
Jan.–Apr.
The Boteh
Feb. 12–Apr. 25
Encountering the New World, 1493–1800
Apr.–July
Turkish Towels
May 14–30
RISD Graduate Students
June 25–Aug. 14
Symbolist and Surrealist
July–Sept.
Bunny Harvey: Works on Paper
July 23, 1993–Feb. 14, 1994
Twentieth-Century Art from the Permanent Collection
Sept. 3–Oct. 24
Ernst Lichtblau, 1883–1963: Architectural and Industrial Designs
Sept.–Dec.
Recent Acquisitions in Photography
Nov. 12, 1993–Jan. 16, 1994
Dress, Art and Society

Permanent Collection

Greek and Roman art; Asian art; masterpieces of European and American painting, sculpture from the early Middle Ages to the present; French Impressionist painting; American furniture, decorative arts. **Architecture:** Includes the Pendleton House, first decorative arts wing built in the United States; 1897 Neo-Romanesque building; 1906 Colonial Revival addition by Stone, Carpenter & Wilson; 1926 Georgian addition by William Aldrich.

Admission: Adults, \$2; seniors, \$1; children 5–18, college students, 50¢. Thurs., 6–8, Sat., free. Handicapped accessible.
Hours: Sept.–Jun. 15: Tues.–Wed., Fri.–Sat., 10:30–5; Thurs., noon–8; Sun., 2–5. June 16–Aug. 31: Tues.–Sat., noon–5. Closed Mon., Jan. 1, July 4, Thanksgiving, Dec. 25.
Tours: Call (401) 454-6534.

Greenville County Museum of Art

420 College St., Greenville, S.C. 29601
(803) 271-7570

1993 Exhibitions

Jan. 7–Feb. 28
**Telling Tales: Nineteenth-Century Narrative Painting from the Collection of the Pennsylvania Academy of the Fine Arts*
Works that tell a story drawn from history or literature; includes works by Cassatt and Chase.
Jan. 19–Mar. 7
Messengers of Style: Itinerancy and Taste in Southern Portraiture, 1790–1861
Examines the Southern aesthetic while surveying the works of some of the nation's premier itinerant portraitists of the pre–Civil War period.
Mar. 23–May 9
Nancy Spero
Work by the contemporary feminist artist.
Apr. 13–June 20
Homecoming: William H. Johnson and Afro-America, 1938–1946
Unique two-dimensional works by the South Carolina artist.
May 25–July 18
Stephen Scott Young
July 27–Sept. 5
Upstate Artists Invitational
Sept. 14–Oct. 24
Greenville Collects: Sporting and Wildlife Art
Paintings and drawings by noted artists.

Permanent Collection

Works document the major themes in American art history; included are several Civil War–related works. Artists represented include Allston, Davies, Healy, Hofmann, Johns, Krasner, Lazell, Myers, O'Keeffe, Warhol. **Architecture:** 1974 building by Craig, Gaulden & Davis.

Admission: Free. Handicapped accessible.
Hours: Tues.–Sat., 10–5; Sun., 1–5. Closed Mon., major holidays.
Tours: For information call (803) 271-7570.

The Knoxville Museum of Art

410 Tenth St., World's Fair Park, Knoxville, Tenn. 37916
(615) 525-6101

1993 Exhibitions

Thru Jan. 24
Elliot Erwitt: Personal Exposures
Black-and-white images of the photographer's travels to locations from New Jersey to Siberia.
Thru Feb. 28
Cindy Blair: Recent Paintings Inspired by Southern Architecture
Feb. 5–Apr. 4
Roland Reiss: Environments of the Mind
Ten theatrical sculptural scenarios that express the humor, mystery, and drama of 20th-century life.
Mar. 12–June 20
Forest of Visions
Contemporary work that addresses environmental concerns.
Apr. 9–June 20
East Tennessee Women Artists

Permanent Collection

Small permanent collection. **Architecture:** 1990 building by Edward Larrabee Barnes.

Admission: Adults, $2; seniors and students, $1. Children under 12, members, free. Tues., 5–9, free. Handicapped accessible.
Hours: Tues., 10–9; Wed.–Sat., 10–5; Sun., noon–5. Closed Mon.
Tours: For reservations call (615) 525-6101.
Food & Drink: Cafe open Tues.–Fri., 11–2.

The Dixon Gallery and Gardens

4339 Park Ave., Memphis, Tenn. 38117
(901) 761-5250

1993 Exhibitions

Thru Jan. 17
Impressions of America: The Warner Collection of Gulf States Paper Corporation
American 19th- and 20th-century paintings by Inness, Cassatt, Sargent, Church, Bierstadt, and others.
Jan. 17–Apr. 4
Treasures of Peter Carl Fabergé from the Gray Foundation Collection
One of the world's finest assemblages of Fabergé, including three Imperial Easter eggs and several floral creations.

Feb. 14–Apr. 25
Frédéric Bazille: Prophet of Impressionism
Sixty works by the little-known but pivotal 19th-century French painter.
June 6–Aug. 8
Masterworks of American Impressionism from the Pfeil Collection
Over 100 works from the 1880s to the 1920s, examining the transition in American painting from the late Barbizon painters to the Post-Impressionist era. Catalogue.
Aug. 15–Oct. 10
Duncan Phillips Collects: Paris Between the Wars
Highlights include the Modernist painting of Bonnard, Braque, Derain, and Soutine. From the Phillips Collection, Washington, D.C.
Dec. 5, 1993–Jan. 30, 1994
**Telling Tales: Nineteenth-Century Narrative Painting from the Collection of the Pennsylvania Academy of the Fine Arts*
Works that tell a story drawn from history or literature; includes works by Cassatt and Chase.

Permanent Collection
Focuses on French Impressionist, Post-Impressionist painting; 18th- and 19th-century British portraits; landscapes, period furniture, decorative arts. **Highlights:** Cassatt, *The Visitor* and *Left Profile*; Corot, *Le Paveur de la Route Chailly*; Degas, *Dancer Adjusting Her Shoe*; Renoir, *Le Livre d'Images*; Rodin, *Young Girl with Flowers in Her Hair*; Stout collection of 18th-century German Meissen porcelain. **Architecture:** 1949 Georgian-style complex designed by Staub; 1977 wing; 1986 Georgian-style addition.

Admission: Adults, $4; senior citizens, students, $3; children under 12, $1; members, free. Handicapped accessible.
Hours: Tues.–Sat., 10–5; Sun., 1–5. Closed Mon., holidays.
Tours: Call (901) 761-5250 for information.
Food & Drink: Can be prearranged for tour groups; call (901) 761-5250.

Memphis Brooks Museum of Art

Overton Park, Memphis, Tenn. 38112
(901) 722-3500

1993 Exhibitions
Thru Jan. 17
Pop on Paper
Thru spring
The Beauty of the Beasts: Animals in Ancient Art

The Melody Haunts my Reverie, 1965, Roy Lichtenstein. Memphis Brooks Museum of Art.

Jan. 31–Apr. 11
African and Oceanic Sculpture: The Henry Easterwood Collection
Mar. 14–May 15
The Levy Print Collection
May 2–June 27
Treasures of Old Russia
June 6–Aug. 15
Memphis Collects: American Decorative Arts
Sept. 5–Oct. 10
Contemporary Clay Works
Oct. 31–Dec. 12
Songs of My People
The regional traditions and lifestyles of African Americans as recorded on film by 50 black photojournalists in summer 1990. Catalogue.
Dec. 19, 1993–Jan. 16, 1994
Ted Faiers Prints

Permanent Collection

Spans eight centuries of art, including core collections of Italian and Northern Renaissance and Baroque paintings and 18th–19th-century English and American portraiture; works by French Impressionists and contemporary American artists; selection of 17th- and 18th-century European decorative arts and Doughty ceramics. **Architecture:** 1916 Beaux Arts building by John Gamble Rogers; 1973 and 1990 renovations and expansions.

Admission: Adults, $4; students and seniors, groups of 10 or more, $2 per person; members, school groups, children under 6, free; Fri., free. Handicapped accessible.
Hours: Tues.–Sat., 10–5; Sun., 11:30–5. Closed Mon., Thanksgiving, Christmas, New Year's Day.
Tours: Sept.–May, daily, 1:30; call (901) 722-3515 for private or group tours.
Food & Drink: Tues.–Sun., 11:30–2:30.

Laguna Gloria Art Museum

3809 W. 35th St., Austin, Texas 78703
(512) 458-8191

1993 Exhibitions

Thru Jan. 17
The Realm of the Coin: Money in Contemporary Art
Examines the images and references to money found in art created during the last 30 years. Catalogue.
Jan. 23–Mar. 14
2 x 2: Exploring Scale in Contemporary Art
Two works that address the concept of scale by each of 12 artists.
Mar. 20–Apr. 25
New American Talent: The Ninth Exhibition
May 1–June 13
Companions in Time: The Paintings of William Lester and Everett Spruce
Retrospective exhibition illustrating the parallels in the artistic development of two Texas regionalist painters.
June 19–Aug. 8
Information Art: Diagramming Microchips
Examines the computer chip as an icon of our technological civilization. Catalogue.
Aug. 14–Sept. 12
Drawing into the 90s

Permanent Collection

The museum presents changing exhibitions of 20th-century American art. Objects from the small collection are not on permanent exhibit. Outdoor sculpture from the permanent collection is displayed on the grounds. **Architecture:** 1916 historic landmark Mediterranean-style villa by Page; building by Venturi planned.

Admission: Adults, $2; senior citizens, students, $1; children under 16, free. Thurs., 10–9, free.
Hours: Tues.–Sat., 10–5; Thurs., 10–9; Sun., 1–5. Closed Mon., holidays.
Tours: Sun., 2; Mon.–Fri., by reservation. Call (512) 458-8191.

Dallas Museum of Art

1717 N. Harwood, Dallas, Texas 75201
(214) 922-1200

1993 Exhibitions

Thru Jan. 10
The Impressionist and the City: Pissarro's Series
Eighty of the artist's paintings from his urban series, united for the first time.

Feb. 7–Apr. 4
**American Prints in Black and White, 1900–1950: Selections from the Collection of Reba and Dave Williams*

Feb. 14–Apr. 11
Gates of Mystery: The Art of Holy Russia from the Russian Museum, St. Petersburg
Features 120 objects from the collection of the State Russian Museum, dating from the 11th to the 18th century, when Peter the Great turned artists toward Western art.

May 16–July 11
Imperial Painters from the Ming Dynasty: The Zhe School
About 100 paintings, mostly on silk, from a professional school of the Ming Dynasty (1368–1644), emphasizing a revival of Sung Dynasty styles. Catalogue.

Tall Clock, 1730–1745, Benjamin Bagnall, Sr. Dallas Museum of Art.

Permanent Collection

Significant holdings of Pre-Columbian and African art; 18th- to 20th-century European and American paintings; decorative arts, including American furniture, English silver; prints, drawings; photographs. **Highlights:** Peruvian gold; Reves collection of Chinese porcelain; antique furniture; ironwork; Impressionist and Post-Impressionist paintings; drawings; watercolors; Brancusi, *Beginning of the World*; Matisse, *Ivy in Flowers*; Oldenburg, *Stake Hitch*; Kelly, *Untitled* (commissioned for sculpture garden).
Architecture: 1984 building of Indiana limestone by Edward Larrabee Barnes; 1985 recreated Mediterranean villa housing Reves collection.

Admission: Free. Entrance fee for selected exhibitions. Handicapped accessible.
Hours: Tues.–Fri., 11–4; Thurs., 11–9; Sat.–Sun. and holidays, noon–5. Closed Mon.
Tours: Introduction to the collections: Tues.–Fri., 11:30; Sat.–Sun., 2; special interest tours, Thurs., 12:15; private tours, $15. Call (214) 922-1313.
Food & Drink: Gallery Buffet open Tues.–Sat., 11–2:30; Thurs. dinner, 5:30–8, by reservation; Sun., noon–2. Bar open Tues.–Sun., 11:30–2:30; Thurs., 11:30–8. For reservations call (214) 922-1260.

Amon Carter Museum

3501 Camp Bowie Blvd., Fort Worth, Texas 76107
(817) 738-1933

1993 Exhibitions

Jan. 16–Apr. 25
Bellows' New York
Graphic works by the Ash Can School artist and his contemporaries illustrate the vital cultural and social environment in New York that influenced his work from 1904–1925.

Feb. 20–May 9
The Paintings of George Bellows
A retrospective of paintings by the artist. Among the gritty, urban views are New York scenes, female nudes, circuses, prayer meetings, his famous prize fighters, as well as lyrical landscapes and coastal views. Catalogue.

May 1–July 25
Bror Utter
A selection of surrealist etchings and gouache drawings from the 1940s by the Fort Worth native.

May 1–July 25
Nineteenth-Century Landscape Photographs
Draws from the museum's collection of mammoth plate photographs by 19th-century masters, including Carleton E. Watkins, William Henry Jackson, and Frank Jay Haynes; accompanied by several smaller-scale stenographs.

May 15–Aug. 1
Theme and Improvisation: Kandinsky and the American Avant-Garde, 1912–1950
Traces the influence of this father of pure abstraction on American artists.

July 31–Oct. 31
Turner's Frontier

Aug. 14–Oct. 10
Laura Gilpin: The Early Work
Gertrude Kasebier, Photographer

Permanent Collection

Art of the American West including work by Remington and Russell; 19th- and 20th-century painting, sculpture, graphic art by Davis, Demuth, Harnett, Homer, Marin, Nadelman, O'Keeffe. **Highlights:** Comprehensive collection of American photography; Heade, *Thunderstorm over Narragansett Bay*; Lane, *Boston Harbor*; Remington, *A Dash for the Timber.* **Architecture:** 1961 building by Philip Johnson.

Admission: Free. Handicapped accessible.
Hours: Tues.–Sat., 10–5; Sun., 12-5. Closed Mon., Jan. 1, July 4, Thanksgiving, Dec. 25.
Tours: Call tour coordinator at (817) 737-5913.

The Cheat with the Ace of Clubs, c. 1630, George de La Tour. Kimbell Art Museum.

Kimbell Art Museum

3333 Camp Bowie Blvd., Fort Worth, Texas 76107-2792
(817) 332-8451

1993 Exhibitions

Thru Jan. 31
Egypt's Dazzling Sun: Amenhotep III and His World
Some 140 works from the reign (1391–1353 B.C.) of a pharaoh who called himself the "Dazzling Sun-disk." Includes a red granite lion, over life-size statues of the royal family and court, jewelry, and colored glass vessels. Catalogue.

Thru Feb. 7
Italian Drawings from the Albertina, Vienna
Eighty Italian Old Master drawings from the world's largest collection of European drawings and prints. Catalogue.

Jan. 23–Apr. 25
Jacopo Bassano: A Quadricentennial Celebration and First American Retrospective
Works by one of the leading masters of late-Renaissance Venetian art on the 400th anniversary of his death. Catalogue.

May 15–July 11
Sir Thomas Lawrence: Portrait of an Age, 1790–1830
About 50 paintings and 20 drawings by the leading society portraitist of the Regency age. Catalogue.

June 5–Aug. 29
Degas to Matisse: The Maurice Wertheim Collection
Rare collection of Impressionist and Post-Impressionist paintings; includes works by Degas, Monet, Cézanne, and Matisse. Catalogue.

July 3–Oct. 10
Louis I. Kahn: In the Realm of Architecture
Drawings, models, and photographs for 60 projects by the American architect. Catalogue.

Sept. 18–Dec. 12
Giambattista Tiepolo: Master of the Oil Sketch
Features over 70 works from this little-known aspect of the 18th-century Venetian artist's career. Catalogue.

Permanent Collection
European painting, sculpture through the early 20th century; Asian paintings, sculptures, ceramics; Meso-American, African, ancient Mediterranean art. **Highlights:** Caravaggio, *Cardsharps*; Cézanne, *Man in a Blue Smock*; Duccio, *Raising of Lazarus*; Fra Angelico, *Saint James Freeing Hermogenes*; Guercino, *Portrait of a Lawyer*; Houdon, *Portrait of Aymard-Jean de Nicolay*; de La Tour, *Cheat with the Ace of Clubs*; Mantegna, *Holy Family with Saint Elizabeth and the Infant Saint John the Baptist*; Mondrian, *Composition No. 7 (Facade)*; Monet, *Pointe de la Heve at Low Tide*; Picasso, *Man With a Pipe* and *Nude Combing Her Hair*; Poussin, *Venus and Adonis*; Rembrandt, *Portrait of a Young Jew*; Rubens, *The Duke of Buckingham*; Ruisdael, *A Stormy Sea*; Titian, *Madonna and Child with Saint Catherine and the Infant Saint John the Baptist.*
Architecture: 1966–72 building by Kahn, set in a park environment with reflecting pools.

Admission: Free. Handicapped accessible.
Hours: Tues.–Fri., 10–5; Sat., noon-8; Sun., noon–5. Closed Mon., holidays.
Tours: Sun., 3. Selected exhibitions: Tues.–Fri., Sun., 2; Sat., 6:30. For group-tour reservations call (817) 332-8687.
Food & Drink: Buffet restaurant open Tues.–Fri., 11:30–4; Sat., noon–4, 5:30–7:30; Sun., noon–4. Reservations recommended; call (817) 332-8451.

Modern Art Museum of Fort Worth

1309 Montgomery St., Fort Worth, Texas 76107
(817) 738-9215

1993 Exhibitions
Thru Feb. 14
Red Grooms: Ruckus Rodeo
The artist's room-sized "sculpto-pictorama," based on the annual Southwestern Exposition and Stock Show, on view for the first time in 10 years.
Feb. 28–Apr. 18
Terry Allen: Youth in Asia
Sixty-three wall constructions combining visual and literary elements that explore the aftermath of the Vietnam War.
Apr. 18–June 13
Julie Bozzi: American Food
The Fort Worth artist's whimsical recreations of a wide range of foods in hand-painted porcelain, representing a study of one aspect of American culture.
May 16–July 25
Sean Scully: The Catherine Paintings
Each year for the past 17 years, the artist has chosen a particularly important work and titled it in honor of his wife,

Catherine Lee; the collection represents a survey of Scully's achievement as well as a moving personal tribute.
Dec. 9, 1993–Feb. 20, 1994
Mark Tansey
Retrospective of the career of the New York figurative painter, featuring works from the late 1970s through early 1993.

Girl with Flowered Background, 1962, Richard Diebenkorn. Modern Art Museum of Fort Worth.

Permanent Collection

Surveys all major developments in 20th-century figurative and abstract art, specializing in American art after 1940 and European art after 1920. Nearly 2,000 paintings, sculpture, drawings, and prints, ranging from Picasso and Miró to Stella and Graves, and works by Texan artists. **Highlights:** Inness, *Approaching Storm*; Judd, *Untitled*; Kandinsky, *Above and Left*; Kelly, *Curved Red on Blue*; Picasso, *Suite Vollard, Reclining Woman Reading* and *Head of a Woman*; Rothko, *Light Cloud, Dark Cloud*; Still, *Untitled.* **Architecture:** 1901 gallery; 1954 first museum building by Bayer; 1974 addition with garden courtyard and solarium by Ford & Associates.

Admission: Free. Handicapped accessible.
Hours: Tues.–Fri., 10–5; Sat., 11–5; Sun., 12–5. Closed Mon. and holidays.
Tours: For group-tour reservations call (817) 738-6811.

Contemporary Arts Museum

5216 Montrose Blvd., Houston, Texas 77006
(713) 526-0773; 526-3129 (recording)

1993 Exhibitions

Thru Jan. 31
Meg Webster: Garden and Sculpture
Works demonstrating the artist's combination of minimalist and earthwork aesthetics.
Jan. 16–Mar. 7
3-D Rupture
Small-scale sculpture by five young Houston artists.
Feb. 20–May 2
On the Road: Selections from the Permanent Collection of the Museum of Contemporary Art, San Diego
Comprehensive examination of the art of the past 20 years; artists include Vito Acconci, Claes Oldenburg, and Martin Puryear.
Mar. 20–May 30
Lorna Simpson: For the Sake of the Viewer
A survey of the artist's conceptual photographs, from 1985 to her most recent series. Catalogue.
May 22–Aug. 22
Krzysztof Wodiczko: Public Address
Survey of works by the Polish-born artist, inlcuding sculpture, drawings, and large-scale interior projections.

June 12–Aug. 1
Liz Phillips: Graphite Ground
Soundscape installation by the audio artist.
Sept. 11–Oct. 31
Agnes Martin
A major retrospective of the career of one of America's leading contemporary reductivist painters.

Permanent Collection

No permanent collection. **Architecture:** 1972 stainless-steel parallelogram building by Birkerts and Associates.

Admission: Donation suggested: $2. Handicapped accessible.
Hours: Tues.–Fri., 10–5; Sat.–Sun., noon–5. Closed Mon., Jan. 1, July 4, Thanksgiving, Dec. 25.
Tours: Group tours available by calling (713) 526-0773.

The Menil Collection

1515 Sul Ross, Houston, Texas 77006
(713) 525-9400

1993 Exhibitions

Thru Feb. 21
René Magritte
A major retrospective featuring 120 paintings, works on paper, sculptures, and objects by the 20th-century Surrealist master.
Mar. 11–May 9
Jean Michel Basquiat
First U.S. exhibition to survey the work of this 20th-century artist.
May 27–Aug. 29
Max Ernst: Dada and the Dawn of Surrealism
An exploration of the artist as a Dadaist, through collages, prints, paintings, and relief sculpture. Catalogue.
Sept. 1993–Feb. 1994
Mark Rothko: Early Work from the Edith Carson Collection
Mark Rothko: The Chapel Commission
Jan. 14–Apr. 3, 1994
Rolywholyover: A Circus
A major exhibition with accompanying performances and events, based on the life of composer, writer, and artist John Cage. Catalogue.

Permanent Collection

Antiquities including Cycladic, Hellenistic, Roman, European artifacts; Byzantine icons; Medieval art; art of tribal cultures featuring extensive surveys of African and Oceanic cultures; 20th-century works with particular strengths in Cubism, Surrealism, Abstract Expressionism; Richmond Hall (1416 Richmond) presenting contemporary and experimental art, performance. **Highlights:** Sumerian

statue of the Prince of Lagash; Ernst, *Day and Night*; Johns, *Voice*; Léger, *Still Life*; works by Brauner, Cornell, Tanguy.
Architecture: 1987 building by Renzo Piano with Fitzgerald and Partners.

Admission: Free. Handicapped accessible.
Hours: Wed.–Sun., 11–7. Closed Mon.–Tues., holidays.
Tours: By special arrangement only.

The Museum of Fine Arts, Houston

1001 Bissonnet St., Houston, Texas 77005
(713) 639-7300

1993 Exhibitions

Thru June 27
The Bayou Bend Museum of Americana at Tenneco
During renovation of the Bayou Bend estate, the museum will house "The Masterpieces of Bayou Bend, 1620–1870" and "The Voyage of Life," on the second floor of the Tenneco building (1010 Milam, Houston).

Feb. 14–Apr. 18
The Ancient Americas: Art from Sacred Landscapes
About 300 objects from 1200 B.C. to 1530 A.D., ranging from small, exquisite gold works to monumental stone sculptures, that offer a glimpse of the world views of 13 distinct cultures. Catalogue.

Mar. 14–June 27
Imperial Austria: Treasures of Art, Arms, and Armor from the State of Styria
Over 250 Baroque and Renaissance objects ranging from rare panel paintings to weapons and suits of armor. Catalogue.

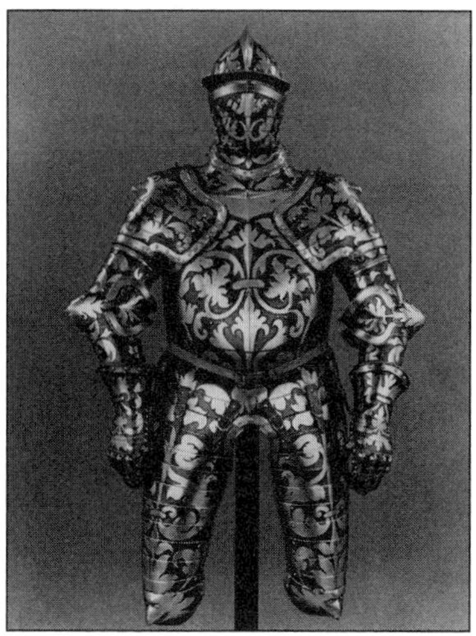

Black-and-white armor for a nobleman, c. 1550, Michael Witz the Younger. From "Imperial Austria: Treasures of Art, Arms, & Armor from the State of Styria." A traveling exhibition.

May 23–Aug. 8
The Lure of Italy: American Artists and the Italian Experience, 1760–1914
Examines the influence of Italian art from antiquity to contemporary times on American 18th- and 19th-century artists. Catalogue.
June 26–Aug. 22
**Donald Sultan: A Print Retrospective*
Surveys the artist's graphic work from 1979 to the present. Catalogue.
Oct. 3–Nov. 28
Two Lives: Georgia O'Keeffe and Alfred Stieglitz—A Conversation in Paintings and Photographs
Tracks the visual and intellectual correspondences in the work of the two artists, who were artistic collaborators as well as husband and wife. Catalogue.
Dec. 19, 1993–Jan. 30, 1994
Annie Leibovitz: Photographs 1970–1990
Images spanning the photographer's career, from early black-and-white portraits for *Rolling Stone* to recent advertising work.
May 1–July 24, 1994
Classical Taste in America 1800–1840
Presents over 225 paintings, sculpture, furniture, and other works that demonstrate America's captivation with the classical or Grecian style.

Permanent Collection

Works ranging from ancient to modern: Straus collection of Renaissance and 18th-century art; Beck collection of Impressionist and Post-Impressionist art; Target collection of American photography. **Highlights:** Greek bronze youth; Bayou Bend collection of 17th- to 19th-century furniture, silver, ceramics, paintings; Brancusi, *A Muse*; Cézanne, *Portrait of the Artist's Wife*; van Gogh, *The Rocks*; Pollock, *Number 6*; Van der Weyden, *Virgin and Child*; Noguchi sculpture garden. **Architecture:** 1924 building by Watkin; 1926 east and west wings; 1958 and 1974 additions by Mies van der Rohe.

Admission: Adults, $3; senior citizens, college students with ID, $1.50; members and children under 18, free. Thurs., free. Handicapped accessible.
Hours: Tues.–Sat., 10–5; Thurs., 10–9; Sun., 12:15–6. Closed Mon., major holidays.
Tours: Daily, noon. Call (713) 639-7324 for groups.
Food & Drink: Museum Café open Tues.–Sat., 11–2.

The Chrysler Museum

245 W. Olney Rd., Norfolk, Va. 23510-1567
(804) 622-1211; 622-ARTS (recording)

1993 Exhibitions

Thru Jan. 17
The Great Age of Sail
Paintings and nautical objects documenting the history and technological innovations of sailing from the 16th to 19th centuries; features works by Turner and Reynolds.
America's Cup: There is No Second Place
Vintage prints and rare photographs of past races.
Hampton Roads, 1920–1930
Documents the scenes, lifestyles, and moods of this coastal Virginia area.
Thru Apr. 1
Peruvian Textiles
Ancient textiles from seven regional cultures over 2,000 miles of coastal Peru.
Jan. 16–Mar. 21
Patrick Tosani
Features 35 large-scale color photographs by the French artist. Catalogue.
Jan. 17–Mar. 28
Jaune Quick-to-See Smith
Works by the artist that draw on storytelling, music, and dance from her Native American heritage.
Mar. 13–May 9
**Telling Tales: Narrative Painting from the Collection of the Pennsylvania Academy of the Fine Arts*
Works that tell a story drawn from history or literature; includes works by Cassatt and Chase.
Apr. 14–May 9
Student Gallery '93
Apr. 25–June 27
Mark Leithauser
Paintings, watercolors, toys, silverpoint drawings, and etchings by the contemporary artist.
June 10–Aug. 8
Clearly Art: The Glass Legacy of Pilchuck
July 18–Sept. 19
Walter Martin
Works by the contemporary sculptor.
Oct. 17, 1993–Jan. 2, 1994
Terry Adkins
Abstract sculpture by the artist and musician.
Oct. 24, 1993–Jan. 3, 1994
With Grace and Favour: Fashion from the Victorian and Edwardian Eras
Represents all aspects of the fashionable woman's wardrobe from 1837 to 1910, including wedding gowns and evening wear. Catalogue.

Permanent Collection
Art of many civilizations, styles, historical periods. Ancient Greek and Roman works; Pre-Columbian and African textiles, ceramics; Asian bronzes; American 19th-century sculpture; contemporary painting, sculpture; glassware.
Highlights: Bernini, *Bust of the Savior*; Cassatt, *The Family*; Gauguin, *The Loss of Innocence*; de La Tour, *Saint Philip*; Lichtenstein, *Live Ammo (Fifth Panel)*; Matisse, *Bowl of Apples*; Rouault, *Head of Christ*; Veronese, *The Virgin Appearing to Saints Anthony Abbott and Paul the Hermit.*
Architecture: 1933 building; 1967 Houston Wing; 1976 Centennial Wing; 1989 renovation and expansion by Hartman-Cox.

Admission: Donation suggested: $3. Handicapped accessible.
Hours: Tues.–Sat., 10–4; Sun., 1–5. Closed Mon., Jan. 1, July 4, Thanksgiving, Dec. 25.
Tours: Sun., 2, 3; Wed., 2.
Food & Drink: Café open Tues.–Sat., 10–4; Sun., 1–5.

Virginia Museum of Fine Arts

2800 Grove Ave., Richmond, Va. 23221-2466
(804) 367-0844

1993 Exhibitions
Thru Jan. 10
Before the Iron Horse: A Selection of British Drawings and Prints from the Paul Mellon Collection
Portrays the utilitarian aspect of the horse before it was replaced by the steam locomotive, or "iron horse."
Feb. 28–Apr. 4
1993 Virginia Youth Art Exhibit
Mar. 2–Apr. 25
**Art of the Himalayas: Treasures from Nepal and Tibet*
Nepalese and Tibetan paintings, sculpture, artists' sketchbooks, textiles, and ritual objects. Catalogue.

The Earthspirit Daka, 15th–16th c., Central Tibet. From "Art of the Himalayas: Treasures from Nepal and Tibet." A traveling exhibition. AFA.

May 11–Aug. 1
Goddess and Polis: The Panathenaic Festival in Ancient Athens
Explores the ancient festival through 67 objects dating from the early 6th to 5th centuries B.C. Catalogue.
Aug. 3–Sept. 26
Sir Thomas Lawrence: Portrait of an Age, 1790–1830
About 50 pictures and 20 drawings by the leading society portraitist of the Regency age. Catalogue.

Permanent Collection
Comprehensive holdings dating from ancient times to the present: Byzantine, medieval, African art; extensive Himalayan collection; American paintings since World War II; Art Nouveau and Art Deco works. **Highlights:** Statue of Caligula; Mellon collections of English sporting art and French Impressionist, Post-Impressionist works; Fabergé Easter eggs from the Russian Imperial collection; Gobelin Don Quixote tapestries; Goya, *General Nicolas Guye*; Monet, *Irises by the Pond*; sculpture garden; Classical and Egyptian galleries. **Architecture:** 1936 building by Peebles and Ferguson; 1954 addition by Lee; 1970 addition by Baskerville & Son; 1976 addition by Hardwicke Associates; 1985 addition by Holzman.

Admission: Voluntary admission: adults, $4; students and children over 5, $2; members, free; groups of 10 or more, $3 per person. Handicapped accessible.
Hours: Tues.–Sat., 11–5; Sun., 1–5; selected galleries open Thurs. 11–8. Closed Mon., Jan. 1, July 4, Thanksgiving, Dec. 25.
Tours: Tues.–Sat., hourly, 11:30–2:30. For reservations call (804) 367-0859 two weeks in advance.
Food & Drink: Arts Café open Tues.–Sat., 11:30–4; Sun., 1–4. Tea in the galleries open Sat.–Sun., 2:30–4:30.

Henry Art Gallery

University of Washington, 15th Ave. N.E. & N.E. 41st St., Seattle, Wash. 98195
(206) 543-2280 (recording)

1993 Exhibitions
Thru Jan. 10
New Works: Carol Sawyer
The artist constructs a world of fictional "alchemical vessels" through photographic techniques.
Jan. 22–Mar. 21
Motion and Document—Sequence and Time: Eadweard Muybridge and Contemporary American Photography
Traces the influence of the 19th-century photographer's ideas and experimental working methods on other artists. Catalogue.

Mar. 31–May 23
Vija Celmins: Mid-Career Retrospective
More than 65 works by the American artist, from the 1960s through the present. Catalogue.
June 4–June 20
Master of Fine Arts 1993
July 6–Aug. 29
Works from the Permanent Collection
Sept. 10–Nov. 14
Northwest Noir
Explores work by regional artists characterized by an off-center, eccentric view of the world.
Nov. 24–Feb. 6, 1994
Lorna Simpson: For the Sake of the Viewer
A survey of the artist's conceptual photographs, from 1985 to her most recent series. Catalogue.

Permanent Collection
Nineteenth- and 20th-century art; Monsen Study Collection of Photography; ceramic works. **Highlights:** 15,000-piece costume, textile collection. **Architecture:** 1927 Tudor Gothic building by Carl Gould.

Admission: Adults, $3; senior citizens, students, $1.50; Thurs., free; children under 13, University of Washington students and faculty, members, free.
Hours: Tues.–Sun., 10–5; Thurs., 10–9. Closed Mon.
Tours: Call (206) 543-2281 for groups of ten or more.

Seattle Art Museum

100 University St., Seattle, Wash. 98101-2902
(206) 625-8900; 654-3100 (recording)

1993 Exhibitions
Thru Feb. 7
The Willam S. Paley Collection
Paintings, drawings, and sculpture by Bonnard, Cézanne, Degas, Gauguin, Matisse, Toulouse-Lautrec, and others. Catalogue.
Mar. 11–May 9
Art of the American Indian Frontier, 1800–1900: The Chandler/Pohrt Collection
Illustrates the close relationship between cultural and artistic changes in 19th-century Native American history. Catalogue.
Apr. 22–June 27
Northwest Jewelers
June 3–July 25
Dutch and Flemish Seventeenth Century Paintings: The Harold Samuel Collection:
Landscapes, genre scenes, townscapes, still-lifes, and portraits are all represented; artists include Frans Hals, Jacob van Ruisdael, and Gerard ter Borch. Catalogue.

Aug. 19–Oct. 10
Helen Levitt and Mary Ellen Mark
Spans the careers of the two distinguished photographers whose work bridges the gap between art and journalism.
Nov. 17, 1993–Jan. 12, 1994
Susan Rothenberg: Paintings and Drawings
A retrospective tracing the career of this American imagist painter, from her early horse images to recent autobiographical, expressionist paintings. Catalogue.

Permanent Collection

Over 20,000 objects, from ancient Egyptian sculpture to contemporary American painting. Internationally known for its collections of Asian, African, Northwest Coast Native American, and modern Pacific Northwest art; other holdings include ancient Mediterranean, medieval and early Renaissance, Baroque, early and late 20th-century art. **Highlights:** Classical coins; 18th-century European porcelain; Chinese jades and snuff boxes. **Architecture:** 1991 building by Robert Venturi.

Admission: Recommended admission: adults, $5; senior citizens, students, $3; children under 12 accompanied by adult, free. First Tues. of each month, free. Handicapped accessible.
Hours: Tues.–Sat., 11–5; Thurs., 11–9; Sun., noon–5. Closed Mon., holidays.
Tours: Tues.–Sat., 2; Sun., 1, 1:30; Thurs., 7, 7:30. Call (206) 654-3123.
Food and Drink: Café open museum hours.

Huntington Museum of Art

2033 McCoy Rd., Huntington, W.Va. 25701
(304) 529-2701

1993 Exhibitions

Thru Jan. 24
Icons: Sacred Images
Explores the identity and purpose of figures depicted through icons.
Recollecting Forty Years: Images and Objects from the Huntington Museum of Art Archives
Thru May 5
The Daywood Collection
American paintings from the late 19th century, including landscape paintings by George Inness and Alexander Wyant.
Thru Oct. 31
The French Countryside and the Barbizon Tradition
Examines the origins of modern landscape painting through the artists of the 19th-century Barbizon school.
Thru June 1994
Figuratively Speaking: The Art of Animation
Highlights milestones in animation and tools of the trade.

Jan. 24–Oct. 31
Four Decades of Collecting
Highlights works from the permanent collection.
Jan. 31–Feb. 28
School Arts of the Area
Mar. 13–June 13
Exhibition 280: Works Off Walls

Permanent Collection
Exceptional range of artistic interests: English portraits, Oriental prayer rugs, Georgian silver, antique firearms, contemporary prints, Appalachian folk art, and holdings of historical glass from the Ohio River Valley and American studio glass; American furniture and decorative arts; contemporary sculpture; nature trails in natural woodland state.

Admission: Suggested admission: adults, $2; seniors and students, $1; children 12 and under, free. Wed., free.
Hours: Tues.–Sat., 10–5; Sun., noon–5. Closed Mon.
Tours: Call (504) 529-2701 at least three weeks in advance; maximum 60 people.

Milwaukee Art Museum

750 N. Lincoln Memorial Dr., Milwaukee, Wis. 53202
(414) 224-3200

1993 Exhibitions
Thru Jan. 17
A Breadth of Vision: The Ritz Collection
Features paintings, drawings, and prints from international artists including Lovis Corinth, Max Beckmann, Käthe Kollwitz, and regional Wisconsin artists. Catalogue.
Made in Milwaukee: Editions from John Gruenwald, Printer
A selection of recent prints by the artist, an established Milwaukee printer. Catalogue.
Thru Jan. 24
Fata Morgana USA: The American Way of Life, Photomontage by Josep Renau
German Expressionism, Dada, and Surrealism, combined with the artist's background in the Communist Party, influence this photomontage series. Catalogue.
Thru Feb. 21
Baroque to Barbizon: French Prints from the Permanent Collection
A selection of the museum's prints and drawings by French artists from the 17th through 19th centuries.
Jan. 22–Apr. 25
Andy Warhol: Works from the Permanent Collection
A review of Warhol's innovations in painting, sculpture, and prints, featuring the renowned images of Campbell's soup cans and the screenprint portrait series of Marilyn Monroe and Mao Tse-Tung.

Portrait of Clara McBride Hale, 1989, Brian Lanker. From "I Dream a World: Portraits of Black Women Who Changed America." A traveling exhibition. AFA.

Jan. 31–Feb. 27
65th Scholastic Art Awards
Feb. 12–Apr. 4
Agnes Martin
A major retrospective of the career of one of America's leading contemporary reductivist painters. Catalogue.
Mar. 12–May 16
Pop! Prints from the Permanent Collection
A survey of Pop Art from the 1960s to 1970s, through the works of Claes Oldenburg, James Rosenquist, and others.
Mar. 26–May 9
Tiffany to Ben Tre: A Century of Glass
A survey of the use of glass as a medium of artistic expression over the past century. Catalogue.
Apr. 3–May 16; May 21–June 27
Dreams, Hopes and Fears: Work by Wisconsin Artists
Apr. 16–June 20
Common Ground/Uncommon Vision: The Michael and Julie Hall Collection of American Folk Art
More than 150 objects, ranging from an 18th-century weather vane to works by Rev. Howard Finster. Catalogue.
May 21–Aug. 22
Recent Acquisitions
May 28–Sept. 21
Currents 22: Felix Gonzalez-Torres
The work of the conceptual artist who stretches the boundaries of sculpture, installation, and editioned multiples.
June 4–Sept. 19
Lucien Clergue: Photographs from the Permanent Collection
Over 40 prints, including the artist's documentation of Picasso and Jean Cocteau, and his recent color prints of bullfights.
July 9–Aug. 29
Master European Drawings from Polish Collections: Fifteenth through Eighteenth Centuries
More than 100 drawings, selected from the Old Master collections of 10 Polish museums. Catalogue.

July 10–Sept. 5
Rugged to Refined: Furniture by Wisconsin Artists
Features a number of styles, from rustic twig furniture to fine woodworking. Catalogue.
Sept. 10–Nov. 2
Mark Tansey
Retrospective of the career of the New York figurative painter, featuring works from the late 1970s through early 1993.
Oct. 9–Nov. 20
**I Dream a World: Portraits of Black Women who Changed America*
Seventy-five portraits by Pulitzer Prize–winning photographer Brian Lanker of Maya Angelou, Shirley Chisholm, Odetta, Rosa Parks, Sarah Vaughan, and others. Catalogue.
Feb. 4–Mar. 20, 1994
Jacob Lawrence's The Migration of the Negro
The artist's 60-panel series depicting African Americans' post–World War I fight from the rural South to the industrial cities of the North.

Permanent Collection

Includes over 25,000 18th- to 20th-century works of European and American art, decorative art, and photography, including works by German Expressionists, American Ashcan School artists. **Highlights:** Archive of Prairie School architecture; Bradley collection of early modern and contemporary art; one of the world's largest collections of Haitian art; Fragonard, *Shepherdess*; Johnson, *The Old Stage Coach*; Zurbarán, *Saint Francis.* **Architecture:** 1957 building by Eero Saarinen; 1975 addition by David Kahler.

Admission: Adults, $4; senior citizens, students, handicapped, $2; children under 12, members, free; Milwaukee County residents: Wed. and Sat. 10–noon, free. Handicapped accessible.
Hours: Tues.–Wed., Fri.–Sat., 10–5; Thurs., noon–9; Sun., noon–5. Closed Mon., Jan. 1, Dec. 25.
Tours: Call (414) 224-3225, ext. 271 for information.
Food & Drink: Restaurant open Tues.–Wed., Fri., 10:30–3; Thurs., Sun., noon–4; Sat., 11–4.

Buffalo Bill Historical Center

720 Sheridan Ave., Cody, Wyo. 82414
(307) 587-4771

1993 Exhibitions

June 18–Sept. 12
Art of the American Indian Frontier, 1800–1900: The Chandler/Pohrt Collection
Illustrates the close relationship between cultural and artistic changes in 19th-century Native American history. Catalogue.

Permanent Collection

Four museums in one: **Buffalo Bill Museum** contains personal and historical memorabilia of William F. "Buffalo Bill" Cody. **Plains Indian Museum** displays materials reflecting artistic expression of Arapaho, Blackfeet, Cheyenne, Crow, Shoshone, Sioux, Gros Ventre tribes. **Whitney Gallery of Western Art** documents beauty of the American West through paintings and sculptures by American artists Bierstadt, Catlin, Miller, Moran, Remington, Russell, Sharp, Wyeth. **Cody Firearms Museum** presents story of development of firearms in America through its comprehensive collection.
Architecture: 1927 log building; 1959 Whitney Gallery building by George Tresler; 1969 Buffalo Bill Museum by Tresler; 1979 Plains Indian Museum by Adrian Malone; 1991 Cody Firearms Museum by Luckman Associates.

Admission: Adults, $7; senior citizens, $6; students 13+, $4; children 6–12, $2; families, $18; children under 6, free. Group rates by request. Handicapped accessible.
Hours: May and Sept.: daily, 8–8; June–Aug.: daily, 7–10; Oct.: daily, 8–5; Mar., Nov.: Tues.–Sun., 10–3; Apr.: Tues.–Sun., 8–5. Closed Dec.–Feb.
Tours: Call (307) 587-4771 for information.
Food & Drink: Luncheon Eatery open May–Sept., 8–3.

Ghost Dance shirt. Buffalo Bill Historical Center.

CANADIAN MUSEUMS

Un coin pour peindre (Painting Place), 1930, David B. Milne. National Gallery of Canada.

Musée des Beaux-Arts de Montréal

1380 Sherbrook Street West, Montreal, Quebec, Canada H36 2T9
(514) 285-1600

1993 Exhibitions
Thru Jan. 10
The Photography Collection of Howard and Carole Tannenbaum
Artists range from 19th-century photographers Peter Henry Emerson and John Thomson to contemporary artists Doug Clarke and Arlene Collin.
Thru Jan. 24
Pop Art
Features 200 major works dated between 1950–1960, organized around "series of episodes" in the evolution of Pop Art.
Thru Mar. 21
Italian Old Master Drawings from the Collection of Jeffrey E. Horvitz
Seventeenth- and 18th-century drawings by artists including Guercino, Canaletto, and Tiepolo.
Thru Mar. 28
Masterpieces of French 17th-Century Painting
Works from the major public collections represent all the genres of painting in France before 1660; artists include Poussin, La Tour, and Claude.
Mar. 11–May 16
Jacques Villon
One hundred prints by the French artist.
Mar. 25–May 16
Living in Style: Fine Furniture in Victorian Quebec
Bacon-Picasso
Features Picasso's *The Crucifixion*, and two paintings by Bacon inspired by the work.
June 17–Sept. 12
Jean Paul Lemieux
Retrospective of the 76-year career of the renowned Quebec painter.
June 17–Sept. 26
Pictures for the Sky: Art Kites
Over 100 world-renowned artists created works designed to be transformed into "art kites" by Japanese artisans; artists include Niki de Saint-Phalle, Arman, and Sam Francis.
Oct. 14, 1993–Jan. 30, 1994
Design 1935–1965: What Modern Was
Over 200 mass-produced and handcrafted objects, including furniture, glassware, fabric, and graphic works.

Jean-Noël Desmarais Pavilion, The Montreal Museum of Fine Arts.

Permanent Collection
Over 25,000 works, including sculpture, prints, drawings, photography, decorative arts; contemporary art, Canadian art. **Architecture:** 1912 Benaiah Gibb Pavilion by Edward & W. S. Maxwell; 1939 Norton wing annex; 1976 pavilion by Fred Lebensold; 1991 Jean-Noël Desmarais Pavilion, incorporating facade of 1905 apartment building, by Moshe Safdie and Associates, Inc.

Admission: Temporary exhibitions and permanent collection: adults, $9.50; students, seniors, $4.75; children 3–12, $2; children 2 and under, Friends of the Museum, free; families, $19; groups of 15 or more, $7.50 per person. Permanent collection only: families, $9.50; adults, $4.75; students, $3; seniors, children 3–12, $1; children 2 and under, Friends of the Museum, free. Handicapped accessible.
Hours: Tues., Thurs., Fri., Sun., 11–6; Wed., Sat., 11–9.
Food and Drink: Tues.–Sun., 11–6; Sat., 11–9.

National Gallery of Canada

380 Sussex Dr., Ottawa, Ontario, Canada K1N 9N4
(613) 990-1985

1993 Exhibitions
Thru Jan. 10
William Kurelek
Installation commemorating the 100th anniversary of the Ukrainians' first coming to Canada.
Women Photographed
Eva/Ave: Woman in Renaissance and Baroque Prints
From the collection of the National Gallery of Art, Washington, D.C.
Thru Feb. 7
Vidéo, Oralité
Jack Shadbolt
Over 100 paintings and drawings by the Canadian artist.
Feb. 19–May 9
Mary Cassatt
Highlights a set of 10 rare color prints, accompanied by works from the permanent collection. Catalogue.

Mar. 12–May 23
The Crises of Abstraction in Canada in the Early Fifties
Features several groups of abstract artists working in the 1950s. Catalogue.
Apr.–May
Daniel Dion
May 14–Aug. 8
Studiolo
June 4–Sept. 6
Masterpieces from the Photography Collection
June 18–Sept. 6
Gandolfi
July 9–Sept. 19
Anish Kapoor
The Bombay-born, London-based artist, whose sculptures are characterized by biomorphic forms and tactile surfaces, will create new works in sandstone. Also earlier work. Catalogue.
Oct. 1993–Jan. 1994
Leon Levenstein
Spans the artist's career, including work produced in Europe, Haiti, India, Mexico, and New York.
Oct. 22, 1993–Jan. 16, 1994
The Earthly Paradise: Arts and Crafts by William Morris and His Circle from Canadian Collections
Oct. 29, 1993–Jan. 23, 1994
Don Wright 1931–1988: A Retrospective Exhibition
Forty works by the influential Newfoundland artist.
Nov. 19, 1993–Jan. 9, 1994
Luke Anguhadlug

Permanent Collection

Most extensive collection of Canadian art in the world; European, Asian, Inuit, American art; international collection of contemporary film, video; Canadian silver; indoor garden court, water court. **Highlights:** Paintings and sculpture by Cranach the Elder, Grien, Bernini, Murillo, Poussin, Rubens, Rembrandt, West, Chardin, Turner, Constable, Degas, Pissarro, Monet, Cézanne, Klimt, Ensor, Matisse, Picasso, Braque, Moore, Bacon, Pollock, Newman; photography by Cameron, Atget, Evans, Sander, Weston, Model, Arbus; completely reconstructed 19th-century Rideau Convent Chapel. **Architecture:** 1988 building by Moshe Safdie.

Admission: Adults, $5; seniors, students, $3; group rates available. Handicapped accessible.
Hours: Summer (May 1–Labor Day): Sat.–Tues., 10–6; Wed.–Fri., 10–8. Winter (Sept.–Apr. 30): Tues.–Wed., Fri.–Sun., 10–5; Thurs., 10–8. Closed Mon.
Tours: Call (613) 990–0570 for reservation and group-tour information.
Food & Drink: Café L'Entrée and Sketches Cafeteria open museum hours but close 15 minutes early.

Art Gallery of Ontario

317 Dundas St. West, Toronto, Ontario, Canada M5T 1G4
(416) 977-0414

1993 Exhibitions

NOTE: Thirty new galleries open Jan. 1993.
July
The Earthly Paradise: Arts and Crafts by William Morris and His Circle from Canadian Collections

Permanent Collection

European, American, and Canadian art since the Renaissance, including Impressionist, Post-Impressionist, Modernist, and contemporary works; Inuit art. **Highlights:** European masterworks by Hals, Rembrandt, Rubens, Chardin, Gainsborough, Degas, Pissarro; largest public collection of sculpture by Henry Moore; Canadian works by Krieghoff, Legare, Peel, Plamondon; religious carvings, paintings; the Klamer Collection, other Inuit holdings. **Architecture:** 1911 home, the Grange; 1936 expansion and Walker Memorial Sculpture Court; 1974 Henry Moore Sculpture Centre and Sam and Ayala Zacks Wing; 1977 Canadian Wing and Gallery School addition; 1993 additions and renovation culminating in a new building by Barton Myers, Architect, Inc., in joint venture with Kuwabara Payne McKenna Blumberg Architects.

Admission: adults, $7.50; seniors, students, $4 (Fri., free); members, free; families (maximum 6 people), $15. Handicapped accessible.
Hours: Spring–fall: Mon.–Sun., 11–5:30, Wed., 11–9. Winter: Tues.–Sun., 11–5:30; Wed., 11–9.
Tours: Daily. Call (416) 977-0414 for information and booking large groups. NOTE: tours interrupted due to construction; call ahead to confirm.
Food & Drink: Cafeteria and restaurant open gallery hours.

Henry Moore Sculpture Center, Art Gallery of Ontario.

Other Important Museums

Glenbow Museum
130 9th Ave. S.E., Calgary, Alberta, Canada T2G 0P3
(403) 264-8300

Edmonton Art Gallery
2 Sir Winston Churchill Sq., Edmonton, Alberta, Canada
T5J 2C1
(403) 422-6223

Canadian Museum of Civilization
100 Laurier St., Hull, Quebec, Canada J8X 4H2
(819) 953-8704

Canadian Centre for Architecture
1920, rue Baile, Montreal, Quebec, Canada H3H 2S6.
(514) 939-7000; 939-7026

Le Musée du Quebec
1 ave. Wolfe-Montcalm, Parc des Champs-de-Bataille,
Quebec, Canada G1R 5H3
(418) 643-2150

Royal Ontario Museum
100 Queen's Park, Toronto, Ontario, Canada M5S 2C6
(416) 586-5551

Vancouver Art Gallery
750 Hornby St., Vancouver, British Columbia, Canada V6Z
2H7
(604) 682-4668

EUROPEAN MUSEUMS

Der Wanderer über dem Nebelmeer, 1818, Caspar David Friedrich. Hamburger Kunsthalle.

Graphische Sammlung Albertina

1010-Vienna, Augustinerstrasse 1, Vienna, Austria
Telephone: 0222-534 83

1993 Exhibitions

Thru Jan.
Johannes Wanke
Thru Jan. 31
Zoran Music
Feb. 11–Apr. 25
Polish Graphic Arts
New Acquisitions of the Albertina
May–June
Morandi
May 5–July 10
Dutch Landscape Drawings
July 21–Oct. 3
Dürer–Cycles
Sept.–Oct.
Beuys in Vienna
Oct. 14, 1993–Jan. 1, 1994
French Drawings of the Albertina from Clouet to Le Brun

Permanent Collection

One of the most important print and drawing collections in the world, including masterpieces by Raphael, Dürer, Rembrandt, Rubens; European drawings, prints from the 15th century to the present. Special collections of architectural drawings, posters, miniatures, illustrated books. **Highlights:** Michelangelo, *Seated Male Nude*; Greuze, *Head of a Girl*; Schiele, *Male Nude with Red Loincloth.*

Admission: Free.
Hours: Mon.–Tues., Thurs., 10–4; Wed., 10–6; Fri. 10–2; Sat.–Sun., 10–1. Closed Sun., July–Aug., holidays.

Musées Royaux des Beaux-Arts de Belgique

Musée d'Art Ancien
Rue de la Regence, 3, Brussels, Belgium
Telephone: 32/2 508 32 11

Musée d'Art Moderne
1–2, Place Royale, 1000 Brussels, Belgium

1993 Exhibitions

Mar. 3–May 30
Belgian Art of the 1980s
Mid-Sept.–Mid-Dec.
Frida Kahlo

Permanent Collection

Museum of Classical Art: 14th–18th centuries. Works from the Low Countries—Dutch, German, Italian, French schools. Van der Weyden, Bruegel the Elder, Cranach, Hals, Lorrain, Massys, Memling, Rembrandt, Rubens, Van Dyck. **Highlights:** Breughel the Elder, *La Chute d'Icare (The Fall of Icarus);* Bosch, *Le Dernier Jugement (The Last Judgement).* **Museum of Modern Art:** Important 19th-century Impressionists; abstract art, CoBrA, Cubism, Dada, Expressionism, Fauvism, Futurism, Surrealism. International scope with emphasis on Belgian art. Works by Alechinsky, Arman, Braque, Bacon, Calder, Cragg, Dalí, de Chirico, Ernst, Magritte, Picasso. **Architecture:** 1880 building by Balat; 1984 below-grade addition by Bastin.

Admission: Free. Handicapped accessible; special entrance.
Hours: Tues.–Sun, 10–5. Closed Mon., Jan. 1, May 1, Nov. 11, Dec. 25.
Tours: Call 32/2-508-3200 for reservations and information.
Food & Drink: Cafeteria open 11–4:30.

Louisiana Museum of Modern Art

DK-3050 Humlebaek (north of Copenhagen), Denmark
45 42 19 07 19

1993 Exhibitions
Jan. 29–Apr. 18
New World Images
Pictures from the worlds of science, architecture, and art; artists include Ilya Kabakov, Bill Viola, and Alfredo Jaar.
May 6–Aug. 22
Alexander Calder
Over 200 works representing the full scale of the artist's production, including sculptures, paintings, drawings, and jewelry.
Sept. 10–Jan. 9
Claude Monet: Pictures from Giverny

Permanent Collection
Twentieth-century masters Giacometti, Moore, Picasso; postwar U.S. and European art by Baselitz, Dubuffet, Dine, Warhol; Constructivism, CoBrA. **Highlights:** Sculpture by Calder, Arp, Serra. **Architecture:** Building by Jorgen Bo and Vilhelm Wohlert; Landscape architects: Norgaard & Holscher.

Admission: DKK 42. Handicapped accessible.
Hours: Daily, 10–5; Wed., 10–10.
Tours: Daily, 9–4. Call 45 42 19 07 19 for reservations.
Food & Drink: Café open Sun.–Tues., Thurs.–Sat., 10–4:30; Wed., 10:30–9:30.

Musée National d'Art Moderne–Centre National d'Art et de Culture Georges Pompidou

(Centre Beaubourg)
31 rue St Nerri, Paris CEDEX 04, France
Telephone: 44 78 12 33

1993 Exhibitions
Thru Jan. 11
Latin American Artists of the Twentieth Century
In-depth examination of Latin American Modernism, encompassing over 300 works by 70 artists.

Thru Jan. 24
Gary Hill
Peter Fischli and David Weiss
Jan. 13–Apr. 5
Daniel Dezeuze
Feb. 25–June 7
Henri Matisse Retrospective
Mar. 3–May 23
Bernard Bazille
Apr. 14–July 5
Jean-Michel Alberola
July 7–Sept. 19
Malcolm Morley

Permanent Collection
Outstanding collection of major 20th-century movements, including Impressionism, Cubism, abstract art, Surrealism, Pop Art. Artists include Brancusi, Braque, Chagall, Dali, Dubuffet, Leger, Kandinsky, Klein, Matisse, Mondrian, Picasso, Pollock, Rouault, Tàpies, Warhol. **Highlights:** Brancusi studio, Niki de Saint-Phalle courtyard fountain sculptures; Braque, *Woman with Guitar*; Matisse, *The Sadness of the King*; Picasso, *Harlequin.* **Architecture:** 1977 building by Renzo Piano and Richard Roger.

Admission: Adults Fr 22; ages 18–25, seniors, Fr 18; under 18, free. Sun., free.
Hours: Mon., Wed.–Fri., noon–10; Sat., Sun., 10–10. Closed Tues.
Tours: One-hour tours continually; call 44 78 46 57.
Food & Drink: Cafeteria and restaurant open summer, noon–9:30; winter, open museum hours.

Galeries Nationales du Grand Palais

3 Avenue du Général Eisenhower, Paris 8e, France
Telephone: 44 13 17 17

1993 Exhibitions
Mid-Feb.–May 31
The Age of Titian, Giorgione, and Veronese
Mar. 2–May 31
Egypt's Dazzling Sun: Amenhotep III and His World
Some 140 works from the reign (1391–1353 B.C.) of a pharoah who called himself the "Dazzling Sun-disk." Includes a red granite lion, over life-size portraits of the family and court, and colored-glass vessels. Catalogue.

Permanent Collection
No permanent collection.

Admission: Varies with exhibition. Handicapped accessible.
Hours: Thurs.–Mon., 10–7:30; Wed., 10–9:30. Closed Tues.
Tours: By reservation. Call 44 13 17 10 for information.
Food & Drink: Cafeteria open 11:30–closing.

Musée du Louvre

34–36 Quai de Louvre, 75058 Paris Cedex 01, France
Telephone: 40 20 50 50

1993 Exhibitions

Thru Feb. 1
Byzantine Art
"Flying Out of This World": The Set Idea of Peter Greenaway
Thru Feb. 15
Pannini
Thru Mar. 29
The Wedding of Cana *by Veronese*
Jan. 29–Apr. 26
French Drawings of the 17th Century
Apr. 23–July 26
At the Louvre, After the Masters
June 1–Aug. 30
Academicians from the Past
June 2–Aug. 30
The French Drawing: Masterpieces from the Collection of the Pierpont Morgan Library
Spans five centuries of French draftsmanship; includes works by Poussin, Watteau, Delacroix, and Ingres. Catalogue.
May–June
Valadier
Oct. 1993–Jan. 1994
Fra Bartolommeo
About 105 sheets from the Museum Boymans-van Beuningen, Rotterdam, by this Florentine artist and Dominican friar, including quick sketches for compositions, carefully finished designs, and figure studies. Catalogue.
Nov. 1993–Feb. 1994
The Birth of Assyriology

Permanent Collection

One of the largest collections in the world; 25,000–30,000 works on display, divided into seven departments: Oriental antiquities; Egyptian antiquities; Greek, Roman, and Etruscan antiquities; paintings, sculpture, objects of art and graphic art through the middle of the 19th century.
Highlights: Leonardo, *Mona Lisa (La Joconde)*; *Hera of*

Samos (570 B.C.); *Venus de Milo* (c. 100 B.C.); Winged Victory of Samothrace; Winged Bulls of Khorsabad; *The Squatting Sribe*; *The Sceptre of Charles V*; Michelangelo, the *Slaves*. **Architecture:** Eight-hundred-year-old building, originally palace of French kings; changed and enlarged over the centuries. The original building was a medieval fortress; moats of this early building, dating from around 1200, can be visited. It became the first museum in Europe in 1793. Central Glass Pyramid (1989) by I. M. Pei acts as museum entrance and reception area. North wing of the former palace restoration as a new museum space opening in 1993.

Admission: Adults, Fr 31; ages 18–25, over 60, Fr 16; under 18, free. Sun, Fr 16. Additional fee for some exhibitions. Handicapped accessible.
Hours: Permanent collection: Mon., Wed.–Sun., 9–6. Closed Tues. Entire museum open Wed., Mon., 9–10. Pyramid Hall, 9–10 (moats of the medieval Louvre, history galleries, shops and restaurants). Exhibition rooms under the Pyramid, 10–10.
Tours: Call 40 20 51 77 for group tours; 40 20 51 66 for individual tours. English tours: Mon.–Sat., four times a day.
Food & Drink: Restaurant Le Grand Louvre, cafeteria, bar under the Pyramid open 10–10.

Musée D'Orsay

1 rue de Bellechasse 75007 Paris, France
Telephone: 40 49 48 14; 45 49 11 11 (recording)

1993 Exhibitions

Thru Jan. 10
Palaces of Money: Bank Architecture 1850–1930
Thru Jan. 18
Hill and Adamson: The First Photographic Reportage 1843–1845
A Family of Artists in 1900: The Saint-Marceaux
Thru Feb. 15
Sisley, Master Impressionist
First major overview of the artist's career, illuminating three phases of his painting: the pre-Impressionist period (1865–70); his Impressionist years on the Seine and Thames (1870–80); and the "new horizons" explored in France and Wales (1880–90).

Permanent Collection

Impressionist works from by Manet, Monet, Renoir, Degas, Van Gogh, Cézanne, Gauguin, Daumier, Derain, Pissarro, Seurat, Toulouse-Lautrec, Marquet; vast collection of 19th-century Neoclassicism; several outstanding works by Rodin. **Highlights:** Daumier, *Caricatures* (busts); Degas, *Au Café, dit l'Absinthe*; Gauguin, *Arearea, Le Bel Ange*; van Gogh, *Bedroom at Arles*; Ingres, *La Source*; Manet, *Le Dejeuner sur l'Herbe (Luncheon on the Grass); Millet, The Gleaners*; Monet, *La Cathedral de Rouen* (five paintings); Renoir, *Bal du Moulin de la Galette (Dance at the Moulin de la Galette); Toulouse-Lautrec, Jane Avril*; Whistler, *Whistler's Mother.* **Architecture:** Railway station with hotel and restaurant; 1986 renovation by Gae Aulenti.

Admission: Tues.–Sat., Fr 31; Sun., Fr 16. Handicapped accessible.
Hours: Tues.–Wed., Fri.–Sat., 10–6; Thurs., 10–9:45; Sun., 9–6. Closed Mon. June 20–Sept. 20: opens at 9.
Tours: Call 45 49 45 46 for reservations; 45 49 49 49 for recorded tour information.
Food & Drink: Restaurant and rooftop café open museum hours.

Musée Picasso

Hôtel Sâlé, 5 rue Thorigny, 75003 Paris, France
Telephone: 42 71 25 21

1993 Exhibitions

Permanent Collection

Extraordinary and enormous collection of paintings, drawings, prints by Picasso that cover many periods of his career, emphasizing later works; works by other artists from Picasso's own collection. **Architecture:** Housed in former private 18th-century elegant private house in the ancient Marais section, near La Place des Vosges.

Admission: Mon., Wed.–Sat., Fr 23; Sun., Fr 12.
Hours: Thurs.–Mon., 9:15–5:15, Wed., 9:15–10. Closed Tues.
Tours: Call 42 71 70 84.
Food & Drink: Restaurant, café in the beautiful erstwhile private gardens of the mansion.

Galerie Nationale du Jeu de Paume

Place de la Concorde, 75008 Paris, France
Telephone: 47 03 12 50

1993 Exhibitions

Thru Jan. 31
Martial Raysse: Retrospective

Feb. 16–Apr. 11
Barré: 1979–1992
David Rabinowitch (sculpture)
Apr. 27–June 20
Eva Hesse: A Retrospective
The first major retrospective for this influential artist who died in 1970, bringing together her sculptures, reliefs, and rarely seen drawings and early paintings. Catalogue.
Thierry Kuntzel (video)
July–Oct.
Takis: A Retrospective (sculpture)

Permanent Collection
No permanent collection. **Architecture:** 1861 building; 1990 renovation.

Admission: Fr 30. Handicapped accessible.
Hours: Tues. 12–9:30; Wed.–Fri,. 12–6; Sat.–Sun., 10–6. Closed Mon.
Tours: Free with entrance ticket. Tues., 3; Wed.–Thurs., 1; Fri.–Sat., 3; Sun., 11.
Food & Drink: Café du Jeu de Paume open museum hours.

Akademie der Künst
Hanseatenweg 10, 1000 Berlin 21, Germany
Telephone: (030) 39 00 07-0

1993 Exhibitions
May 2–June 13
"Universal Peace–Youthful Happinness": Olympic Festival Exhibition
Aug. 22–Oct. 31
Hans Scharoun: Architect (1893–1972)
Dec. 1993–Jan. 1994
Fragments

Permanent Collection
Information not available.

Admission: Information not available.

Berlinische Galerie

Museum Für Moderne Kunst, Photographie und Architektur
Martin-Gropius Bau, Stresemannstrasse 110, 1000 Berlin 61, Germany
Telephone: (030) 2 54 86 0

1993 Exhibitions

Thru Jan. 31
Naum Gabo–Der Wettbewerb für den Palace of the Soviets, 1931
Thru Jan.
Hermann Rückwath/Architectural Photography Berlin 1860–1920
Jan. 15–Feb. 28
History of Modern Photography in Berlin
Apr.
Einrichtung eines Georg Frietzsche-Raumes zum 90. Geburtstag
Sept. 9–Dec. 13
Puni–Retrospective in conjuction with Le Musée d'Art Moderne, Paris

Permanent Collection

Features Dadaist works, Modern art, Russian avant-garde, photography, architecture after 1945. **Highlights:** Höch, *The Journalists*; Dix, *Portrait of the Poet*; Grosz, *Self-Portrait*; Gabo, *Torso Construction*; *Hell, It's Me*; Middendor, *Natives of the Big City*, *Salomé*, *Judith and Holofernes*; Killisch, *The Artist's Atelier*; Sonntag, *Little Oedipus Head.* **Architecture:** 1881 building destroyed in 1945; 1981 reconstruction by W. Kampmann.

Admission: DM 6; groups, senior citizens, students, DM 3. Special exhibits: DM 8; groups, senior citizens, students, DM 4. Handicapped accessible.
Hours: Tues.–Sun., 10–10. Closed Mon.

Die Versammlung, 1984, Brigitte and Martin Matschinsky-Denninghoff. Berlinische Galerie.

Staatliche Kunsthalle Berlin

Budapester Strasse 42-46, 1000 Berlin 30, Germany
Telephone: (030) 261 70 67 68

1993 Exhibitions

Information not available at press time.

Permanent Collection

No permanent collection.

Admission: Adults, DM 4; students, senior citizens, DM 2.
Hours: Tues.–Sun., 10–6; Wed., 10–10. Closed Mon.
Tours: Call for information.
Food & Drink: Café open museum hours.

Museum für Moderne Kunst

Domstrasse 10, D-6000 Frankfurt am Main, Germany
069 212 37 882

1993 Exhibitions

Information not available at press time.

Permanent Collection

Features contemporary art, including Pop Art, other works from the 1960s to the present. **Architecture:** 1991 building by Hans Holbein.

Admission: Free.
Hours: Tues.–Sun., 10–6; Wed., 10–10. Closed Mon.

Hamburger Kunsthalle

Glockengieberwall, 2000 Hamburg 1, Germany
Telephone: 40-2486 2612

1993 Exhibitions

Thru Jan. 17
Goya: Desastres de la Guerra
Jan.–Feb.
Rolf Nesch; Karl Muck-Zyklus
Feb. 5–Apr. 4
Ingo Günther
Feb. 12–Mar. 28
Axel Hütte: Photography I
Mar. 19–May 23
Max Beckmann: Self Portraits
Apr.–May
Candida Höfer: Photography II
June 18–Aug. 29
Pablo Picasso: Paintings and Sculpture, 1937–1973
Sept. 17–Oct. 31
Hermann Finsterlin

Sept. 24–Nov. 28
Thomas Schütte

Permanent Collection
Paintings from Gothic to contemporary; 19th- and 20th-century sculpture; drawings, graphics. **Highlights:** paintings by Meister Bertram, *The Creation of the Animals*; Rembrandt, *Simeon and Anna Recognize Jesus as the Lord*; Claude, *The Departure of Aeneas from Carthage*; Friedrich, *The Sea of Ice*; Runge, *Morning*; Beckmann, *Ulysses and Calypso*; Hockney, *Doll Boy*. **Architecture:** 1869 building by Hude und Schirrmacher; 1919 annex; building by Oswald Mathias Ungers planned for 1996.

Admission: DM 3. Handicapped accessible.
Hours: Tues.–Sun., 10–6. Closed Mon.
Food & Drink: Café Liebermann open 1–5.

Staatsgalerie Stuttgart

Konrad-Adenauer-Str. 32, Postanschrift: Urbanstrasse 35, 7000 Stuttgart 1, Germany
Telephone: 0711 212 5074

1992 Exhibitions
Feb. 22–Apr.
Masterworks of Art—10th Anniversary of the Founding of the Baden-Würtenberg Museum
May 23–July 26
Kandinsky—Watercolors and Drawings
Dec. 18, 1992–Feb. 14, 1993
Juan Gris
May 5–Aug. 8
To Draw, to paint, to sculpt...Schwabisch Classicism between Ideal and Reality
Sept. 11–Nov. 14
Oskar Schlemmer
Der Folwang–Cycle: Metamorphosis in Space
Oct. 10–Dec. 12
Architectural Drawings from Bernini through Piranesi
Dec. 11, 1993–Feb. 13, 1994
Henri Matisse: Drawings and papiers collés

Permanent Collection
Focus on early German, Italian, Neoclassical painting, prints, drawings; contemporary art. **Highlights:** Ratgeb, Altar from Herenberg of 1519; Italian works by Fra Bartolommeo, Bellini, Carpaccio, Vasari, Carracci, Tiepolo; Memling, *Bathsheba*; Rembrandt, *Paul in Prison*; works by Bouts, Rubens, Hals; Monet, *Fields of Spring*; Burne-Jones, *"Perseus"* cycle; 19th-century painting by Friedrich, Menzel, Böcklin, Corot, Courbet, Manet, Pissarro, Renoir, Cézanne, Gauguin; Modern, contemporary works by Schlemmer, Picasso, German Expressionists,

Constructivists, Italian Futurists, Dadaists, Surrealists, Dubuffet, Giacometti, Pollock, Segal, Warhol, Fontana, Yves Klein; extensive documentation of Happenings, Fluxus events. NOTE: Due to remodeling, the Italian, Medieval German, Netherlandish, Swabian, and Neoclassical painting departments will be closed until the end of 1992. **Architecture:** 1843 Old Staatsgalerie by Georg Gottlob Barth; 1984 addition by James Stirling.

Admission: Free; charge for some temporary exhibitions. Handicapped accessible.
Hours: Tues.–Wed., 10–8; Thurs.–Sun., 10–5. Closed Mon., Good Friday, Dec. 24–25.
Tours: Call 0711 212 5050 for information.

National Galleries of Scotland

Telephone: 031 332 4939

National Gallery of Scotland

The Mound, EH2 2EL Edinburgh, Scotland, Great Britain
Telephone: 031 556 8921

1993 Exhibitions

Jan. 1–31
Turner Watercolors
Mar. 5–28
Drawings from Holkham
July 22–Sept. 26
Holbein Drawings from the Royal Collection
Oct. 7–Dec. 19
Barbizon Prints
Treasures of the Merdag Museum

Permanent Collection

Masterpieces from the Renaissance to Post-Impressionism by Raphael, Titian, El Greco, Velázquez, Rembrandt, Turner, Constable, Cézanne, van Gogh; Scottish paintings including works by Ramsay, Raeburn, Wilkie, and McTaggart. **Architecture:** 1859 neoclassical building by William Playfair.

Scottish National Portrait Gallery

1 Queen St., Edinburgh, Scotland, Great Britain

1993 Exhibitions

Mar. 20–May 23
Eugene Impeys Photographs of India
May 29–Aug. 1
Children: A Photographic Portrait

Summer
Howard Gilman Paper Company Collection
Oct. 15, 1993–Jan. 1994
Daguerrotypes

Permanent Collection

Subjects include Mary, Queen of Scots; Bonnie Prince Charlie; Robert Burns; Sir Walter Scott; Charles Rennie Macintosh; Queen Elizabeth. Scottish Photography Archive, including work by Hill & Adamson and contemporary photographers.

Scottish National Gallery of Modern Art

Belford Rd., Edinburgh, Scotland, Great Britain

1993 Exhibitions

Jan. 30–Mar. 28
John Heartfield
May 15–June 24
Recent British Sculpture
Aug.–mid-Oct.
Russian Avant-Garde Art
Oct. 29, 1993–Jan. 1994
William Wilson and the Society of Artist Printmakers

Permanent Collection

Twentieth-century paintings, sculpture, graphics, including works by Picasso, Matisse, Giacometti, Moore, Hepworth, Lichtenstein, Hockney. National Collection of Scottish art, from the Colourists to contemporary artists.

Admission: Free. Charge for some loan exhibitions. Hours: Mon.–Sat., 10–5; Sun., 2–5. During Edinburgh International Festival: Mon.–Sat., 10–6; Sun., 11–6.
Food & Drink: Gallery Cafés open Mon.–Sat., 10:30–4:30; Sun., 2:30–4:30.

Courtauld Institute Galleries

University of London, Somerset House, The Strand, London WC2R ORN, Great Britain
Telephone: 071-873-2526; 873-2538

1993 Exhibitions

Jan. 25–Mar. 8
Montreal: Views, Maps, and Plans
Mar. 15–May 2
Boudin at Trouville
Late Spring–Summer
Thomas Gambier Parry as Artist and Collector
Oct. 15–Nov. 28
The Liverpool Manuscripts

A Bar at the Folies-Bergère, 1882, Edouard Manet. Courtauld Institute Galleries.

Permanent Collection
Western European art from the 14th century to present day. Courtauld Collection of Impressionists and Post-Impressionists, including works by Bonnard, Degas, Gauguin, Utrillo, van Gogh. Princes Gate Collection of Old Master paintings; artists include Rubens, Tiepolo, Daddi, Van Dyck. Fry Collection includes works by Roger Fry, Vanessa Bell, Duncan Grant. **Highlights:** Cézanne, *Lac d'Annecy, The Card Players, Mont Ste. Victoire;* Manet, *Le Déjeuner sur l'Herbe*; Renoir, *La Loge*; Monet, *Antibes.*
Architecture: 1776–80 Neoclassical "Fine Rooms" of Somerset House by Sir William Chambers; 1987–90 renovation by Firmstone & Co.

Admission: Adults, £3; seniors, students, children, £1.50. Handicapped accessible.
Hours: Mon.–Sat., 10–6; Sun., 2–6; last tickets, 5:20. Closed Jan. 1, Good Friday, Dec. 24, 25, 26.
Tours: Group tours available for 25 or less; call 071-873-2549 for reservations; no group tours on Sunday.
Food & Drink: Coffee shop open Mon.–Sat., 10–5:30; Sun., 2–5:30.

Hayward Gallery

The South Bank Centre, Belvedere Road, London SE1 8X, Great Britain
Telephone: 071-928-3144

1993 Exhibitions
Jan. 21–Mar. 14
Gravity and Grace: The Changing Condition of Sculpture 1965–75
Apr. 8–June 20
Georgia O'Keeffe

July 22–Oct. 10
Aratjara: Australian Aboriginal Art

Permanent Collection

Base for Arts Council Collection of postwar British art, but no permanent collection on view. **Architecture:** 1968 building by G.L.C. Department of Architecture and Civic Design.

Admission: Adults, £5; concessions, £3.50.
Hours: Daily, 10–6; Tues.–Wed., 10–8. Closed between exhibitions.
Tours: Call 071-928-3144 for information.
Food & Drink: Café open gallery hours.

The National Gallery

Trafalgar Square, London WC2N 5DN, Great Britain
Telephone: 071-839-3321

1993 Exhibitions

Thru Feb. 7
Edvard Munch: The Frieze of Life
Jan. 20–Mar. 28
Brief Encounters: Campin
Mar. 24–July 11
Masterworks from Lille: Old Master Paintings and Drawings from the Musée des Beaux Arts, Lille
An alternative view of French painting and drawing during the 18th and 19th centuries; includes works by David, Delacroix, Courbet, and others from the Musée des Beaux-Arts, Lille, France.
Apr. 28–June 20
Paintings from the Bowes Museum
A selection of paintings by El Greco, Goya, and others from the Bowes Museum, Barnard Castle, County Durham.
Sept. 15–Dec. 12
Making and Meaning: The Wilton Diptych
The first of a series of exhibitions examining a major work from the gallery's collection; focuses on this rare painting of the presentation of Richard II to the Virgin and Child.

Permanent Collection

National Collection of Western European painting from the 13th to early 20th centuries. **Highlights:** Van Eyck, *The Arnolfini Marriage*; Rubens, *The Judgement of Paris*; Monet, *Waterlilies*; Renoir, *Umbrellas*; della Francesca, *Baptism of Christ*; Seurat, *The Bathers, Asnières; Velázquez, The Rokeby Venus*; da Vinci, *Virgin of the Rocks,* Titian, Tintoretto. **Architecture:** 1838 Neoclassical building by William Wilkins; 1975 northern extension by PSA; 1991 Sainsbury Wing by Venturi, Scott Brown Associates.

Admission: Free. Charge for special exhibitions. Handicapped accessible.
Hours: Mon.–Sat., 10–6; Sun., 2–6. Closed Jan. 1, Good Friday, May Day Bank Holiday, Dec. 24–26.
Tours: Mon.–Sat. Times vary according to season. For group reservations, call 071-389-1744.
Food & Drink: Café in main building, brasserie in Sainsbury Wing, open Mon.–Sat, 10–5; Sun. 2–5.

Royal Academy of Arts

Burlington House, Piccadilly, London WIV ODS, Great Britain
Telephone: 071-439-7438

1993 Exhibitions

Jan. 15–Apr. 11
The Great Age of British Watercolours, c. 1750–1880
Mar. 12–June 6
Georges Rouault: Early Work 1903–1920
June 6–Aug. 15
225th Summer Exhibition
July 2–Oct. 10
Camille Pissarro
Sept. 17–Dec. 12
American Art in the 20th Century
Oct. 9, 1993–Jan. 23, 1994
Master Drawings from the Getty Collection

Permanent Collection

Works by Constable, Gainsborough, Michelangelo, Turner; *The Marriage Feast of Eros and Psyche* (ceiling painting); Ricci, *Juno and Jupiter on Olympus, The Triumph of Galatea, Diana and Attendants* and *Bacchus and Ariadne; West, The Graces Unveiling Nature (ceiling painting); Kauffman, Genius, Painting, Composition, and Design; Reynolds, Self-Portrait*; Gainsborough, *Self-Portrait,* landscapes, sketches. The first president of the Academy was Benjamin West, followed by Joshua Reynolds; among the early students were Constable, Lawrence, and Turner.
Architecture: 1660 building; 1717 Palladian style redesign by Colin Campbell; 1815 renovation by Samuel Ware.

Admission: Adults, £1.50–£4.50, varies with exhibition; reduced rates for seniors, students, children.
Hours: Daily, 10–6.
Tours: Call for information.
Food & Drink: Restaurant open daily, 10–6:30.

Tate Gallery

Millbank, London SWIP 4RG, Great Britain
Telephone: 071-821-1313

1993 Exhibitions

Thru Jan.
Richard Serra
Thru Jan. 3
The Swagger Portrait
Feb. 10–May 17
Turner: The Final Years
Feb. 17–Apr. 25
Robert Ryman
Thru Feb.
Modern Collection Exhibition
Mar. 3–June
Georges Braque
June 2–Sept. 12
Turner's Painting Techniques
June 9–Sept. 5
Art and Liberation: Painting and Sculpture in Postwar Paris, 1945–1955
July–Nov.
Burne-Jones
Sept. 29, 1993–Jan. 23, 1994
Turner's Vignettes
Oct. 13, 1993–Jan. 9, 1994
Ben Nicholson

Permanent Collection

Houses the national collection of British painting from the 16th century to the present day; also the national gallery for modern art, encompassing British, European, and American painting and sculpture and works on paper since 1945. **Highlights:** 1987 Clore Gallery houses the Turner Bequest, comprising the paintings, watercolors, drawings and sketchbooks of J. M. W. Turner; works by Blake, Cézanne, Constable, Gainsborough, Gauguin, Giacometti, van Gogh, Hepworth, Hogarth, Lichtenstein, Moore, Picasso, Pollock, Rodin, Warhol. **Architecture:** 1897 Neoclassical building overlooking the Thames by Sidney J. R. Smith; Clore Gallery by James Stirling, Michael Wilford and Assoc.

Admission: Free to gallery; fees for three loan exhibitions per year. Handicapped accessible.
Hours: Mon.–Sat., 10–5:50; Sun., 2–5:50. Closed Jan. 1, Good Friday, May 1, Bank Holiday, Dec. 24–26.
Tours: Mon.–Fri., 11 (British Art Before 1900), noon (Highlights of Early Modern Art), 2 (Highlights of Later Modern Art), 3 (Turner Collection).
Food & Drink: Coffee shop open Mon.–Sat., 10:30–5:50; Sun., 2–5:50. Restaurant open Mon.–Sat., 12–3; closed Sun. Call 071-834-6754 for reservations.

Branches:
Tate Gallery Liverpool
Telephone: 051-709-3223
Works from the Tate Gallery's 20th-century collection, with temporary exhibitions.

Tate Gallery St. Ives (Opens Spring 1993)
Works by artists associated with St. Ives, Cornwall, from the gallery collection.

Victoria and Albert Museum

South Kensington, London SW7 2RL, Great Britain
Telephone: 01-938-8361

1993 Exhibitions
Thru Feb.
Prospects, Thresholds, Interiors
Thru Feb. 14
Sporting Trophies

Permanent Collection
The most important decorative art museum in the world, known fondly as the "attic," including enormous collections of applied art in all media worldwide. Art and Design Galleries from the Middle Ages to the Renaissance; Mannerism to Art Nouveau in British Art; The Arts of the East; special collections such as Raphael cartoons, musical instruments, sculpture by Rodin, tapestries, jewelry, furniture, interior design, ceramics and glass, dress, Indian art, textiles, prints and drawings. **Architecture:** 1891 building by Captain Francis Fowke; 1899–1909 south front by Aston Webb.

Admission: Voluntary donation. Handicapped accessible.
Hours: Mon.–Sat., 9–5:50; Sun., 2:30–5:50.
Tours: Mon.–Sat., 11, 12, 2, 3. Sun., 3.
Food & Drink: Millburns Restaurant open museum hours.

Museum of Modern Art, Oxford

30 Pembroke St., Oxford OX11BP, Great Britain
Telephone: 0865 722733

1993 Exhibitions
Thru Jan. 17
A World of Difference: Oxfam Photography
Bill Jacklin: Urban Portraits 198
Jan. 24–Mar. 28
Sol LeWitt

Apr. 4–June 20
Marcel Broodthaers
Flags of the Fante Asafo
Exhibition of large, brightly colored, appliquéd flags from the Fante Asafo people of south central Ghana. Catalogue.
Robert Crumb
June 27–Sept. 12
Chinese Graphics
No Turning Back—Chinese Avant-Garde
Sept. 19–Nov. 21
Kalighat Mukherjee
Nov. 28, 1993–Jan. 30, 1994
Peter Campus
Gary Hill

Permanent Collection
No permanent collection.

Admission: £3. Handicapped accessible.
Hours: Tues.–Sat., 10–6; Thurs., 10–9; Sun., 2–6. Closed Mon.
Food & Drink: Café MOMA open Tues.–Sat., 10–5; Sun., 2–5.

Museo Nazionale del Bargello
Via del Proconsolo 4, 50125 Florence, Italy
Telephone: 055 21 83 41

1993 Exhibitions
Spring 1993
Recent Gifts: 1987–1992

Permanent Collection
Treasure house of Italian sculpture; Islamic tiles, ceramics, Italian Renaissance medals, sacred goldworks, seals, coins. **Highlights:** Giambologna, *Mercury*; Donatello, *St. George*; Michelangelo, *Apollo*; works by Brunelleschi, Donatello, Ghiberti, Luca della Robbia, Verrocchio. **Architecture:** 1280 medieval palace by Arnolfo di Cambio; 1860 restoration by Francesco Mazzei.

Admission: 6,000 lire; children under 18, senior citizens over 60, free.
Hours: Tues.–Sat., 9–2; Sun., 9–1. Closed Mon.
Tours: Call for information.

Galleria degli Uffizi

Loggiato degli Uffizi 6, 50121 Florence, Italy
Telephone: 055 21 83 41

1993 Exhibitions

Works from the permanent collection on display.

Permanent Collection

One of the world's most important collections of Italian painting, including galleries of the Sienese School, Giotto, Botticelli, Leonardo, Pollaiuolo, Lippi, Michelangelo and Florentine masters, Raphael, Andrea del Sarto, Titian, Caravaggio; also salons of Rembrandt, Rubens. **Highlights:** Botticelli, *Birth of Venus*; Da Fabriano, *Adoration of the Magi*; Giotto, *Madonna and Child*; Leonardo, *Annunciation*; Michelangelo; *Holy Family*; Raphael, *Madonna of the Goldfinch; Titian, Venus of Urbino.* **Architecture:** 1560–81 building by Giorgio Vasari and others; created by Francesco I de' Medici to house key Medici collections.

Admission: 10,000 lire. Ticket sales stop 45 minutes before closing.
Hours: Tues.–Sat., 9–7; Sun., holidays, 9–1. Closed Mon.
Tours: Call for information.
Food & Drink: Snack bar and terrace café open museum hours.

Monumenti Musei e Gallerie Pontificie

00120 Città del Vaticano, Rome, Italy
Telephone: 066 988 3333

1993 Exhibitions

Works from the permanent collection on display.

Permanent Collection

Egyptian, Etruscan, classical and near Eastern antiquities; paintings and tapestries; modern religious art; ethnology; Church history. **Highlights:** Newly restored Sistine Chapel; *Apollo Belvedere*; *Praxiteles*; *Laocoön*; *Belvedere* torso; School of Athens; Raphael rooms; Gallery of Maps; works by Leonardo, Caravaggio, Giotto.

Admission: 12,000 lire. Handicapped accessible.
Hours: Weekdays, last Sun. of month: 8:45–1:45; no entrance after 1. Easter period and summer: 8:45–4:45; no entrance after 4. Closed Jan. 1, Feb. 11, Mar. 19, Easter, Easter Mon., May 1, Ascension, Corpus Christi, Thurs., June 19, Aug. 15, 16, Nov. 1, Dec. 8, 25, 26.
Food & Drink: Cafeteria open museum hours.

Palazzo Grassi S.P.A.

San Samuele 3231, 30124 Venice, Italy
Telephone: 041 523 1680

1993 Exhibitions

Information not available at press time.

Permanent Collection

No permanent collection. **Architecture:** 1986 renovation of the 18th-century Grassi family palazzo on the Grand Canal by Gae Aulenti and Antonio Foscari.

Admission: 10,000 lire; reduced price, 7,000 lire. Handicapped accessible.
Hours: Daily, 9–7, including holidays.
Food & Drink: Cafeteria open daily, 9–6:30.

Peggy Guggenheim Collection

Palazzo Venier dei Leoni, 701 Dorsoduro, 30123 Venice, Italy
Telephone: 041 520 6288

1993 Exhibitions

Works from the permanent collection on display.
Spring
Photographs of Hans Namuth

Permanent Collection

Focus on Cubism, Futurism, European abstract art, Constructivism, De Stijl, Surrealism, early American Abstract Expressionism; postwar European artists also represented. **Highlights:** Picasso, *The Poet* and *On the Beach*; Kandinsky, *Landscape with Red Spots*; Léger, *Men in the City*; Mondrian, *Composition*; Brancusi, Maiastra; de Chirico, *The Red Tower*. Sculpture garden contains works by Duchamp-Villon, Giacometti, Arp, Moore.

Admission: 7,000 lire; students, 4,000 lire. Sat. 6–9, free admission.
Hours: Daily, 11–6; Sat., 11–9. Closed Tues., Dec. 25.
Tours: Call 041 520 6288 for information.

Rijksmuseum Amsterdam

Stadhouderskade 42, Amsterdam, The Netherlands
Telephone: 020 673 2121

1993 Exhibitions

Thru Jan. 10
Clair-obscur Woodcuts
The complete collection of clair-obscur woodcuts by Hendrick Goltzius (1558–1617) in all known prints.

Thru Feb. 14
Fans and Leaves (1690–1820) from the Collection of the Rijksmuseum
Works in lacquer, ivory, mother-of-pearl, gold, and silver.

Thru Feb. 28
Discarding the Brush: Gao Qipei and the Art of Fingerpainting
Large-scroll and album paintings by the Chinese artist (1660–1734) and his followers.

Thru Mar. 15
In the Service of the Kingdom
A series of photographs by Dutch artist Werry Crone on the theme of the monarchy.

Jan. 23–May 2
Art, Expertise, and Trade: Art Dealer J. H. de Bois
Behind-the-scenes view of the 20th-century art dealer's international exhibitions; includes works by van Gogh, Redon, Ensor, and Toorop.

Apr. 4–May 23
Meeting of Masterpieces III
Series that brings together a pair of closely related paintings; this installment features Vermeer's *Street in Delft* and de Hooch's *The Courtyard of a House in Delft.*

May 8–July 25
The Collection of Jacob Klaver: Drawings

July 31–Oct. 31
Acquisitions of Prints and Drawings

Sept. 11–Nov. 7
Meeting of Masterpieces IV

Nov. 6, 1993–Jan. 30, 1994
The Royal Ottens Atlas *"Rediscovered"*

Dec. 11, 1993–Mar. 7, 1994
The Dawn of the Golden Age
Paintings, applied art, sculpture, drawings, and prints.

The Hassan Tabbard, c. 1647. Rijksmuseum Amsterdam.

Permanent Collection

Unrivaled collection of 16th- and 17th-century Dutch masters including Rembrandt, Hals, Vermeer, Steen; textiles, ceramics, glass, furniture, Asiatic art, paintings, prints by Italian, Spanish, Flemish, and Dutch artists. **Highlights:** Hals, *The Merry Drinker*; Rembrandt, *The Night Watch* and *The Jewish Bride*; *The Draper's Guild*; Vermeer, *Young Woman Reading a Letter* and *The Kitchen Maid.*
Architecture: 1885 Neo-Renaissance building by P. J. H. Cuypers.

Admission: Adults, Fl. 10; seniors, students, and children 6–18, Fl. 5; groups of 20 or more, Fl. 8. Handicapped accessible.
Hours: Tues.–Sat., 10–5; Sun., 1–5.
Tours: Reservations required; introductory film.

Rijksmuseum Vincent van Gogh

Paulus Potterstraat 7, 1071 CX Amsterdam, The Netherlands
Telephone: 020 570 5200

1993 Exhibitions

Thru Feb. 7
Glasgow 1900
Paintings, drawings, watercolors, and crafts.
Feb. 12–Apr. 18
From Pissarro to Picasso
French color etchings.
Feb. 26–May 31
Walter Sickert: Retrospective
June 11–Aug. 29
Van Gogh Museum 20th Anniversary: The Potato Eaters
Presentation on van Gogh's famous work, compiled by the Van Gogh Research Project.
Sept. 10–Nov. 14
Three Unknown 19th-Century Masters
Features the works of Philippe Rousseau, Félix Braquemond, and Louis Welden-Hawkins.
Nov. 4, 1993–Feb. 6, 1994
Colenbrander
Ceramics and textiles by the artist.
Nov. 26, 1993–Feb. 13, 1994
Puvis de Chavannes

Permanent Collection

Paintings, drawings from each period of van Gogh's life; background materials; works of contemporaries, including Toulouse-Lautrec, Gauguin, Redon, French Impressionists, Japanese printmakers, 19th-century Dutch painters.
Highlights: Works by van Gogh: *The Potato Eaters; Old*

Church; Tower at Neunen; Pieta (after Delacroix); Self-Portrait with Old Felt Hat; Bedroom at Arles and *Crows in a Wheatfield (his last painting).* **Architecture:** 1973 building by Gerrit Rietweld and Ivan Billen.

Admission: Fl. 10; seniors, students Fl. 5. Group rates available. Handicapped accessible.
Hours: Mon.–Sat., 10–5; Sun., holidays, 1–5.
Food & Drink: Restaurant open museum hours; terrace restaurant open summer months.

Stedelijk Museum

Paulus Potterstraat 13, 1071 CX Amsterdam, The Netherlands
Telephone: 020 573 2737

1993 Exhibitions

Thru Jan. 3
Jeff Koons
Thru Feb. 7
Anthon Beeke: Graphic Design
Acquisitions 1985–1992
Jan. 15–Mar. 7
Annie Leibovitz: Photos
Jan. 16–Mar. 7
Benno Premsela as Collector
Jan. 29–Mar. 28
Ilya Kabakov: The State of Russia
Dec. 1993–Feb. 1994
Vladimir Tatlin: Retrospective

Permanent Collection

Modern, contemporary art including works by Beckmann, Chagall, Cézanne, Kirchner, Matisse, Mondrian, Monet, Picasso; unique collection of Malevich and major postwar artists including Appel, de Kooning, Newman, Judd, Stella, Lichtenstein, Warhol, Nauman, Long, Kiefer, Polke. **Architecture:** 1895 Neo-Renaissance building by A. W. Weissman; 1954 addition by J. Sargentini and F. A. Eschauzier.

Admission: Adults, Fl. 7.50; seniors, groups of 15 or more, children 7–16, Fl. 3.75; children 6 and under, free. Fee for special exhibitions. Handicapped accessible.
Hours: Daily, 11–5.
Tours: Written request two weeks in advance or scheduled tours daily.
Food & Drink: Restaurant open museum hours.

Museum Boymans-van Beuningen Rotterdam

Museumpark 18–20, 3015 CB Rotterdam, The Netherlands
Telephone: 010 441 9400

1993 Exhibitions
Jan. 14–Feb. 28
James Tissot: Prints
Jan. 14–Mar. 7
Edmé Bouchardon
Features a drawing recently acquired by the museum.
Jan. 15–Mar. 7
French Paintings, 17th–18th Centuries
Feb. 21–Apr. 18
Ger van Elk, 1991-1992
Feb. 28–Apr. 25
Leen Quist: Ceramics
Feb. 28–May 9
Kees Timmer: Paintings, Watercolors, Drawings
Mar.–June
Joost van Rooyen
Mar. 14–May 30
Collected Works 5
Recent acquisitions of the city collection.
Mar. 21, 1993–Mar. 21, 1994
People Through the Looking Glass: Van Beuningen-de Vriese Collection
Apr. 18–May 9
Donald Judd: Furniture
May 9–July 4
Bob Wilson
July–Sept.
Ap Sok: Prints
July 25–Sept. 12
Bas Jan Ader: Photographs and Films
Aug. 8–Nov. 7
1928 Design: A Farewell to W. H. Crouwel
Sept.–Dec.
Saints and Sex, 1250–1550: Religious and Profane Insignias
Sept. 9–Nov. 7
Roos Theuws
Sept. 12–Nov. 14
Chaim Soutine
Oct. 3–Nov. 28
Richard Prince
Nov. 12, 1993–Jan. 1994
Ben Zegers
Dec. 1993–Feb. 1994
Cornelis Cort: Prints
Dec. 28, 1993–Jan. 15, 1994
C. A. Lion Cachet: Applied Art and Design

Permanent Collection
Old Masters, sculpture, drawings, paintings, applied art, industrial design, Modern, contemporary art. **Highlights:** Bosch, *The Prodigal Son.* **Architecture:** 1935 building by A. van der Steur; 1972 addition by A. Bodon; 1991 pavilion by H. J. Henket.

Admission: Adults, Fl. 3.50; groups of 15 or more, Fl. 1.75 per person. Handicapped accessible.
Tours: Call 010 441 9471.
Hours: Tues.–Sat., 10–7; Sun., 11–5. Closed Mon., Jan. 1, Apr. 30.
Food & Drink: Open museum hours.

Rijksmuseum Kröller–Müller

6730 AA, Otterlo, The Netherlands
Telephone: 08382 1241

1993 Exhibitions
Jan. 1–Mar. 7
A Selection from the Sculpture Collection of the Rijksmuseum Kröller-Müller
Mar. 6–May 2
Juan Gris: Retrospective
English catalogue.
Mar. 11–Apr. 25
Designs for the Museum
May 12–June 6
A Selection from the 19th-Century Collection of Drawings from the Rijksmuseum Kröller-Müller
Fall
Artists of the Netherlands

Permanent Collection
Painting by Corot, Fantin Latour, van Gogh, Seurat, Signac, Ensor, Picasso, Léger, Gris, Mondrian; sculpture by Rodin, Maillol, Lipchitz, Moore, Hepworth, Snelson, Ricky, Oldenburg, Serra, Merz, Penone; 60-work sculpture park. **Architecture:** 1938 building by Henry van der Velde; 1977 wing by Wim Quist.

Admission: National Park including museum: Fl. 7.
Hours: Tues.–Sat., 10–5; Sun, 1–5 (Nov. 1–Apr. 1), 11–5 (Apr. 1–Nov. 1). Closed Mon.
Tours: Call 08382 1241 for information.

Fundació Joan Miró

Parc de Montjuïc, 08038 Barcelona, Spain
Telephone: 93 329 19 08

1993 Exhibitions

Thru Jan. 10
Gilbert and George
Jan. 21–Mar. 28
Wilfredo Lam
Apr. 20–Aug. 30
Centennial of Joan Miró's Birth

Permanent Collection

More than 200 paintings, sculptures, works on paper, textiles (1917–70s) donated by Miró to his native city. Foundation is dedicated to conserving and showing his work, work by all contemporary artists, and work by young artists. **Highlights:** Major works by Miró; "To Joan Miró" (works dedicated to Miró by major artists).

Admission: 300 pesetas. Handicapped accessible.
Hours: Tues.–Sat., 11–6; Thurs. 11–9:30; Sun., holidays, 10:30–2:30. Closed Mon.
Tours: General public, weekends; schools, weekdays.
Food & Drink: buffet and restaurant with outdoor café.

Museu Picasso

Montcada, 15-17, 08003, Barcelona, Spain
Telephone: 10 315 47 61

1993 Exhibitions

Information not available at press time.

Permanent Collection

Graphics and early works installed in a former private mansion.

Admission: Not available at press time.
Hours: Tues.–Sat., 10–8; Sun., 10–3. Closed Mon. No entrance one-half hour before closing.

Fundació Antoni Tàpies

Aragó 255, 08007 Barcelona, Spain
Telephone: 93 487 03 15

1993 Exhibitions

Feb.–May
Tàpies: A Celebration of the Honey
Ninety-two works from between 1953 and 1992 that center around the use of varnish.

May–July
Mario Merz
Sept.–Nov.
Africa Explores: 20th Century African Art
African artists who confront and reinterpret Western images in light of their own culture. This exhibition features 133 works from 15 countries. Catalogue.

Permanent Collection

Over 300 paintings, drawings, and sculptures representing every aspect of the artist's work; library collections on Tàpies, modern art history, and art of the Orient. **Architecture:** 1885 building by Lluís Domènech i Montaner; 1990 renovation by Roser Amadó and Lluís Domènech Girbau.

Admission: Adults, 400 pesetas; students, 200 pesetas. Handicapped accessible.
Hours: Tues.–Sun., 11–8. Closed Mon.
Tours: Groups by appointment; call 93 487 03 15.

Museo del Prado

Paseo del Prado s/n., 28014 Madrid, Spain
Telephone: 420 28 36

1993 Exhibitions

Thru Jan. 6
Caspar David Friedrich
Thru Jan. 17
Sánchez Cotán
May–July
Victorian Painting
Nov. 1993–Feb. 1994
Goya Requeño Formato

Permanent Collection

Master paintings from Italian Renaissance, Northern European, Spanish Court Painters collected by Royal family since the 15th century. At the Cason del Buen Retiro is Picasso's *Guernica*, returned following the demise of Franco. Works by Brueghel, Van Dyck, Goya, El Greco, Giorgioni, Rubens, Titian, Tintoretto, Velázquez, Zurbarán. **Highlights:** Fra Angelico, *The Annunciation*; Titian, *Danae*; Bosch, *The Garden of Delights*; Breughel, *The Triumph of Death*; El Greco, *The Nobleman with his Hand on His Chest*; Velásquez, *The Surrender of Breda, Las Meniñas*; Goya, *Nude Maja, Clothed Maja, Third of May*; frescoes; works by Rubens, Titian, Tintoretto, Veronese. **Architecture:** 1780 Neoclassical building by Juan de Villanueva.

Admission: 400 pesetas.
Hours: Tues.–Sat., 9–7; Sun., holidays, 9–2. Closed Mon.
Tours: Call 420 06 70.
Food & Drink: Cafeteria, Restaurant open 9–5.

Museo de Arte Contemporáneo de Sevilla

Santo Tomás 5, 41004, Seville, Spain
Telephone: 95 421 58 30

1993 Exhibitions

Information not available at press time.

Permanent Collection

Spanish art of the 1970s: Gordillo, Guerrero, Millares, Sempere, Tàpies; young Andalusian artists. **Architecture:** 1770 building by Pedro de Silva; 1972 restoration and new wing by Rafael Manzano.

Admission: 250 pesetas; students, free.
Hours: Oct.–June: Thurs.–Fri., 10–6; Sat.–Sun., 10–2. July–Sept.: Tues.–Sun., 10–2. Closed Mon., holidays.

Moderna Museet

Box 163 82, Skeppsholmen, 10327 Stockholm, Sweden
Telephone: 08 666 42 50

1993 Exhibitions

Thru Jan.
Léger and the North
Jan. 30–Mar. 21
Robert Mapplethorpe
Apr. 3–June 6
Arne Jones

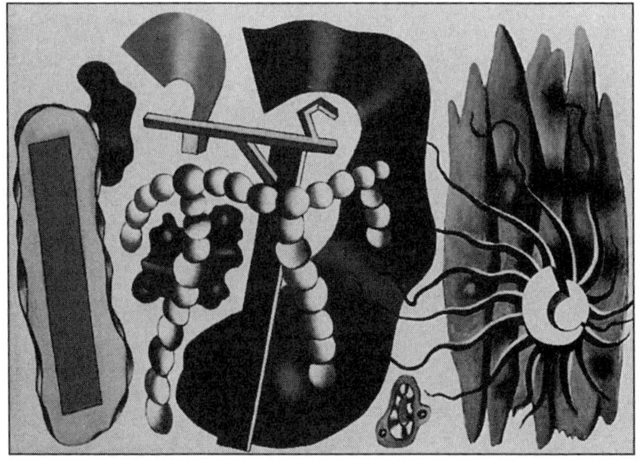

Contrasting Compostition, 1932, Fernand Léger. From "Fernand Léger." Moderna Museet.

Permanent Collection

More than 4,000 works by Swedish, international artists; Modernist works by Balla, Braque, Dali, Duchamp, Ernst, Giacometti, Kandinsky, Picasso; American art of the 1960s and 1970s. **Highlights:** Brancusi, *Le Nouveau-né*; de Chirico, *Le Cerveau de l'enfant*; Rauschenberg, *Monogram*; Duchamp room. **Architecture:** 1852 former naval drill hall by Fredrik Blom; 1958 and 1975 renovations by Per-Olof Olsson.

Admission: Adults, 40 SEK; seniors, students, military, 20 SEK; groups of 15 or more, 15 SEK per person. No handicapped access.
Hours: Tues.–Thurs., 11–8; Fri.–Sun., 11–5. Closed Mon.
Tours: Call 08 666 43 56.
Food & Drink: The Restaurant of Moderna Museet open museum hours.

Öffentliche Kunstsammlung Basel

Telephone: 061 271 08 28

Kunstmuseum Basel
St. Alban-Graben 16, Basel, Switzerland

1993 Exhibitions

Information not available at press time.

Permanent Collection

Features the development of painting and drawing in the upper Rhine region from 1400 to 1600. **Architecture:** 1936 building by Rudolf Christ and Paul Bonatz.

Museum für Gegenwartskunst
St. Alban-Rheinweg 60, CH-4010, Basel, Switzerland

1993 Exhibitions

Information not available at press time.

Permanent Collection

Twentieth-century art. **Architecture:** 1980 building by Katharina and Wilfrid Steib.

Hours: Tues.–Sun., 10–5. Closed Mon.

Kunstmuseum Bern

Holderstrasse 8–12, CH-3000 Bern 7, Switzerland
Telephone: 041 31 22 09 44

1993 Exhibitions

NOTE: The museum is under renovation and will not feature special exhibits; works by Klee from the permanent collection will be on view.

Permanent Collection

Also known as the Klee-Museum, with an extensive collection of the artist's work; portraits by Anker; altarpieces by Deutsch; old panels by di Buoninsgna, Angelico; works by Beuys, Byars, Chagall, Dalí, Matisse, Kirchner, Picasso. **Architecture:** 1879 Classical building by Eugen Stettler; 1983 ultramodern annex by Karl Indermühle and Otto Salvisberg.

Admission: SFr 4.0; fees for temporary exhibits. Handicapped accessible.
Hours: Tues., 10–9; Wed.–Sun., 10–5. Closed Mon.
Tours: Public tours (free with admission) usually Tues. Individual tours by reservation only; call 041 31 22 09 44.
Food & Drink: Cafeteria open museum hours.

The Thyssen-Bornemisza Collection

Villa Favorita, 6976 Lugano-Castagnola, Switzerland
Telephone: 091 52 17 41

1993 Exhibitions

NOTE: Museum reopens April 1993; works from the permanent collection including new acquisitions will be on view.

Permanent Collection

The private collection of Baron Hans Heinrich Thyssen-Bornemisza, featuring paintings from all European and American schools and periods; masterpieces include works by Bierstadt, Benton, de Chirico, Demuth, Munch, Schiele, and Wyeth.

Fondation Pierre Gianadda

Rue du Forum 59, 1920, Martigny, Switzerland
Telephone: 026 22 31 13

1993 Exhibitions
Thru Jan. 31
Ben Nicholson
Feb. 5–Feb. 28
Georges Borgeaud
Mar. 6–June 13
Jean Dubuffet
June 19–Nov. 21
Edgar Degas
Nov. 26, 1993–Mar. 6, 1994
Marie Laurencin

Permanent Collection
Three permanent galleries: le Musée Gallo-Romain, featuring statues, coins, jewelry, and other artifacts from a first-century Roman temple discovered in 1976 (museum is constructed around the site); le Musée de l'Automobile, a collection of vehicles from 1897–1939; and a sculpture garden, featuring works by Miró, Arp, Moore, Brancusi, and others. Adjacent to the museum is an excavated Roman ampitheater.

Admission: Adults, SFr 12; children, students, SFr 5; senior citizens, SFr 9; families, SFr 25. Groups of 10: adults, SFr 9; children, students, SFr 4; senior citizens, SFr 7.
Hours: Open daily.
Tours: Reservations required; call 026 22 39 78.
Food & Drink: Seasonal outdoor restaurant.

Hallen für neue Kunst

Baumgartenstrasse 23, CH-8200
Schaffhausen (near Zürich), Switzerland
Telephone: 053 25 25 15

1993 Exhibitions
Information not available at press time.

Permanent Collection
Key large-scale works of the '60s and '70s housed in converted textile factory on the banks of the Rhine.
Highlights: Installations by André, Beuys, Flavin, LeWitt, Long, Mangold, Nauman.

Admission: SFr 10; students, SFr 5.
Hours: May 2–Oct. 31: Tues.–Sat., 3–5; Sun., 11–3. Winter: by appointment.
Tours: First Sun. of the month, 11. Group tours by appointment.

Kunsthaus Zurich

Heimplatz 1, 8024 Zürich, Switzerland
Telephone: 012 51 67 55

1993 Exhibitions

Information not available at press time.

Permanent Collection

Features Old Master paintings; works by Swiss artists; 20th-century works by Chagall, Giacometti, Hodler, Johns, Mondrian, Rauschenberg, Rothko. **Architecture:** 1910 building by Karl Moser.

Admission: Special exhibitions: adults, SFr 4; students, groups over 20, senior citizens, SFr 3; school and university groups, free. Sun., free. Special exhibitions: adults, SFr 8–12; students, groups over 20, senior citizens, SFr 4–6; groups of 20 or more, SFr 7–11.
Hours: Tues.–Thurs., 10–9; Fri.–Sun., 10–5. Closed Mon., holidays.
Tours: Public tour, Wed., 7; call 01 251 67 55 for individual tour reservations.
Food & Drink: Café-bar and restaurant; Miró garden café open in summer.

Photo Credits

The Capricorn Trust, lender, 21
Grant Mudford, photo, 27
Michael Wilson Collection, lender, 31
Amon Carter Museum, lender, 31
Marco Bischof, lender, 43
Lloyd Rule, lender, 45
Julie Ainsworth, photo, 51
©The Barnes Foundation, lender, 53
©Helen Frankenthaler, Tyler Graphics Ltd., photo, 54
Campbell-Thiebaud Gallery, San Francisco, ©AFA/Ken Cohen, 58
Courtesy Monticello, Thomas Jefferson Memorial Foundation, and National Portrait Gallery, 58
Pence Fine Art, Los Angeles, lender, 59
National Museum, Colombo, lender, 61
Rosaline and Arthur Gilbert, lenders; courtesy Los Angeles County Museum of Art, 66
Lee Brian, photo, 69
San Diego Museum of Art, lender, 75
©Brian Lanker/Courtesy AFA, 78
Lisson Gallery, London, lender, 81
Audrey Flack, lender, 83
The Museum of Modern Art, lender, 87
Musées Nationaux des Chateaux de Versailles et de Trianon, lender, 100
©Detroit Institute of Arts, 1991, photo, 101
Chuck Fedorowicz, photo, 102
San Francisco Museum of Modern Art, lender, 105
Pennsylvania Academy of the Fine Arts, lender, 114
Reba and Dave Williams, lenders; Dwight Primiano/AFA, photo, 116
Ursula von Rydingsvard, lender; Jerry L. Thompson, photo, 124
Tazio N. Lombardo, lender, 125
Robert E. Mates, photo, 130
The National Gallery of Ireland, lender; courtesy The Art Institute of Chicago, 131
National Archaeological Museum, Athens, 135
Paula Goldman, photo; courtesy The Museum of Contemporary Art, Los Angeles, 142
Timothy H. Raab, photo, 145
Tony Walsh, Cincinnati, photo, 153
Pennsylvania Academy of the Fine Arts, lender, 163
Joanneun Graz, Landeszeughaus, lender; Robert E. Mates, photo, 184
©1989 Brian Lanker/courtesy AFA, photo, 189
Brian Merrett, photo, 194

Color Section

Rose Art Museum, lender; courtesy AFA (Davis)
Grant Mudford, photo; courtesy The Museum of Contemporary Art, Los Angeles (Kahn)
The Brooklyn Museum, lender (Bazille)
Mr. and Mrs. Thomas E. Worrell, Jr., lenders; ©estate of Jean Michel Basquiat (Basquiat)
Hermann Kiessling, photo (Baselitz)
Courtesy The Museum of Contemporary Art, Los Angeles (Rosenquist)
The Metropolitan Museum of Art, lender; courtesy Museum of Art, Fort Lauderdale (Monet)
Courtesy the Phillips Collection (O'Keeffe)
Museo Antropológico del Banco Central, Guayaquil, lender; Dirk Bakker, photo (*Sun Mask*)
Galleria Nazionale d'Arte Moderna e Contemporanea, lender; courtesy AFA (Balla)
National Museum of American History, lender; Joe A. Goulait, photo; courtesy Cooper-Hewitt. (map)
Courtesy Museum of Contemporary Art, San Diego (Bozzi)
Courtesy the Phillips Collection (Lawrence)
The Pfeil Collection, lender; courtesy Phoenix Art Museum (Frieske)
©1992 The Barnes Foundation; courtesy National Gallery of Art (Cézanne)
Spencer Museum of Art, lender; courtesy Phoenix Museum of Art (Rossetti)

Index of Museums

Index of Cities

NOTES

1993 TRAVELER'S GUIDE TO ART MUSEUM EXHIBITIONS

☐ Please send me ________ copy(ies), at $12.95 each, of the **1993 Traveler's Guide to Art Museum Exhibitions** (plus $1 per copy for postage and handling). Enclosed is my check for $____________.

PLEASE SHIP TO:

Name ____

Address ____

City ______________________ State __________ Zip________________

☐ Please reserve ________ copy(ies) of the **1994 Traveler's Guide toArt Museum Exhibitions.** Bill me when ready to ship.

Mail this coupon with check to:
Museum Guide Publications, Inc., P.O. Box 25369, 1619 31st St., NW, Washington, DC 20007.

- -

1993 TRAVELER'S GUIDE TO ART MUSEUM EXHIBITIONS

☐ Please send me ________ copy(ies), at $12.95 each, of the **1993 Traveler's Guide to Museum Exhibitions** (plus $1 per copy for postage and handling). Enclosed is my check for $____________.

PLEASE SHIP TO:

Name ____

Address ____

City ______________________ State __________ Zip________________

☐ Please reserve ________ copy(ies) of the **1994 Traveler's Guide to Museum Exhibitions.** Bill me when ready to ship.

Mail this coupon with check to:
Museum Guide Publications, Inc., P.O. Box 25369, 1619 31st St. NW, Washington, D.C. 20007.